FINDING
HOME

FINDING
HOME

A MEMOIR

DENISE NICHOLAS

A BOLDEN BOOK

AGATE

CHICAGO

First printing November 2025
Printed in the United States of America

10 9 8 7 6 5 4 3 2 1   25 26 27 28 29

Library of Congress Cataloging-in-Publication Data

Names: Nicholas, Denise, author
Title: Finding home : a memoir / Denise Nicholas.
Description: Chicago : Agate Bolden, 2025. | Identifiers: LCCN 2025019163
(print) | LCCN 2025019164 (ebook) | ISBN
9781572843530 hardcover | ISBN 9781572849020 epub
Subjects: LCSH: Nicholas, Denise, 1944- | Television actors and
actresses--United States--Biography | Novelists, American--21st
century--Biography | LCGFT: Autobiographies
Classification: LCC PN2287.N47 A3 2025 (print) | LCC PN2287.N47 (ebook)|
DDC 791.4502/8092 [B]--dc23/eng/20250507
LC record available at https://lccn.loc.gov/2025019163
LC ebook record available at https://lccn.loc.gov/2025019164

Unless otherwise indicated, all photos courtesy of the author.

Bolden Books is an imprint of Agate Publishing. Agate books are available in bulk at discount prices. For more information, visit agatepublishing.com.

To Emmett, Kim, Marcia & Mom
and the memory of
Otto Nicholas, Sr.

"The privilege of a lifetime is being who you are."

—Joseph Campbell

I KNOW THIS. I DO NOT KNOW MY MOTHER. SHE HAS LIVED her 104 years in a citadel of silence, guarding her life's secrets with an iron commitment to an opaque mythology. I barely know the shadows of her secrets, have spent years stumbling around in the dark trying to find the keys because I needed those keys to understand parts of myself. The keys were not available. She held herself away emotionally most of the time, even when dictating how we'd live in any particular moment.

With dementia, all has changed. Her struggles to maintain secrecy are no more. Everything is a secret now and it's devastating. The expressed love that I needed from her years ago was rarely available to me. As difficult as it is to watch this beautiful woman with impressive brains disappear into that disease, her heart is now available. It's a tradeoff that should be banned from human existence. She kisses me, reaches her arms to hug me, tells me she loves me. She is my child now. It is as has been described by a multitude of dementia researchers: *once an adult, twice a child.*

For Mom, that need to secrete, to cloister her inner self, begins before my birth and lives through all the years of my life. She swore me to secrets indirectly. She left tiny crumbs that I stumbled over as if they were boulders in my path, a generalized closeting of life's most cruel moments and intimate details, hiding those nuggets of power that can inform the coming generation, keep them safe.

I made my home into a place of peace, a place of refuge, a place that feeds not only my body but my heart and soul. I feel safe and protected here. I haven't felt safe in too many places in my life. I often feel as if I wasn't "planted" correctly and have spent years trying to create the best soil for my soul. Certainly, turning this house into my soul's home has helped me thrive. Mom lives here now too, with dementia caregivers coming and going. I resisted this move for as long as I could, but it became clear that my mother could no longer care for herself and that it was on me to step up. I continue to do so even when I feel like running down my street screaming at the top of my lungs. My home is now a refuge with issues. It is partially a care facility for a person who loved me from a distance.

My mother and her sister, my aunt Ruby, were two beautiful women born into a level of poverty that even Charles Dickens may have shied away from. Especially during the Great Depression, they struggled to survive. They went to school hungry. They were placed into foster care when life became too difficult for my widowed grandmother to bear. She was forced into live-or-die survival mode, doing whatever to keep living, including being an elevator operator in Birmingham, Alabama. The thought of her in that place at that time makes my arm pits sweat with anger. The never-ending insults, the racism of that place amplified in the days of the Great Depression haunts me as if I, too, lived it with her, as if I hid in the back corner of the elevator watching and listening to the horrible treatment she received.

My mother and her sister's emotional limbs foreshortened, causing them to teeter, to live stingy lives as love and physical security were never sure things. The stress on all three of these women—my mom, my grandmother Ethel who has a chapter in this book, and my Aunt Ruby who died young and worn out from poverty and bad relationships—make my life stresses seem nearly benign.

Of the three, it is my mother who was/is one of the strongest people I've ever met. She kept picking up the pieces of her struggled life, marching forward. She suffered. She never spoke of it. She's a real teeth clencher, a whisperer. She sealed her struggles and her mistakes so tightly they became useless for me to learn from, for my sister Michele to learn from. Mom wanted a different narrative, so she lived to the best of her abilities a better narrative shoving the dreadful into lock boxes and tossing them into dumpsters on some highway in Michigan. I understand now. But that did not help my sister survive nor did it help me sidestep some of the nightmares I've lived through. I needed the lessons, the secrets she held close, I needed the unrestricted love of a mother.

When my brother and I were young children and Mom a single working woman raising us, we were evicted from an apartment on the west side of Detroit for nonpayment of rent. My memory of it is smokey, filtered. I remember the incident at all because of the confusion and somehow, I have a flitting memory of her embarrassment, her pain. As a child, when I saw my mom suffering, even when she tried to hide it from us, I would suffer with her. I would cry. I tried to hold on to her in my childish death grip. She was not that kind of mother. Not old school Southern as we see in films or read in stories about elder women pulling all the young children to their ample breasts to rock them in their laps. I know none of that. Years later, I asked Mom about the eviction. She said,

"That didn't happen." My brother remembered it but he was a child, too, and could offer no details. Mom had *un-historied* the entire event.

There have been times since moving Mom in here that I've wanted to run away from home and never come back. Dementia is like a crawling thing that sucks up every good feeling, every hope and dream. I struggle now for peace in this place I created to be peaceful. We go on. I'm called a trooper, a workaholic, a strong woman. I am. I am also scrambling for sanity in this place that takes so much from everyone, this dementia place.

Mom pushed all three of her children to get not a good education but an excellent one, the education that race and poverty robbed her of until she was a mature woman and comfortable enough to go back to school. These are the overwhelming goals she set for us: *You will be educated. Ignorance is not an option. You will have good manners, saying please and thank you as if you were born with those words on your lips. You will look good at all times. You will be quiet. You will not discuss our family issues, ever. Pretend they don't exist then you're safe. Keep the secrets.*

1.

It feels like a twisted urban myth, but its feet are planted firmly in the black tar and concrete of Detroit's West Side. I still shake my head in disbelief.

July 12, 1944, I am born at Henry Ford Hospital. I've lied about my age so often I have to research it to get it right. Mom, Louise C. Nicholas, née Jones, is in her hospital bed holding me. It's war time, and it's also racial-high-dudgeon time. Memories of the previous year's race riot persisted. The riot rumbled beneath the surface many years before it exploded onto the streets in June 1943. Detroit had embraced multitudes of poor Blacks escaping the furious racism of the South and multitudes of poor whites seeking employment in the auto industry and the war industries who'd suffered mightily during The Great Depression of the 1930s. At its core, the riot was a response to in-your-face racism in housing, transportation, education—every walk of life imaginable was drenched in an unrelenting racism. It exploded on the picnic and recreational playground island, Belle Isle.

I imagine Mom was not in a private room but rather in a small ward, her bed surrounded by sheet-like white curtains, the humidity though windows were flung open, with one or two electric fans moving a lazy breeze that died before it went three feet.

1

Though Henry Ford welcomed his plant workers and their families to use Henry Ford Hospital, that didn't mean there was any parity between the treatment of whites and others at that time. This ward was for Black women.

Mom had given birth three years earlier to my late brother, Otto Nicholas, Jr., born at Henry Ford Hospital in 1941, a few months before the Japanese attack on Pearl Harbor. He was of medium-brown skin, had a head full of looping dark hair, and was quite chubby. At first glance, this new baby, me, appears more Caucasian than Black, has practically no color at all, wisps of straight blond hair, and hazel-blue eyes.

Is there an issue here? After all, Mom's appearance is not specifically Negro but more . . . *ethnically ambiguous.* Years later, when Mom worked on the University of Michigan campus in Ann Arbor and I was a student there, we'd go for lunch, and strangers would invariably ask her openly about her ethnicity. Was she Italian, Greek, Spanish? She was a dark-haired, dark-eyed, slightly olive-skinned beauty.

But hazel-blue eyes and wispy blond hair?

I've created this scene in my mind more than once. The progenitor of the baby, a tallish, thin-lipped man with movie-star, *ethnically ambiguous* looks, enters the ward. He has the kind of appearance that might cause a small stir when he enters a room—little nods and whispers, grunts, studied staring at other things. He glances at Mom and me, perhaps says something or other. Then walks out, never to be seen again.

A short time later, Otto Nicholas, Sr., the husband, walks in to see his new baby. Of medium height, he is brown as well-done toast and obviously Black. He sees me. Maybe he clears his throat to cover his surprise. Was he thinking, *Well, well, what have we here? A whose child is this* moment? Or, did he just accept me on first viewing with no questions asked? He was a man with a good eye and a lot of street sense. I have no idea what he thought in that moment and regret profoundly never asking him that specific question many years later when we finally discussed the drama.

What about the doctor and the nurses? Did they witness any of this unfolding drama? Did they make judgmental comments, or treat Mom hatefully? Henry Ford Hospital in those days was not a bastion of forward thinking relative to "race." Old Man Ford himself was clear in his infatuation with Hitler. How did Mom feel in that space at that time? Terrified, I'm sure.

Whatever the tension in that hospital nook, Otto and Louise began the parental negotiation on a name for me—*sotto voce*. Mom's vote was for *Angela Lynn*. Dad disagreed. His choice was *Donna Denise*. From where he'd either heard, learned, or conjured those two names, I'll never know. My original birth certificate reads *Angela Lynn Nicholas* with the *Angela Lynn* crossed out and *Donna Denise* handwritten in. It occurred to me that *Angela Lynn* may have come from the phantom dad, if you will, during his brief visit to Mom's bedside. *Donna* is Italian, a woman or a lady. That's a part of me. *Denise*, a French name, means to be devoted to Bacchus, the Roman god of wine and pleasure. That's *definitely* me.

Otto Nicholas signed my birth certificate and that was the end of that. To him, for all time, I was his daughter, and he never behaved as if anything else could possibly be true. But it was also the beginning of a profound mysterious exchange that rumbled around in my head for most of my life.

The drama emanating from this event grew slowly, festered, and eventually exploded onto the main stage of my life. The phantom dad remained a phantom—a person I did not know—lurking in the interstices of my life. Years later, when

Mom confessed her truth, the phantom refused to leave my mind and even the man with the hook couldn't pull the apparition behind the curtain again. The phantom is in me, half of my DNA is from a human being I never laid eyes on.

My mother had a fling when her marriage to Otto went sideways. She dealt with it in a kind of across-the-board, zipped-lip silence. She didn't want to be judged for bringing a love child into the world, so she denied the truth. She sealed her secret in an envelope that gradually aged and browned and lost its adhesive. The secret began to dribble out of its enclosure in big and small ways. In time, the light of day shone on all of it. But the slow leak of truth took time and brought hurt and confusion with it.

For years before I knew the whole truth, I walked around unmoored, free floating, lacking much sense of a self. I knew something was wrong but couldn't figure it out. My near-life-long restlessness was born here. I could not attach. I roamed through men, through love-ships and friendships. I was constantly working to find some way to concretize my life, make it stable. I failed so many times. From that inauspicious beginning, I slowly and hesitatingly built this Denise.

In my utter confusion, I lined my failures against a wall and killed them. Unfortunately, I did the same with my successes. I received three Golden Globe nominations for my work on *Room 222*. I put the certificates in a box and there they stayed until very recently. Now they're beautifully framed and up on the wall. I see them. I'm proud and grateful. The same with my four NAACP Image Awards and the local Emmy awards I received for co-producing (with my friend Charles Floyd Johnson) and acting in the PBS show, *Stories of My People, In Celebration of Black Poetry*. My sense of self was utterly elusive through the years of *Room 222*, through working with the great Sidney Poitier three times in *Let's Do It Again, A Piece of the Action,* and the ill-fated *Ghost Dad.* Even during my years on *In the Heat of the Night,* Carroll O'Connor and his wife, Nancy, surmised that I had emotional issues and took it upon themselves to draw me closer to them. Most folks could not tell that I was in turmoil. As I have often felt about acting: it's about looking good when you're feeling bad.

For the longest time, I had no real sense of why people responded to me the way they did. For men, it was nearly always a prowl; for women, it was anxiety. I found a baby picture in my mother's things from the 1940s. The baby is chubby, blue-eyed, as one friend said, a perfect Gerber baby with a very slight suntan. I sent my older brother a copy of the photo to see if he knew who it was. "That's you, dummy," he said. I did not see myself in that baby's face.

In photo session after photo session over all the years of my public career, I'd stare at the photos trying to find myself. What I looked like and what I felt inside couldn't have been farther apart. Compliments focused on my looks, and I'd say *thank you* for something I had nothing to do with. My words felt empty, though I tried to sell them as I'd been taught to do. *Thank you.*

My instincts whispered to me that people congratulating me for being *beautiful* separated me from my soul. It began to coalesce in my mind that connecting my looks to my brains and my soul might go a long way toward gluing me together into one human being. Was that even possible? It wasn't anyone else's job or work that needed to be done. It was on me to make the leap to wholeness. It has taken nearly a lifetime.

There were times when I had the slightest feeling that from a very young age, I'd been thrown to the wolves. I remember my mother saying to me, "Nobody owes you anything because you're cute." Now I understand what she meant—get ready to work hard, girl, and being pretty can cause you pain. I was a teen when those words went straight from her mouth into my insecure brain. Was the lesson then "cute" is nothing—it doesn't matter? She didn't fill in the blanks of what *is* owed and for what reason. Never said a word about how to deal with men coming at me. I did glean, though, that education was uppermost in her mind, as with others of her generation who were not able to attend university, mainly because of poverty and racism. That message I got.

Only now do I see the wisdom of her admonishment. Underneath it is this lesson: Yes, you're a pretty girl, but you live in a country that will neither celebrate your looks nor your brains unless you work hard all the time, and even then, it may not be enough. America doesn't value your look or your thought. Things have changed slowly but profoundly.

Underneath all of that was the horrifying thought free-floating in my heart and mind that Otto Nicholas, Sr., was not my father. I didn't look like him at all. Who did I actually look like in my family? I stare at a photo of Mom's father, John Jones. He looks like a handsome white man standing next to my tiny beautiful brown Grandma Ethel.

My Grandma Ethel's father, a man she took me to meet near the end of his life, also appeared to be an older white man to my child eyes. He had too many cats, which didn't endear him to me. I saw this man one time in my life when I was a wee child. I have never forgotten him. I stare at his photo. These biracial elders on Mom's side were Ohioans and Kentuckians. The entire lot of them were born into mind-numbing poverty. They are all in appearance more white than Black. There's an old family tale that one of those white-looking relatives went to live in a retirement facility in Ohio, passing for white to even get a place, and none of the members of the family were allowed to visit her for fear she'd be ejected.

If I remove the DNA of the phantom dad I never laid eyes on, but now have photographs of—thanks to his niece, Shelly Mullins, and her son, Adam—what I'm left with is Mom's side of my DNA profile. Nearly every photo I have of those relatives pretty much shows a more-white-than-Black-looking human being. John Jones, Mom's father, passed for white in Ohio during the Great Depression. He fought in France during WWI. I'm assuming, based on the miniscule amount of knowledge I have about Black soldiers in WWI, that he joined as a Black man. I imagine the racism of that situation where Black soldiers were given the crap jobs and white soldiers treated them pretty much as they treated Black men at home. He would've been safer with the Black troops.

My great-grandfather, my Grandma Ethel's father, a man with too many cats, has that same biracial look. When I finally saw the photos of the phantom, it made sense. He appears to be taller than the shorties in my family, so my height definitely comes from him. I'm 5 feet 7 inches and Mom is 5 feet 4 ½ inches tall. It could well have jumped back a generation to Mom's father, John Jones, but it's hard to tell his height from the only photo I have. Standing next to my seated Grandma, he looks of average height. Grandma Ethel was petite. I say all this to help me understand the quagmire of racial genetics in America. I often wonder how many white people yelling racist blather have DNA from the Black side. In this country? Probably quite a few.

2.

I imagine the response when Mom brought me—a baby with hazel-blue eyes, blond streaks of hair, and very pale skin—home to a house of brown-skinned, dark-eyed people who probably knew at first glance that I did not belong to Otto Nicholas, Sr. Mom and Dad lived in his parents' home in those days because it was financially untenable for him to support his family elsewhere.

From that moment on, there was a tension between my grandparents, Mom, and me. The tone was set. There was no place to go and no place to hide. It all had to be lived.

Perhaps it was male ego that prompted my dad to embrace me as his own, a way to brush any taint away. Perhaps he saw that as his best option for making things right—at least to the gawking world, to his buddies, and to the rest of his family. I was his and he dared anyone to say differently. By his actions and attitude, Dad laid down the law. No one was to dismiss me or treat me as anything but his daughter. That worked well as long as he was in the house. He was my protector. But, after a brief stint working at Ford Motors, the in-your-face racism of the white management and other workers forced this proud man into the streets. He became a gambler, a bar owner, a hustler, and an active participant in the Detroit Race Riot of 1943.

Years later, when I was voted Best Dressed Girl in my high school senior class, my classmates (and even I) didn't completely understand that my high school wardrobe consisted of boosted clothing that came out of paper bags that appeared in the trunk of one of my dad's Cadillacs. I dared not have silly conversations with girlfriends about what store or boutique was my favorite for finding those clothes, since I never shopped in any.

My parents' marriage had largely failed before Mom's fling. My surmise is that Mom, maybe in a romantic flurry over the phantom, somehow miscounted her days—no birth control pills then—and *voila*, here comes Denise. I do not know if she and the phantom discussed potential marriage, or the far-off possibility of an abortion—something reserved in those days for the very rich or those willing to risk death at the hands of the minimally trained.

Mom was a married woman with one child already, and I made two. It was complicated. When I try to think through the nightmarish anxieties she must have tussled with during those days, I'm happy her decisions were not mine to make. Perhaps there was no decision to make: phantom dad took that one look at me and walked out the door of the hospital ward. But maybe, just maybe, that was her decision. She was going to ride that rough wave until she sank or made it to shore. It was years until her confession to me, years of watching me bond with the man who was not my biological father, in a state of nervous collapse that her lie would be revealed.

The fact that Otto Sr. treated me as his own made his parents, particularly his father, Samuel, seethe with anger. The big lie demanded everyone participate in it to protect the family name. The anger roiling the house also was based on our—Mom, Dad, Otto Jr., and me—not only living in their home, at their expense, during the period when my dad was redefining his life in the streets. I absorbed the angst as a child and gradually came to realize that I was the cause. No matter how he embraced me or tied me to my brother Otto Jr., I felt I was outside the protective shield of family. I didn't understand the things I felt. I was too young to figure out the distance family members placed between me and them, but I felt it. I was *otherized*. When I look back, except for my grandfather's hatefulness, everyone else did the best that they could to hold me inside the family unit. But I felt the emotional distance because that's how I'm made.

When I was four years old, my grandfather, out of the corner of his thin-lipped mouth, called me a fool. He was standing near the dining room bay window that faced the well-tended backyard. I loved that room, and as child spent hours staring at the stained-glass windows high up on the side wall. That day I was scampering around the house as he lurked, watching me through hate-filled eyes. I didn't even know what "fool" meant, but I still felt, as a small child, his hatred and disdain. Years later, that word would light up my mind as if he'd spoken it again, in my ear so no one else could hear the quiet hatefulness. I knew then what he'd meant all those years before —that I was a child of shame.

Mom's anxiety—an offshoot of her guilt—became the foundational energy between us. Her guilt and embarrassment every time she looked at me, I believe, made me who I am to this day. Years later, after the truth was revealed, I asked her about the phantom and she, of tight lip and few words, snarled, "You look just like him!" And that was it. I didn't know her to be a snarler, which led me to believe that the entire affair had dug a pothole of guilt in her consciousness—or maybe even left a crater of longing. I never learned more. Her guilt and fear of being outed never rested. So it was that every time she looked at me, she saw him. Years later when I managed to get photos of phantom dad, I sat with her at my kitchen table one day and laid the photos out. She became very agitated and pushed the photos to the side. He was deceased by then and someone in his family had called to tell her. I never knew if that reaction to the photos meant she'd loved him long after he was gone or whether the anxiety of the situation had worn her out and she wanted nothing to do with it.

These Black Kentuckians named Nicholas, my fabricated family, migrated to Detroit around 1918. Kentucky had been a slave state, with many more slaves living within the state's boundaries than whites. My curiosity about the story of my dad's family began years ago when, at my grandparents' dining room table, I heard stories about "my family" in the mid-South. There were periodic visits from those who'd decided to stay in Kentucky. There was the Detroit contingent. And, as history would have it, there was the Chicago group. One visitor from Kentucky to the house in Detroit came with a classic Southern story. This man escaped a lynch mob because his white lady friend and he had become an item. They ended up living in Chicago but visited the house in Detroit on more than one occasion.

My Kentucky research is more literary, more general than pedagogical and is available on line. I've read of slave revolts, of slaves being sold South to plantations in Mississippi and other labor-intensive plantations where cotton was the wealth crop and brutality common and horrifying. I visualize that time and place, the auctions of human beings, the horror of snatching babies from their mothers, the whip-lashed back, the amputated hand or arm.

The institution of slavery made Kentucky a wealthy state. Lexington was a rich slavery city. Harrodsburg was a slavery city. Nearby was a smaller town—Nicholasville. I do not know for sure that my dad's people evolved from a plantation at Nicholasville, but where else would they have come from with that oh-so-European name? As a child I heard the names Harrodsburg, Lexington, Louisville constantly. My grandad Samuel told us stories of "walking the horses" from Lexington to Louisville for the Derby. I never heard anyone say the word "Nicholasville," which is only fifteen miles from Lexington. Was that on purpose? Were they pushing memories or stories of slavery so far back in their minds in order to forget it? It's possible that at the end of slavery, slaves held in Nicholasville migrated to Harrodsburg or other places in the state to find work that paid. The goal was to become stable enough financially to get out of that place.

Dad was born in Detroit to these Kentuckians who were strong as acid and aspirational in their presentation of themselves—immaculately dressed and with excellent language skills, working-class folks tipping into the middle class with no looking back. They were property owners who understood the importance of same well before most folks of whatever ethnicity. At some point, it clicked in my brain that my dad had a German first name. Where'd that come from? The Kentuckians of my family read the newspapers of the day. Europe was in the news. Russia was in the news. Germany was in the news. Of course, slave-owning whites gave European surnames to slaves. Otto and Nicholas as names have rich European histories.

Dad's mom was named Waddy Bridgett, and we called her Waddy B. She was a grand lady who loved *The Lawrence Welk Show*, *Amos 'n' Andy*, *The Ed Sullivan Show* and the other popular shows of the 1950s. She would talk directly and openly to the television screen as my brother and I rolled around on her much-vacuumed, pristine, living room carpet, giggling in spasms. In this living room, nothing was ever out of place—not a mote of dust, a scrap of lint, a smudge of a glass ring on an end table. Even with its undercurrent of anxiety for me, this house gave me something I needed and loved as a child—my own bedroom, a backyard with flowers and trees that made me feel I was in a small park, a front porch for sitting on summer evenings, physical security.

That house was in our family from the early 1940s until 2024. When I visited Detroit over the years, I went there. My feet hit the front porch steps and memories flooded in. My brother set up his first Lionel train tracks under the dining room table. My favorite thing to do was to put anything on the tracks to get his attention. I got his attention all right and a sock to my upper arm after being warned to not put debris on the tracks. I picked apples in the backyard. We dyed Easter eggs and made Easter baskets. New Year's Eve was eggnog and noisy company. Of course, it's much smaller than my memory would have it. Compared to where we later lived with Mom, this was a house of abundance. Things felt easy there.

As time passed, Waddy B.'s disdain for Mom's predicament softened and she drew me closer. On her deathbed, she told me how proud of me she was, especially my academic achievements and my manners. In her eyes, I saw the apology for Grandad's brusque treatment of me over the years. I loved this woman—her class, her grit, her work ethic. She wore mink stoles, lovely dresses, jewelry, all of which my dad *purchased* for her. She hosted teas for her social clubs and hauled Otto Jr. and me with her to St. Stephen African Methodist Episcopal Church on a regular basis.

The comfortable-looking old brick building that housed St. Stephen AME seemed huge to our child eyes with its nave, multiple doors to the interior hall, a full basement for children's Sunday school classes, a kitchen, bathrooms, meeting rooms. The music here burrowed into you, the chords stirring you and your emotions toward service to God. We watched in rapt silence as nurses in white uniforms fanned those who were overtaken by the music and the scriptures. To my little eyes and brain, it was theatre, excellent theatre, at times scary, other times so joyful we knew God heard us and gave us leave.

God also saw us, the children of the church, escaping out the side door heading down the block to the candy store.

Mom, on the other hand, attended the very quiet Lutheran church where we were baptized. At Mom's church, we sat quietly listening, minds wandering.

These two churches, these two radically different approaches to Christianity, came to symbolize something in me—studious, calm, and quiet on the one hand and borderline holy roller on the other. I prefer to think of them as having expanded my cultural palette. I'm comfortable in either world.

Only recently has it become clear to me how much Waddy B. taught me by her example, and by her insisting that I apply what I was learning, right down to the flowers in the yard. She taught me the fine points of using and cleaning silver, of bone china, lace cloths, cloth napkins, crystal. She set a beautiful table. To this day, I love that part of entertaining most of all. Once I set the table the way I like it, I'm usually ready to go to bed. She taught me to pay attention to all the accoutrement of the home.

Waddy B. did domestic work for well-heeled Jewish women and brought home her own personal gentrification notes, with which she indoctrinated me. She taught me how to make everything beautiful. One day, when my dad picked her up from work in one of his new Cadillacs, the woman she worked for fired her, saying, "Anyone who can afford that car doesn't need this job."

Mom's contributions to my development overlapped in some areas, but Mom was a working mother with two small children to feed and educate. She and Dad divorced in 1950 and my brother and I lived with her after. She was and is a petite woman with an iron spine. Good manners and good grades were expected every day all the time. Trips to the library came every Saturday morning. She didn't have time, energy, or money for at-home entertaining. We struggled financially and lived in apartments. To keep us in good schools, she moved whenever she had to, trying to help our small itinerant family to survive.

Mom enrolled me in a nursery school. My one memory of that was being forced to stand behind the door because I refused to eat spinach for lunch. Years later, Mom told me the teacher resented me because I didn't look Black and wanted to punish me for my looks. Mom took me out of that nursery school soon after the spinach incident. This nursery school teacher was Black herself, which made Mom even more angry.

For a long time, I thought that the distance at which Mom seemed to hold me started to grow when I hit puberty. It's not uncommon for women to have jealous feelings toward their daughters based on youth and looks, life's ever-changing possibilities, comparisons to the mother's more difficult early life, and so on. When I learned more about my paternity, I realized it probably happened in the confusion of emotions the moment I was born. Maybe, in my mother's mind, I was the newborn embodiment of the man she'd had a passionate fling with, the man who fathered me and then left her to deal with it all by herself. Or maybe that leaving was her decision—she chose to push him away and try to fold me into her existing marriage. I have no doubt that she loved me; but how she loved me always felt uneasy, tempered, mitigated. For that I can only point to the facts of my birth and the extraordinary stress that it brought to her life, and my own.

My birth was an event that created stress for our whole family, a shameful event that necessitated a symphony of deceptions I couldn't know or understand as a child. What I did have were inklings, little flits of anxiety, the sense I was living in half-light. I became a bookworm, a very good student, a wallflower, content to be the quiet one. I lived somewhat inside myself for fear of causing some kind of displacement or discomfort for those around me.

The fact that I didn't look at all like my dad or my brother or Dad's relatives lodged in the back of my mind and haunted me for years. I would stare at his wonderfulness, trying to squeeze his DNA into my little face. He had warm brown skin. I was born with very pale skin. He had big dark eyes. I had big hazel-blue eyes. We both had expressive eyes. In my mind, this was cause for hope. I kept stretching reality, trying to be his physical progeny. When I moved to California to work on the new series, *Room 222*, I began soaking in the sun trying to darken myself. I had curly permanents put into my hair. Even Black pals told me I had a problem.

So much of the drama of my personal life stemmed from this hide-and-seek quality to the way people dealt with me and the way I responded to them, which I didn't understand. Family members and close friends behaved strangely around me at times, saying quiet things about my looks that sank in because they felt like cuts. I couldn't really understand these things, yet I felt them deeply. These whisperings, and the push and pull of some family members who simply didn't know what to do with me, lodged deep.

Many years later, after I'd become a television star, I understood clearly that as one of the first Black women to have a lead TV role, I had at the same time become a very prominent role model for young Black girls.

The work one does on a television series is not nine to five. It's more like six a.m. to whenever you finish the work for that particular day. You may finish at five, six, or 10 p.m.

This includes a lot of promotional responsibilities. At a promotion event for that series, I visited a high school and as always, I talked up the virtues of staying in school, of going to college, of making a good life for oneself. A teen walked up to me and with a turned-down mouth yelled, "She don't even look Black!"

It felt like a knife in my heart—because it once again *otherized* me. I tried to ride above my anger and confusion in that moment by embracing that teenager. Around that time, I also wrote my first book—a little manual for young girls with tips on how to take care of oneself—called *The Denise Nicholas Beauty Book.*

Experiences like this highlighted how so much of my life has felt as though I was somehow outside of myself, looking in. Life seemed at times to pick me up and drop me down, unanchored and unmoored. Eventually, I began the long process of anchoring myself, of tending my own garden, sending down my own roots. These roots are real as well as metaphorical—I've lived in this house for decades, much of that time alone, and I've made it into my refuge. Even now, at times, those roots loosen. Nothing frightens me more. I have seen the evidence when someone walks in my garden at night, breaking the fragile leaves and stems of new plantings. I see the footprints in the morning. I wonder who is trying to break down what I've worked so hard to build up. I am alone here. I removed the grass on a wide swath of the front yard and planted a wide gravel path. Now I can hear any footsteps because it's so quiet in this house.

Whatever the turmoil of those earliest years, Otto Nicholas, Sr., adored me and gave me his heart and dared anyone to challenge him. I think my public career gave him as much joy as it gave me. He simply loved it. That feeling that you get from a parent who shows pride in you is powerful. I don't recall getting that same kind of emotional support in any consistent way from anyone else. That isn't to say it was not there. The difference is that he let you know in no uncertain terms that it was there. His chest was out. He didn't give a damn who knew it. That's unconditional love, foundational love.

After their divorce, Mom went to work at the Detroit Arsenal as a single mom until she married Robert E. Burgen. He was a well-educated solid citizen from an upper-middle-class Detroit family who worked for the U.S. Bureau of Prisons for many years. I don't remember when the clarity of Mom's choices hit me: Her first husband was a numbers man who loved jazz, always drove a new Cadillac, was a cool *race man,* much loved wherever he went. Her second husband was the polar opposite—didn't like music, never swore and rarely laughed, was quiet, stable, and domesticated.

Looking back, I see my mother as the first truly independent woman I knew, at least for a few years. With little help, she maneuvered through her difficulties and challenges, quiet but fiercely unrelenting. She made it to a place that gave her the dignity and standing she'd always wanted.

3.

HENRY FORD'S $5 A DAY WAGE CREATED AN IMMIGRANT STAMpede to Detroit in 1914—whites from Southern, Central, and Eastern Europe, and Blacks and whites alike from the Jim Crow South. Detroit's population continued to soar as defense plants scooped up all the labor they could find during World War II, pushing the population to nearly two million, by 1950, when it was the richest city in the country per capita. Detroit had the fifth largest population of U.S. cities, and one of every six jobs in the country was related to the auto industry.

After the World War II, white residents, armed with GI benefits and FHA loans, began fleeing Detroit for the newer, segregated suburbs, first in a trickle and later in droves. At the same time, the second wave of the Great Migration was still going full force, carrying thousands of Southern Blacks north to find relief from the absolute in-your-face racism and racial violence of so many places in the South.

Detroit had mushroomed into a booming metropolis, bustling and muscular. As a little girl, I remember well the feeling of living in the city—cars, buses, and streetcars zooming the streets, pedestrian traffic like a slow tide rolling in and out of Hudson's, the second-largest department store in the country, and Kern's, with its landmark clock. The restaurants and coffee shops bustled like a mini New York City. My dad would take my brother and me on his runs to Henry the Hatter, and to Van Boven's on Grand Circus Park. For a brief moment a Black Detroiter could perhaps believe that the sky really was the limit.

Before emancipation, enslaved people fled north on the Underground Railroad, where Detroit was an important stop. Fugitives were ferried across the Detroit River to Canada and freedom. A century later, high auto plant wages had taken many Black families from the pre-industrial South to the ranks of a highly educated middle class. Sharecroppers' children and grandchildren became teachers, politicians, entrepreneurs, home owners, fine artists, writers, and musicians. There was Motown, of course, and the city also nurtured a deep pool of talented, influential jazz musicians.

There's a sweet spot in the history of my home town in the 1950s when the excitement of advancement, of future stability and success ran through the city's veins. But the negative hits kept coming. As more and more Black people arrived, jobs that had served as the first step out of their rural poverty were disappearing. Detroit had become almost totally dependent on the automobile industry. And as that industry began to decentralize and eliminate jobs through automation, many folks were left in the lurch. Those job losses left the city with an increasing population needing more services.

Even before then, the Race Riot of 1943 had made audible the rumbling racist thunder underneath the city's prosperity and growth. Southern racism brought Black people to Detroit and northern racism met them at the door. So much of what happened to Detroit had to do with racism. It's duplicitous of the white people to carp about Black lack of progress while failing to acknowledge the extraordinary progress that was made in the face of racial antagonism and violence. They miss the salient facts.

Whites still lived in most of the quiet houses, the mini-mansions on tree-lined La Salle Boulevard when we lived nearby. The elm trees formed shady tunnels in summer and the maples exploded in rich colors in fall. Later, we swept them into piles and burned them at the curb, the aroma sealing an emotional memory deep in a powerful place in my brain.

Dark-windowed cars disappeared into garages, doors closing quietly, leaving our staring child eyes to wonder. They may have been behind the heavy drapes in those lavish mini-mansions, drinking dry martinis or Jack Daniel's neat, complaining about how "niggers" had taken over the city of Detroit. There was white anger about the changes in Detroit, just as there is white anger now about this country "getting a bit of a tan." Soon, all the white people had left the city, taking a chunk of the tax base with them.

After her divorce, Mom, my brother Otto, my Grandma Ethel and I lived on Euclid between La Salle and 14th Street on the West Side. Mom worked, so Grandma Ethel was the live-in sitter. I attached to my Grandma Ethel like a barnacle to coral. Love there was sure and never failing.

As children, we ran up and down the nearby streets, our voices pitched high and our little fannies shaking to the music that evolved into the Motown sound. Summer evenings of hide and seek, roller skating, porch sitting, and music humming. We imitated the songs of the doo-wop groups with our childish voices, trying to produce those tight harmonies. I dressed in my mother's clothes, smeared her lipstick on my little lips, put on her high heels, and tripped down Euclid with the other girl children on our block. I played with dolls, all of them white, which at the time didn't bother us.

The world we traveled through was peopled with European Jews, Poles, Greeks, and all manner of Black people from varying economic and educational backgrounds. There definitely was variety. Our elementary school—Thirkell—was integrated. All the teachers were white even as the student body began shifting to primarily Black.

During our tenure at Thirkell, my brother and I received free music lessons. My brother played drums, and I tried, unsuccessfully, to play violin. We had excellent science labs and were taken on field trips to Detroit Symphony Orchestra concerts, the main library on Woodward Avenue, and the Institute of Arts with its Diego Rivera murals, where we heard the names Degas, Cezanne, Monet as we were marched through the galleries. As the tax base for the city declined, so did those wonderful educational perks.

It's fair to say that my mother tried to follow Jewish people all over the West Side of Detroit in her attempt to keep us in good schools. She believed then, as I do today, that generally speaking, Jewish people demand the best education for their children, and my mom wanted the same for us. Education was the way. That desire, that longing, had a nearly religious connotation, harking back to slavery, when teaching a Black person to read could get you an amputated hand, lashes across your back, and whatever other horrid punishments the "master" had up his cruel sleeve.

Mom insisted on scholarship, reading, and proper English usage at all times. There was no *ain't*, no mismatched nouns and verbs and tenses. Consonants at the end of sentences were pronounced clearly, not mumbled or left unspoken. She laid in her platform for survival and success from early on. If, in her exhausting struggle to maintain our household single-handedly for a time, she said the word *damn,* it sounded like a thunderbolt from the heavens. *Shit* was cause for great alarm and was mumbled under the breath, not hollered out. My brother and I laughed and took cover when she marched into the living room with the kitchen broom to smack us across our fannies for making too much noise. She didn't have the energy for spanking us after working all day, then coming home to cook and clean. We laughed and she laughed with us. She returned to the kitchen and soon we'd hear her singing Jo Stafford's "You Belong to Me" or "Where or When" by Patti Page. Mom had a good singing voice. Family lore told us that she also loved Duke Ellington, Count Basie, and other big bands, and had been known to dance in the aisles with Dad when she was a few years younger.

As the city's decline accelerated, working families struggled to push their children into the remaining good schools. Some of their children went to Wayne State, or to the University of Michigan or Michigan State University— all public universities with extremely low fees. Did I find out what a blessing that was years later when I entered the University of Southern California to complete my undergrad degree? I could've paid cash for an apartment building in the 1980s with what I gave them for my tuition. I finished USC with honors and began grad school, but it was time to go back to work, my bank accounts looking quite pitiful after USC took my money.

During one of our lean years before Mom remarried, my brother got a BB gun for Christmas. The next summer, our evening pastime adventure was rat hunting in the back alley. No, we didn't live in a ghetto. This was a working-class neighborhood. In those years, we lived on tree-lined streets with a mix of single-family homes, duplexes, and fourplexes, all with grassy front yards, garages, and small back yards. All the buildings were brick and had porches. The last of the whites lived scattered amongst us for a brief time; then they too disappeared.

My job when rat hunting was to kick the side-opening garbage can and Otto would shoot the beasts as they scampered out. One evening, I kicked the garbage can and didn't move out of the way fast enough. A rat ran over my foot, and I went tearing into the house screaming at the top of my lungs. That ended my sidekick-to-the-great-rat-hunter days. Back to reading books.

Detroit's glory was its parks, its close-by lakes, and the Detroit River, which is actually a strait that flows from Lake St. Clair to Lake Erie. In fact, the word "Detroit" is French for "strait." Our favorite during those years was the Boblo Boat ride to the Boblo Amusement Park on an island on the Canadian side of the Detroit River. I found out I had a fear of heights on the upper deck of that boat, a dizzy girl leaning over the side.

Another favorite were huge family picnics on Belle Isle, the city's jewel, an island park in the Detroit River. My Grandma Waddy B. reigned as queen of summer picnics, cooking and packing an entire day of food for God only knows how many people. Belle Isle in those days was a kind of heaven for kids. There was a zoo, Shetland pony-drawn buggies, hiking, biking, canoeing. If you sought deep relaxation, you might grab a lounge chair and park yourself on the east side of the island and wave at the white boats of summer sailing by.

After library time every Saturday morning, we escaped to one of the grand old theatres from the gilded age of movie palaces. We sat in the dark eating candy, stuffing popcorn into our little mouths, watching *Them, House of Wax, The Creature from the Black Lagoon,* loving our 3-D glasses as we sat there terrified out of our minds. Some years later, when

Alfred Hitchcock's *Psycho* came out, I was in high school. It took quite a few weeks before I ventured into the shower again after seeing that film.

In our early years, my dad pushed Otto Jr. and me to try new things, to live outside the box of expectations. He took us ice skating at Northwestern High School on a snow-banked ice enclosure. He'd been a good skater in his younger days. He'd also been all-city in track and was an excellent swimmer. I had wobbly ankles, and my ice-skating ability disappointed him.

When indoor roller-skating rinks became popular, I learned to skate but anybody with an ounce of rhythm skated me right off the floor when the music got bouncy. It was bouncy most of the time. I got better but not by much. I have rhythm and love to dance, but not on skates.

We went to Joe Louis's farm to learn horseback riding. I was worse on a horse. I sat in the saddle screaming my head off the entire time as the horse walked calmly around the track.

We went to the Black resort at Idlewild, Michigan, and we attended Green Pastures, the Urban League camp—another low point for my behavior, as I threw myself down in the dirt when my dad got in his car after dropping us off. I didn't want to be there. I cried, pitching a fit and embarrassing my brother. I hated it. There wasn't anything wrong with it; I just did not like dust, bugs, singing camp songs, the lack of privacy, what I'll call the rough behaviors of some of the kids.

My brother and our cousins did their best to drag me into their social world, and I went kicking and screaming the entire way. They whooped and hollered playing bid whist and I, terrified of making a mistake, did my best to join in, afraid of being discovered as the interloper. The kind of interloper I later learned I was, sort of.

As a teen, I imbibed too much fantasy, too many wonderful but emotionally silly stories by world-renowned writers, watched too many movies that fed romantic nonsense to women particularly. The kind of nonsense that will trip us up for life, or until we get a clue that romantic fiction, regardless of the beauty of the storytelling, is not real life. This was, though, a grand way to spend an early life provided there's enough balance, ballast, leavening from teachers and parents to keep one from sinking into emotional despair every five minutes. *Wuthering Heights, Jane Eyre, The Scarlet Letter, Tess of the D'Urbervilles.* I inhaled these books, as they assuaged my loneliness.

Consider that exquisite film, *The Red Shoes*. I had not a clue what the symbolism meant the first time I saw this film. I was far too young to understand the emotional horror that was going on. I saw a beautiful dancer devoted to her art tied to a brilliant man who had the power to make her a star. A man who becomes obsessed, dictatorial, and crazy jealous, finally pushing her to her death. *To die for love? To die for art?* That's what swirled through my young brain, and I'm thinking in quite a few other young female brains at the time. I love this film with every fiber of my being, but it's practically a blueprint for every emotional tangle that plagued my adult life. There's no other film that betrays women more, all of us women, of all ethnicities. Like so many of us, I seem to be a mash-up of a *Gone with the Wind* drapery fantasy and a dream of being a conductor on an Underground Railroad.

4.

By the mid to the late 1950s, it was clear even to those of feeble mind that things had been going in the wrong direction for far too long. Detroit was dying and evidence of that impending death was everywhere to see. Job losses, population shifts to the suburbs, resistance to school integration, resistance to the burgeoning Black and brown populations, all sent whites racing toward the outskirts of town. The city itself headed toward a cliff.

Mom remarried and gave birth to baby sister, Michele. My stepfather, Robert Burgen, called Bob, had been born in 1909 and was 12 years older than Mom. He'd never been married and had no other children. He doted on his beautiful baby Michele, her big dark eyes, mountains of hair, and very pleasant baby personality. Bob had been the rare Black student at Michigan State University in the 1930s, graduating in 1936. He served in the United States Army during World War II and was honorably discharged in 1945. He was a walking security blanket. I came to understand that Mom had earned every ounce of the security he offered. But, beneath that security blanket, the same old lies festered, often creeping close to the latches that locked them away. I imagine Bob knew the particulars of my fragile position in the family unit long before I did. We were not fond of each other. I felt outside the unit and no one seemed to care about making my place more secure.

Soon we moved from Detroit to Milan, a small bucolic village 15 or so miles south of Ann Arbor. Though I begged to remain in Detroit with relatives, only my brother Otto was deemed old enough to stay in the city to finish high school, living in our grandparents' home, the same house we'd lived in years earlier as tiny tots, the same house I was born into. During those years, I had inklings, little flits of concern that something was amiss, but I had so bonded with Otto Sr., my mind would not allow the thought that he wasn't my biological father. One consistently creepy thought refused to lay down: my brother, Otto Jr., looked very much like our dad. I did not. In a general way, I looked like my mother. But where were Otto Sr.'s looks in me? They were only there in my imagination.

Though Ann Arbor and the University of Michigan seemed to loom over Southeast Michigan, there were many folks in the small towns of that area who seemed to ignore the importance, the value of being so close to a world-renowned university. It was as if Ann Arbor was not even there. Of course, there were others who felt that Milan was merely a slightly distant suburb of Ann Arbor. We certainly used Ann Arbor for everything from movies to books to restaurants to museums. I began to feel that though I was living in a tiny place, the grandness of the nearby University of Michigan made up for the isolation. Those quick trips to the city of burr oaks and arbors, coupled with periodic weekends in Detroit, saved my sanity. But for those breaks from village life, I may have lost my mind. By that I mean I was a city girl transplanted to a tiny village just as I was reaching the age when a city pushes one to take many leaps into unknown territories. You live, you learn, you fall, you stand, you learn how to survive in a city because you must.

Bob had a sister, Fanette Norris, who was a guidance counselor in the Detroit Public Schools. Just before the big move to Milan, Aunt Fanette had me tested for grade placement in the new school I'd be attending. I scored high on the tests and was put up a full grade, landing in Milan High School a full academic year ahead of the other kids my age. Aunt Fanette was a successful psychologist and a card-carrying member of Detroit's Black bourgeoisie. Her elegant, large home had no aromas and no noise. It was so quiet you could hear your heart beating and when you entered the house, you automatically lowered your voice.

Aunt Fanette decided I needed a more upscale social profile. She proceeded to encourage me toward the social clubs catering to Detroit's middle- and upper-middle-class Black teens, all of whom were college bound. One of the clubs she pushed me toward used a paper bag test for new members: if you were browner than a brown paper bag, you could not belong to the club. I declined membership. Thankfully, this kind of *colorism*—another of slavery's handmaidens—has been ploughed into the dirt, not totally but definitely on the road to extinction.

I respected Aunt Fanette's intelligence, her education and her professional success. I knew I wanted some of the trappings of that life but not all. I believed my journey would be more adventuresome and less about clamped-down protocols. What I didn't grasp back then was that most of the social clubs were the first step to finding an appropriate husband. Being a dutiful, educated, attractive wife meant everything. That was not my lane but at that time, I couldn't identify another lane. It took years to disengage from that thinking, to change lanes in search of one's own lane, to discover one's value beyond a man, separate and apart from a man. I was a slow learner but eventually got it.

Aunt Fanette became the model for my guidance counselor character for the five seasons I co-starred on the ABC television series, *Room 222*.

One lovely late spring day, a student gal pal whose family owned a farm with horses, invited a few classmates to go horseback riding. As I was agreeing to go, two issues took up residence in my brain: I was the only Black girl in the group and my memories of screaming my head off at Joe Louis's farm as the horse did a lazy circle walk. It felt like yesterday.

I'm sure the horse sensed my fear when my left foot first hit the stirrup. I swung my right leg over and found the stirrup, settled into my saddle seat, my heart pounding in terror. The other girls galloped away as I slowly ambled out of the barn. I managed what can best described as a terrified ride around the countryside—very slowly.

Suddenly, the sly devil took off, heading toward the barn. I could see the exterior barn doors were open as my horse galloped full tilt toward his home, me so discombobulated that a stroke wouldn't have been out of the question. The stall doors were open, but I could see that the slat of wood above the stall door was closed. The horse was racing toward his stall and that slat of wood was positioned to hit me right in the forehead. God gave me the good sense to duck and that saved my life. The horse skidded to a stop in his stall, his nose grazing the back wall. By then, the other girls had rushed back to the barn to get me off the horse and onto something that didn't move.

There were precious few moments like the horseback riding day. Most of the time, I was displaced and felt it.

Basically, I was on a kind of social lockdown. My social life felt stuck, small, dull, missing variety, missing color, music and warmth. Imagine, you're a Black person whose parents have moved you to an all-white town that's not particularly forward thinking. People are nice. But the spirit of discovery, the feeling of a cohesive social pod that teenagers live by, that comfortability of knowing by experience what others are thinking? We were to a great extent behind walls of culture and ethnicity that had no cracks, no breaks. Everybody's smiling, saying "hello," but not really engaged. Not really committed. Not really comfortable.

Mom seemed completely comfy with me on lockdown in the tiny village having little to do but study. However, after I nagged her half to death about being bored and socially isolated, Mom, in conversation with a neighbor lady, volunteered me to babysit for the daughter in that household. The child had the mind of a three-year-old in a ten-year-old's body. Her contorted, twisted body and mind, crippled by cerebral palsy among other ailments, required her to live life in a baby crib that was a kind of cell. I sat beside her as she fought the crib's blockade, making gut-wrenching noises, moving around constantly unable to change anything. It will go down as one of the most horrifying experiences of my life. In no way with my fragile mental makeup should I have been in that space. But there I was with my nightmares to remind me for the rest of my life. To this day, I can see that child in her crib struggling to free herself from her condition. I quit that job after three visits.

In high school, I fussed my way through American History. The textbook gave American slavery one paragraph. Of course, I argued against that blasphemy. My stepfather began recommending books for me with emphasis on the works of recognized Black scholars, W.E.B. Du Bois among them. When I group together this reading with the robust cultural input from Detroit itself, my intellectual frame of reference broadened to include the scholars of my own ethnicity, regardless of what was in our textbooks and regardless of where I lived.

My English studies became my passion as I struggled with chemistry and advanced math. I participated in the junior class play. I sang with a quartet at a school function. I put my best foot forward trying to make the situation work. That paid off when the National Honor Society extended an invite to me to join. I joined. And, the National High School Institute at Northwestern University reached out with an invitation to attend that prestigious program the summer before my senior year. Dad was over the moon and delivered me to my dorm in Evanston with my new suitcases packed full of wondrous pretty things purchased off the rack rather than yanked from a bag in his trunk. He'd played a number corresponding to my name and hit. Of course, I didn't run around telling my friends that my dad was a gangster. I saw him as a businessman who'd owned a lucrative bar in Flint, Michigan, which had been true but was no longer.

Though the National High School Institute focused on academics, there was a cultural component to the program. We visited Ravinia, The Art Institute, and Johnson Publishing Company, the only Black institution on our schedule.

Looking back, I see that even in my relative isolation, I was ready to be a person of the world, to know different kinds of people, to understand different cultures. The white students there were all smart and moved through the program with self-assurance. They were warm to me but also subtly distant.

During that trip to Johnson Publishing Company, someone there took sufficient note of my presence to photograph me. That photo ended up on the cover of *Jet,* their weekly pocket-sized magazine that at that time had a circulation of nearly a million. That cover became the first of quite a few *Jet* covers featuring me over the years. Dad carried that *Jet* in his pocket until its tattered pages fell out and the cover itself began to fade.

Back in high school, I kept reading and writing fairly good papers. A year or so later, at sixteen, I graduated from Milan High School and was accepted by the University of Michigan.

5.

I entered the University of Michigan in September 1961, a newly minted 17-year-old who was expanding intellectually but still very much an emotionally stunted near-child. Ann Arbor picked me up by my bootstraps and shook me silly.

My first roommate in Jordan Hall hailed from Grosse Pointe, Michigan, a wealthy suburb of Detroit. She made it known to me before she'd even unpacked her suitcases that the only Black person she'd ever known was her maid. That got things off to a challenging start. I knew already I had no interest in educating people like her about the world they themselves had created. I realized that I had to change my living situation quick or my time in Ann Arbor would be miserable.

Before long, a group of girls on my floor—all of them white and at least a year ahead of me—figured out the situation in my room and began a campaign to either get my Grosse Pointe roommate out of the room or me into an emotionally safer location. They staged their own Civil Rights Movement on my behalf and I was grateful. The campaign was successful. She moved to a sorority house, which was exactly the right place for her.

All of these white young women took up my cause with no urging from me. When I think back, to a one, they were all from New York and its suburbs. They were well-off, well-educated, well-traveled, and beautifully dressed. But the changing times relative to racial issues bubbled to the surface in that dorm in that moment, and I benefited. The fierceness of the coming Civil Rights Movement began to change the air in the country.

Martha Prescod, Black and brilliant, became my new roommate. Before Martha and I moved in together, the three Black girls in Jordan Hall were separated, spaced out one to a floor. Not sure of the thinking behind that arrangement but something tells me it wasn't benign. *Keep 'em separated so they don't stir up trouble.* As it turned out, trouble had been stirred up on my behalf, and white girls did it. That had the house mother scratching her head. Martha became my first Civil Rights Movement guru by her passion for what was going on in the Deep South. She laid the groundwork for my eventual journey in Mississippi and Louisiana. Years later, Martha edited *Hands on the Freedom Plow,* a volume of essays by women who participated in the Civil Rights Movement.

I took a job in the Jordan Hall dining room to make spending money. There I was—the only Black girl, working in the dining room cleaning up after a large group of what seemed to me to be very spoiled white girls who were not only messy, but also seemed unconcerned about the messes they made, with an attitude that reminded me of my first roommate. They were quite comfortable treating me as a maid. In this instance, the other girls working the dining room were white and they pretty much got the same treatment that I got.

But let me be very clear: with my history in this country, there is no parity in this situation. What I felt in that space is not what the white girls felt. And that's as it should be. My history is slavery followed by years and years of poorly paid domestic work for white people just like the ones in that dining room. At a certain point in my history, every Black woman who had any job had that kind of job—being disrespected, underpaid, and treated basically as if you had no value whatsoever beyond carrying out the wishes of a white boss-lady. I didn't last long in that job in the Jordan Hall dining room.

My other close pal in the dorm, another woman who's still a part of my life, was the brainy, Jewish Avis Lang. Avis came from Chicago. Her parents migrated to the US in the late 1930s from Romania. She was and is a serious reader-thinker-writer having co-authored, with Neil DeGrasse Tyson, the book *Accessory to War*. Avis was an editor at *Natural History* magazine for years editing Tyson's column.

Avis and I had healthy curiosities about people beyond our own ethnicities—including men. Avis dated a Trinidadian engineering student who played the bongos. I dated a white artist who taught on campus and rode around on a motorcycle. He was in his late 20s at the time. I was 18.

We were out of touch for years after I left Ann Arbor, but we did have one last contact in the Bay Area in late 1974. I'd gotten a small role in *Mr. Ricco*, a Dean Martin project that was filming in the Bay Area. I was in my trailer waiting to be called to the set when there was a knock on my door. It was the artist, older but still handsome. He'd seen a notice in the *San Francisco Chronicle* that we'd be filming in Oakland and around San Francisco. We chatted briefly before I was called to the set and had to go. That was the last time I saw him.

Years later, I found his phone number in some old papers and called to see how he was doing. The lady who answered told me she was his landlord. He'd lived and painted there for years but had died of ALS a year or so before my phone call. It struck me that he was the first person I'd had an emotional relationship with as an adult who died. That he'd passed from some crippling disease stayed with me—he'd been a star on campus, so handsome he ran through women like branch water after a spring rain. We women didn't seem to mind; women wanted to bed him or maybe it was have him bed them. He had the quality of a celebrity—everyone wanted to be around him, to talk with him, to be painted or drawn by him. He made a drawing of me that I can no longer find. The only comment I recall him making about it was that my face was too balanced to be interesting artistically. I'm not sure I understood that then. I do now.

When it came to me and Avis and the men we dated, we were young, curious, fearless. Dating outside the confines of one's ethnicity while we're young and open-minded should be encouraged. How else will we ever mend the madness that runs through this country relative to race and ethnicity? While the longest and certainly the most profound relationship of my life was with a Black man, I've dated outside of my own ethnicity over the years. I think in my young brain, his being an artist translated into him being a separate, more precious kind of human being. I still feel that way about artists.

We were pushing boundaries and felt good doing it. We pushed against pillars that needed to fall. The house mother of Jordan Hall grew weary of our lust for freedom and pointed her creaky, accusatory fingers at us, announcing that we were corrupting the moral order of the other girls. The fact that I dated a white artist who was a star on campus stood out. I was searching, growing, leaning against old goblins that stood as barriers to a fuller, more interesting life. The house mother conveniently missed the fact that 99 percent of the girls seeking abortions at that time were white and from moneyed families. There was no comment from her on those young ladies corrupting anything. In her mind, because we dated outside our own ethnicities, we were corrupting the moral order of the universe. Because I was Black, I was to blame for the "corruption." On that basis, Avis and I were able to move off campus before reaching the required age and academic standing.

We found a lovely old Victorian house at 311 E. Ann Street, owned by an eccentric Black gentleman who owned other properties in the city. He'd divided the house into three separate units. Avis and I rented the larger main-floor apartment. A dance student occupied a smaller apartment across the hall. Upstairs, in the largest unit, lived the only woman student in the architecture school. To this day, I can barely imagine the pressure she lived with; I don't know that I could've stood it, the pressure of men trying to hinder rather than help, of men doing anything and everything to throw you off your game. We volunteered to help her build her models. She played cello beautifully, and so began my life-long love for Bach's cello music, especially the recordings of Pablo Casals.

During those years, Ann Arbor bustled, electric with the possibilities of change. You could get anything you wanted—a world-class education, top-shelf athletics, theater, foreign films. An abortion. A few very conscious professors crushed the Ivory Tower feel of the place by opening the entire world to us. My interest in the Middle East began there in a Near Eastern Studies class; my interest in art began here, as I studied art history and traveled to Detroit and to the Art Institute of Chicago to study paintings; my passion for the works of the great Spanish writer Federico García Lorca began here. On campus, or near it, there were artists of note like Al Loving—my first exposure to abstract art by a living Black artist. I was later able to acquire some of his exquisite work, which hangs in my home to this day. My connections to my experience in Ann Arbor remain strong in so many ways. My time there pushed me forward, feeding into my need to better understand the truth of this big country and our journey within it.

The Civil Rights Movement was gaining ever more momentum, and there was an actively engaged chapter of the NAACP and regular appearances by campus-hosted speakers. My first involvement in anything of that nature was a tutoring program for junior high-aged children that Martha and I took on. Soon after, a political science professor gave me a copy of C. Vann Woodward's *The Strange Career of Jim Crow* as I'd asked questions in class about what was happening in the South. The campus was also alert to the evolving Vietnam War. Tom Hayden and Students for a Democratic Society's Port Huron Statement landed in 1962. The mushrooming consciousness in student populations all over the country energized organizing and petitioning. We became righteously indignant.

The furor over the horrors going on in the Deep South spread through American college campuses like oil slicks. The Black students who began desegregating lunch counters across the South were on the news. Their calm demeanor in the face of violent white cops with snarling dogs lit a fire under our behinds. Black and white students integrating interstate buses were beaten senseless. We saw that on the news and heard more via loud whispers spreading from people with contacts in the Deep South.

New powerful voices emerged. Bob Moses, Stokely Carmichael, Ivanhoe Donaldson, John Lewis, Diane Nash, Bill Strickland, Ella Baker, Mrs. Fannie Lou Hamer. These and other Civil Rights Movement honchos visited campuses, gathering up volunteers who wanted to be involved in making the changes that were so desperately needed. These volunteers were desegregating lunch counters, libraries, and public transportation and—the *pièce de résistance*—getting Black folks out to register and then to vote without being violently attacked for trying.

Students who'd never even thought about the Black folks in the South started volunteering to join the Civil Rights Movement. Students like me.

6.

THE EARLY PART OF THE 1960S PULLED INTO SHARPER FOCUS what had already happened in the "sleepy" 1950s—Emmett Till's horrific lynching in Mississippi, Rosa Parks and the Montgomery Bus Boycott, the Greensboro Woolworth's lunch counter sit-ins by Black college students in North Carolina, Eisenhower's Civil Rights Act of 1957, and Martin Luther King's ascension to a place of international prominence. Some folks felt it. Some tried to ignore it. Many pressed their weight against the future, resisting it, but the future rolled in anyway.

American cultural and political energy among young people of all ethnicities was shifting and shifting fast. Swaths of students—white and Black—were migrating away from things they'd historically been drawn to and embracing new sources of energy: the Civil Rights Movement and the anti-war movement.

John Kennedy, perhaps because of his youthful college-boy looks, fooled us into believing he was much more liberal than he actually was. He was an Irish Catholic Bostonian—a people not known for their warm fuzzy feelings regarding Black folks, which everyone would witness during the school integration madness in Boston in the 1970s. Kennedy basically was caught politically between the white Southern politicians he needed in Congress and the unrelenting push toward some level of enlightenment regarding race and civil rights. He had to be dragged to the moments playing out before his eyes, but he slowly got it. Thank God. It seems the country was moving faster than he'd ever thought possible— than vast numbers of folks ever thought possible.

The summer of 1963 was a watershed year for this country. Medgar Evers was murdered in front of his own home in Jackson, Mississippi in June. More than 200,000 people took part in the March on Washington in late August. Then, in Birmingham, Alabama, the 16th Street Baptist Church bombing murder of four little girls in September. This was no time to dawdle.

The trajectory of my own life was deeply affected by all of these events. I wasn't sure of my direction, but I had interest, passion, and a deep sense of right and wrong where race was concerned. I wanted to go deep but I was also terrified by the violence, the constant unrelenting violence perpetuated by so many Southern whites. Their profound hatred gave me pause. I dawdled and tap danced for a while.

Spending a summer in New York City sans parental supervision was and still is a rite of passage for hordes of college students. Those coming from families with deeper pockets travel to Europe or to other places of their dreams. But something was smoldering in America and the eruptions started coming fast and furious. It felt like many folks awakened in the early 1960s as if they'd been sleeping under a huge and beautiful tree with multicolored flowers surrounding their prostrate bodies.

I took a hiatus from the University of Michigan and went to New York City over the summer of 1963. This sojourn brought me the key to life-changing experiences, a way to cohere my many loud inner voices relative to what was going on in the country.

I found a place in a tiny apartment on West 82nd Street near West End Avenue, one bedroom with twin beds and one pull-out sofa. It was tight. My two roommates were strangers to me but soon enough we were situational pals. I remember one of these girls was Irish Catholic, pregnant and seeking an abortion. She ultimately was forced to fly to Puerto Rico for the procedure. She came back a worse mess than before she left, her guilt nearly stultifying. We did our best to comfort and encourage her forward.

J. Walter Thompson was, at the time, one of the largest advertising agencies in the world. They hired extra clerical workers during the summer months, the majority of whom were female college students. I got one of those jobs, in the International Department. My Spanish was near-fluent then, and I was asked to meet, greet, and schmooze with persons from Spanish-speaking countries upon their arrival at JWT. Otherwise, it was straight, boring clerical work all day, every day

On workday mornings, I dressed in my office-girl clothes—summer dresses, skirts and blouses, pumps, nothing provocative—and headed to the subway. The agency was located in the Graybar Building on Lexington Avenue with a client list that read like a dissertation on massive corporate success—Kraft, Johnson & Johnson, Ford Motor Company, Avon, Kellogg's, and many more. I surreptitiously scouted for any other Black employees. I found none. For the most part, my social life that summer centered around my two roommates and new pals at the agency. All were white.

We walked the city, tasting its pleasures, sidestepping its dangers. On weekends, we'd meet in front of one museum or another, meander through the galleries, then window shop on

5th Avenue before walking down 6th Avenue to Washington Square Park to hang out with other students from everywhere on the planet. There were after-work stops at high-end bars on Lexington Avenue to purchase one martini, then hog the bar seat eating free hors d'oeuvres while flirting with the well-dressed men, then high-tailing it out the door before things got touchy.

Some nights were spent standing in the summer mist in front of the Americana Hotel on 7th Avenue, as Harry Belafonte or Sarah Vaughn or some other major celebrity slow-walked the red carpet with cameras flashing and we, pretending to be in the entourage, walked up the carpet right behind them waving and smiling on into the hotel lobby. We were marched right back out the door. We couldn't afford the price of the dinner show, and even worse, we looked like San Francisco hippies, with our black tights, brogan-looking shoes, varying colored hats, and cloth shoulder bags that smelled like old damp wool in the humidity of summer. Songs from Bob Dylan's *Freewheelin'* seemed to play on a continuous loop in my mind—"Corina, Corina," "Oxford Town," "Masters of War," "Girl from the North Country."

I met a man named Gil Moses at a party that summer. No one at the party appeared older than 25. They may well have been over that age, but the lights were so dim, you couldn't read anyone's age nor could you see much of anything unless it moved.

While sitting on a too-low sofa, a few bars of the jazz playing in the party space crawled into my ears. I very coolly nodded my approval of the music, trying desperately in my mind to identify the musicians on the recording. The conversations that night touched all the bases of my youthful indignations from the Civil Rights Movement to the burgeoning

Vietnam War. We were so "in the know" about everything. We'd already convinced ourselves we were just shy of brilliant.

Gil walked up and introduced himself to me with a small puff of cigarette smoke exiting his mouth. He sat down, close. I coughed lightly and commented on how strong his cigarettes seemed to be. How could he stand it? He nodded as he showed me his Gauloises. I soon after began smoking them too, imagining myself in Paris every time I looked at the pretty blue package. At each puff, I tried to bury my cough in my chest as I leaned into what I hoped would be an acceptable version of sophistication. I was young.

Gil's nonstop smoking and talking translated in my young mind to brilliance and sensitivity. He talked because he knew so much, and his smoking meant he was nervous. While I'd been attending speeches on campus, digging for a deeper understanding of America and trying to keep up with what was going on in the South, Gil had cracked the code of America's racism in the creative arts and by extension all life itself by studying and living in France, where Black artists had been welcomed with opened arms since the days of Josephine Baker. Black American writers like James Baldwin, Richard Wright, Langston Hughes and Chester Himes found in Europe a place where they could live with dignity and pursue their art without the constant emotional, mental, and even physical duress of homegrown racism.

Gil had studied at the Sorbonne and did an apprenticeship under Jean Vilar, director of the Theatre National Populaire who was foundational in Gil's growth as an artist. Vilar took drama to the French countryside, outlying areas where folks had no easy access to a theater and often no money for tickets. Vilar charged only those who could afford to pay. That experience became the bedrock for the Free Southern Theater, founded by Gil, John O'Neal, and Doris Derby,

under the auspices of The Student Nonviolent Coordinating
Committee (SNCC), that same year in Jackson, Mississippi.
All three of those founders have since passed.

The film *Black Orpheus*, which had won the 1960
Academy Award for Best Foreign Film, among other prizes,
had eventually made its way to America's precious few art
film houses. Gil Moses revered the film and was definitely the
center of attention at that party praising it, telling us of his
adventures in France, moving easily from English to French,
blowing everybody's mind. More than likely, he was madly
in fan-love with Marpessa Dawn, the female star. Every man
I've ever met who's seen the film responded to her. She was a
true stunner—and she'd been expertly lit and photographed
to show off her natural beauty. Often in Hollywood films
you can barely see the Black people clearly, if any were even
there to be seen. It takes skill and time to light multiple skin
tones in one scene. In Hollywood, the first rule is that time is
money. In those days, if you were a Black actor, you weren't
expected to be present for long anyway, so why waste time
giving you good lighting?

When he stopped talking, Gil picked up his guitar, playing and singing to my and everyone else's delight. When
he paused, he lit another cigarette and spoke eloquently of
the power of Black images on the screen when Hollywood
still largely trafficked in stereotypes of one sort or another.
I sat there thinking, *was there anything this man didn't know,
couldn't do?*

For Gil in that moment, life was all about building a theater and driving greater involvement of Black people in the
theater arts, and on the screen, in ways that went far beyond
the images of Black people Broadway and Hollywood had
been selling since *Birth of a Nation*, with rare exceptions. Gil
spoke that night of a way of being in the world, of participat-

ing in it as full human beings. He presented a possible future without me fully understanding the ramifications of it at the time. I absorbed the words and, eventually, gnawed some clarity of purpose out of it all. Gil was a brain feeder. He was that smart, that sophisticated, that creative. If you were around him for even just a bit of time, you'd definitely learn something. All of this talk about a theater in Mississippi fit neatly into my growing anxiety about what was going on in the South. I wanted to be there. This was a way in.

Gil was unlike any Black man I'd met to that point— brilliant, creative, pushy in a good way, exacting. I was entranced. I was attending a university that had perhaps 300 Black students in an overall student body population of about 20,000 at that time. The majority, though not all, of the Black male students were athletes. I do remember being the only Black person in most of my recitation classes. In the large lecture halls, I'd see a couple of Black faces in the crowd. Gil invited me to join him on his journey to found the Free Southern Theater. His discipline, his unrelenting passion for the project became the theater's guiding force and certainly pushed me out of whatever nest I'd been in.

As I hover over my past, I think buried deep in my psyche I knew I wanted to live a life of adventure, of change, of barrier-breaking not only in terms of the issue of racism in America but also as a woman. I was terrified of living a humdrum life. I glommed onto Gil's ambition to build a traveling theater in the Deep South. The very real threat of death there receded in my mind, allowing space for the idealistic, somewhat romantic notion of building a theater for folks who'd never seen live theater before, and all of it hand-in-hand with the Civil Rights Movement. I fell in love with the man and his ideas. My love was definitely founded on the anvil of pushing rocks out of the way to build a garden. It was an intellectual love rather than a sensual love. I believed the work would take me to a future that I wanted.

I returned to Ann Arbor in the fall of 1963 a couple of weeks before John F. Kennedy's assassination. We students converged on campus, many of us crying, totally unsettled. We with our dark thoughts and premonitions thought the world itself was heading for its final chapter. For the few Black students and our sympathizers, President Johnson was a Southerner and could not be trusted. We had much to learn. Come January, I registered for a full schedule for the spring semester. When I finished my finals at the end of May, it was time to go to Mississippi.

Before my journey to the Deep South, Gil came to Michigan to meet my family. Dad was compelled to buy him new clothes, something he joked about for years after. He wasn't particularly partial to the student-as-revolutionary look on Gil or on me. My dad was a fine dresser even when he relaxed. Gil may have been the only guy I ever dated with whom my dad couldn't find a comfortable playing field. Dad wasn't impressed with fluent French or acoustic guitar. And talking about going to the Deep South only gave him anxiety.

When my mother learned that I was heading south, she basically stopped speaking to me. I was leaving the University of Michigan to go where? To do what? I'd surely lost my mind. I was about to kill a dream she'd had for herself and then sacrificed in the hope it would be fulfilled by me and her other children.

Gil and I married in New York City at the American Place Theatre with an African dance and drum troop leading us down the aisle. After the ceremony, we ate cake and danced to a recording of Miriam Makeba singing "The Click Song." We danced and danced. Gil left for Mississippi and I took one more trip home, and in mid-June I boarded a train for Jackson.

What I didn't know initially was that I was an artist, too—an artist who hadn't yet found her space. At Michigan, I'd moved toward the arts, tepidly—never letting go of political science. I tiptoed in by taking art history classes, performing a play in Spanish in the Romance Languages department, eagerly seeking out European films when they made it to America. Francois Truffaut's *Jules and Jim* marked a key place in my development. I'd never seen or read of a character quite like the female lead played by Jeanne Moreau. I'm sure many others had the same response to this exquisite film.

We were young, idealistic, thirsty to grow beyond whatever confines, obvious or more subtle, might hem us in. We wanted to be free and we wanted to create, and we were willing to put our lives on the line for those things. As important, we wanted Black people in the Deep South to have that freedom as well. Very soon the music in my ears and in my spirit was Freedom songs and even more so, Curtis Mayfield's "Keep on Pushin'" and Sam Cooke's "A Change Is Gonna Come"— my anthems of that period and with good reason.

And Gil, well, Gil did it all: acting, directing, writing, singing, guitar playing. His creative energy was the centrifugal force of the Free Southern Theater. He certainly was my creative model. Gil literally pushed me into acting and, by example, writing, back in the middle 1960s. I was absorbing, learning, growing in this new world of the theater. Gil pointed me in the direction of a career that excited me.

But somewhere in my overly romantic mindset, I began to learn a hard lesson—loving someone's creativity or intelligence isn't necessarily the kind of love that stabilizes a marriage when things go sideways. I have loved what a man created rather than actually loving the person himself.

7.

It was the beginning of Freedom Summer in Mississippi. June, 1964. The disappearance of Michael Schwerner, James Chaney, and Andrew Goodman added a profound urgency to the work of the Free Southern Theater, to the entire Civil Rights Movement. Early on, some Movement veterans whispered that they knew the three were already dead. The event put the fire in our bellies and the anxiety in our hearts. We had to ride on top of our fear and keep going.

Learning to act reminded me of when I was learning to drive. My dad sat me behind the wheel of his ginormous Cadillac and guided me to the expressway in Detroit.

"Aim the front of the car toward the white line and you'll stay in the center of your lane. Now drive." That made little sense to me, but I did it. Dad remained cool and calm. Cars whizzed by as I clutched the steering wheel for dear life. My head was stuck in the facing forward position. That's pretty much what I felt like going on stage as a novice.

The Free Southern Theater's first 17-city tour of Martin Duberman's *In White America* was in the planning stages, heading into rehearsal. Working in that play was my first complete creative immersion on the road to becoming an artist. Granted, I'd imagined myself in films, novels, writing, painting, being in love with Heathcliff, García Lorca (who wasn't even into women), and on and on. I made myself dizzy with my own imaginings.

Gil Moses's dedication to the work—acting, writing, building the theater, the discipline of the work—began to seep into my brain during our incredible journey in the South. We performed before audiences who'd never seen live theater before. Many had no radio and certainly no television. This little beacon of hope, the Free Southern Theater, operated in the midst of the Civil Rights Movement with the violence and insanity of Mississippi swirling around our heads. We were a mixed (integrated) group of young people, some with more theater background than others. We pulled it all together and got on the road. When a female actor scheduled to perform with the theater didn't show up, Gil pushed me onto the stage in her place.

Aside from a small role in a high school play and an even smaller role in a play performed in Spanish in the Romance Languages department at college, my entrance into the theater begins when I walked onto the stage in Mississippi for the first time. I had been rehearsing as an understudy, believing I'd never make it onto the stage during the run of that play. We were a tight knit group and my co-actors encouraged me and helped me conquer my terror.

We hit the road.

In McComb, a bomb was thrown at the stage during an outdoor performance. I was on that stage.

In Indianola, a 20-man contingent of the White Citizens Council (the Klan but in suits) came to our performance, scaring the daylights out of all of us. I was on that stage, terrified.

In Ruleville, we slept on the floor in Fannie Lou Hamer's house because bullets flew through there so frequently. I was on that floor.

In the village of Mileston, in Holmes County, we performed in a half-finished community center being rebuilt by three white contractors from California who had to be protected the entire time they were there. The original center had been burned to the ground because the Black people in that town aligned themselves with the Civil Rights Movement. The Black men of Mileston sat on their porches with shot guns across their laps so that we in the Free Southern Theater could get a night of sleep. They wanted to vote. What a hell to live in. What a cauldron to learn in.

The experience required a searing level of attention to survive, taught deep lessons about our history, about the core of this country. That experience lodged itself in my mind never to leave again. Concrete knowledge of the blood and bones of this country is survival material. There is an eternal war, I still feel, between the history of slavery and our present, whenever that is. Racism is still breathing in America.

I worked with the Free Southern Theater from June 1964 to September 1966. One brief break had me in the northern suburbs of Chicago, balancing an elegant teacup on my knee as I tried to convince a group of wealthy white women to support our theater. Another had me in Alabama eating curried goat under a massive tree with Movement folks and our theater members swapping tales and singing freedom songs.

In Mississippi, I was an apprentice actress, set-hauler, public relations helper, teamster, after-performance discussion assistant, prop girl. We carried our lights, sets, props, costumes, and selves around in a small truck and a station wagon. We printed new programs in each town. We'd check into the COFO office (Council of Federated Organizations)—

an amalgamation of SNCC, CORE, NAACP and any local organization involved in the fight for voting rights. We'd use their mimeograph machine to print programs, get schooled on the local situation—how voter registration was going, how the Klan behaved, were there Deacons for Defense and Justice in that town, who were the real bad guys and who were the good ones (were there any good ones)? What should we absolutely steer clear of under threat of death? Was there a soft spot in that town—a few whites who'd stepped out from behind the wall of hatred, people who wanted to be free of that burden they'd been carrying around for years? They did exist and when the theater came to town, those few white people would sneak into the back of the church for our performances and for our after-performance discussions. They were as terrified as we were. At the end of the program, they disappeared into the Mississippi night, sneaking and hiding their way home. They could not discuss with their neighbors that they'd been to a performance of the Free Southern Theater with Black and white people working together, singing Freedom Songs together, praying for safety and peace, praying for the vote for Black people in 1964, 100 years after the end of the Civil War.

Often, we'd end an evening at a local Dew Drop Inn for great jukebox music, fattening and wonderful soul food, dancing in our sweat-drenched jeans and shirts. Those jukeboxes featured soul music as in Black music, a gospel or two and gutbucket blues, too. We were full of idealism, wanting so much to make this world a better place for everyone. We knew and didn't know how profoundly hated we'd be, how entire groups of people find no issue with holding raw unabridged hatred in their hearts as they waved their Bibles in your face. That shocked me then and still does.

Jackson, Mississippi proved to be so oppressive that Gil and John O'Neal decided to move the Free Southern Theater to New Orleans so we could at least breathe a little easier. After Jackson, New Orleans felt like paradise—with a catch or two. Our apartments in the French Quarter were watched by the New Orleans Police Department. Their favorite shoeshine stand was across Burgundy Street from our two old smelly apartments complete with slave quarters in the back. When three SNCC photographers came to town and hung out at our apartments, the police went into action, manhandling the photogs, destroying their cameras and film, throwing them into the back of a squad car, and whisking them away. When I tried to intercede on behalf of the photogs, one of the officers put his gun to my head and threatened to blow my brains out if I moved an inch. I did not move. There I was, in the doorway of the building I lived in, with the barrel of a police revolver pressed against my right temple. I was shaking as I tried to keep an eye on the SNCC photographers, who'd been thrown into the back seat of the squad car. This moment that felt like a century never left my mind. I was as close to death as I've ever been.

The patrol car with the photographers pulled away from the curb. The cop lowered his gun from my head and told me to get lost. I ran up the stairs, shaking, to tell my theater pals of the arrest and of the gun to the head incident. Many years later, when writing my novel, *Freshwater Road*, I was able to use that incident when the voter registration group goes to the courthouse for their first attempt to register to vote.

When I see police persons with guns to people's heads who are on their knees, or any of the other horrendously terrifying behaviors that cops engage in, I remember my experience on a street in the French Quarter during the Civil Rights Movement.

Around that same time, a few of our Free Southern Theater members—Black and white—went to a famous

French Quarter restaurant for lunch. The waiter took orders from the Black folks. He said the law required him to serve us—but no law said he had to serve whites seated with Blacks. We were stunned. It took a few minutes to untangle our minds. We decided to head over to Dooky Chase's restaurant—home of some of the best authentic Creole cuisine in New Orleans and also a somewhat protected space for Civil Rights Movement workers.

During a Free Southern Theater rehearsal in a hall we rented, two young Black men came in and stood watching us. The entire energy in the hall subtly shifted. We actors openly stared at the two young men. We didn't know if we should be cautious, afraid or not. I had a distinct feeling of a blend of appreciating their extraordinary beauty mixed with a kind of low-level fear. They were Jerome Smith and Rudy Lombard. Rudy came to play an important role in my life until his death in 2014.

Both men had good looks. But what they had that most stirred me and the others, I think, was their extremely powerful sense of themselves as Black men. The energy they exuded was the polar opposite of the oft-spread image of Black men shuffling, jiving, ducking, and kissing behind to survive. Many of the young men in the Civil Rights Movement, I realized, had that same powerful quality. It signaled a profound change in the ethos of Black men specifically and Black people generally.

I couldn't identify what caused my anxiety that day. In fact, it took years of me going back in memory to that moment trying to figure out the complexity of what I felt. They presented themselves as men in possession of themselves, not owned by anyone including the system of racism they both lived in. They were not a bit threatening but they were not in any way frightened either. I identified something in them that became, in time, an important measure of how I thought a person was handling all that we as Black people have to handle on a daily basis. Emmett Till, I knew, was a self-possessed young man. Other Black men who present themselves to the world as self-possessed, conscious, clear about their manhood and their right to be in the space they occupy, have been murdered. The imperative had always been for Black men to "take low" to white men and white people generally. When they *didn't* do that, they were standing, more often than not, at death's door. And that is the terror Black women have felt over years and years each time a son, nephew, husband, lover who had a sense of himself as a man walked out the door. I know this because I have felt that terror.

Rudy's eyes were the kindest I've ever seen on a human being. Behind those eyes, there was a mind of steel, a dedication to Black people so strong that it made me afraid for him.

He reminded me some years later that our first meeting was in the Greenwood, Mississippi COFO office when the Free Southern Theater performed there. I'd come into the office parched, looking for water to drink. I soon learned that Rudy was a Civil Rights Movement veteran who did voter registration work in Louisiana's Plaquemines Parish and who eventually had to be clandestinely carried out of that place hidden in a coffin because the Klan wanted him dead. I wouldn't see him again for a couple of years.

Many folks bought into the mistaken notion that New Orleans was appreciably different from the more rabidly racist South. It's true there were pockets of relief in New Orleans. Pockets. Overall, lunch counters were yet to be desegregated, schools and libraries as well. Black people couldn't sit down in those famous restaurants for a meal prepared by the Black folks in the kitchen. Yes, there were scads of mixed-race people. Perhaps this presentation of local racial habits was even more pernicious than life in, say, Mississippi, because it made it so easy to let your guard down enough to make a life -threatening mistake. Try to imagine living your entire life on guard as if "one false move" could mean your total demise. That was life in the Deep South, and it still is in many back-wood places. Racism never seems to run out of steam.

The Free Southern Theater experience in Mississippi and Louisiana during the war for Civil Rights carved a layer of profound seriousness into my mind. I was metamorphosing into an artist, trying to shed that *a girl has to be a teacher, maybe a lawyer, certainly a wife* dictum of those days. I certainly had one foot tied to the past. My other foot was heading straight toward the future. My future. I wanted so much to believe that the Civil Rights Movement diminished racism in this country. I wanted the job to be done, finished, over. I was a bit delusional.

Even at the end of my journey with FST, I still didn't really know myself as an artist. I was struggling to get there. I knew I had a darkness, a profound sadness living in me. Some of that darkness grew with the knowledge that though my will to be free powered parts of my life, society had not readied us for the truly free woman. I ducked and dodged, trying to grab a lifeline for the free woman I was becoming, but there was nothing there. Or if there was something there, I couldn't find it. We grew up believing that women were less than men, that the Bible gave us all the space we needed. I felt my soul needed fuel, and I was digging for it. I found it extremely difficult, impossible, to be ruled by a man, or anyone for that matter. I paid a heavy price for that, then and since, but I'd do much of it all again in my will to be my own person. My internal struggles regarding my identity waned for a bit but they did not die. I slowly was carving out a place for myself but there were no straight lines. It has always been three steps forward, two steps back.

Gil and I went our separate ways. He had a fling with an actress in the company and I had a relationship with an actor. We separated in 1965 after one year of marriage. We divorced two or so years after that. In digging for things while writing this memoir, I found a smattering of correspondence with Gil from the early 1970s. I was by then working in television and he was directing theater in New York. We had come back around to friendship. I'd forgotten that, and liked the fact that we communicated a bit after the divorce.

My experiences in the Deep South during those years formed the emotional foundation for my novel *Freshwater Road*. It took me a little over three years to write that book, the hardest and most agreeable work I've ever done. When I look back, it feels like it poured out of me because of my passion both for the writing process and for the period of my life that evoked that story. It was grueling work; I composed it as I was learning the craft of fiction in a workshop with seven other writers of enormous skill and intelligence. However, writing the book so many years after the experiences that inspired it gave me a better understanding of the nature of my time in the Deep South. To understand Mississippi was and is to know our journey in this too often unfriendly place.

As I wrote in *Freshwater Road*:

> What difference did it make where in Mississippi she was? Emmett Till had been in Money, Medgar Evers in Jackson, Herbert Lee in Liberty. Ambushed and shot, beaten to death and thrown into a river for organizing for voter registration, standing up to

any white man for any reason, accusations of wink-
ing, eyeballing, whistling, raping a white woman
whether proven or not . . . Pineyville was in no way
special.

I speak of my time in the South as a kind of branding,
surrounded by dark-eyed people and too many ghosts to
name. Shallow graves erupting with memories of lynching,
rape, forced amputations, separated families, fear and anger
stacked on top of one another like a wobbly chimney reaching into the sky. And somewhere in that agonizing stew, there
was beauty—in the trees, in the souls of folks, in their eyes,
in their hesitant speech, in the magnolias and the hydrangeas
and the crepe myrtle trees.

Back in the day, I believed guilt raged beneath the surfaces of America. Now I see there is no guilt—there's only
a hatred that ebbs and flows like a river that has no end,
a hatred that never stays under wraps for very long. On
the news the day before I wrote these lines it was reported
that a Kansas City police officer, while arresting a Black
woman, called her an animal as he brutalized her. That's
straight from the slavery playbook. Of course, there's nothing unique about that news story—these stories of the
demented violence some police officers use in dealing with
Black people keep coming, and they tell any sane person all
one needs to know about racism in America. Police do what
they do in that regard because its acceptable to the powers
that be, no matter who they are.

I keep digging for the undertow, the deepest universal
reason for this unrestrained, never-ending hatred and violence against a people who helped to build this country.
The rationale, the undertow, may well be that white people
know when they mix with other ethnicities, they tend to

disappear *as white people*. If you see Black people as equal, the barriers crumble. Some whites circle their wagons to keep those barriers in place. The goal seems to be to protect their *whiteness*, the place of privilege they've created for themselves based on ethnicity. As I see it, that's pretty much the definition of racism.

8.

After two years of ducking the Ku Klux Klan, the White Citizens Councils, and the raw-boned hatred of far too many people—all as I hovered at poverty's door—my life's clock ticked me out of the Deep South. During the days of the Civil Rights Movement and to this day, Black lives, in far too many places, did not and do not matter at all.

The Free Southern Theater's poetry show, *Ghetto of Desire*, had been filmed and aired in New York City on CBS's Sunday morning show, *Look Up and Live*. Soon after, an invitation from Hungarian writer George Tabori and his Swedish actress wife Viveca Lindfors landed. The Taboris saw me in the televised show and reached out, asking me to join them in the production/tour of his new play, *Three Boards and a Passion*. That was my ticket out of the South. I cashed it in and departed. New York here I come! Again!

The play, compiled and developed by Tabori, was an elegant vanity piece for Ms. Lindfors who was a respected member of both the Hollywood and New York show business communities. The play featured duet pieces from classic plays. They brought in Harris Yulin to play opposite Ms. Lindfors on the mature side, with me and Free Southern Theater alum Roscoe Orman on the younger side. Roscoe later became a star on the television series Sesame Street. I thought the pairings clever. We rehearsed in New York and prepared to hit the road.

My first exposure to marijuana was smelling it as I walked across the quad in Ann Arbor. I did not know what it was until told by a fellow student. It was in the air. Later, a few of the Free Southern Theater crew were in Chicago to raise money for the theater. At a party of young like-minded folks, I actually inhaled marijuana for the first time. I then slid down the wall onto the floor, where I stayed for quite a while sleeping.

On the *Three Boards and a Passion* tour, one of the crew guys shared his marijuana. I, Denise Nicholas, took a few puffs one afternoon, sure that by curtain later that evening, I'd be fine. I wasn't. I wandered around the stage like a lost puppy. I managed to say my lines, though my eyes were at half-mast and my energy quite sleepy.

If your brains are not with you when you step onto a stage in front of an audience, more than likely, you're in trouble. If not for Roscoe Orman leading me around the stage, nodding and encouraging me to speak up, to move, to do anything to get through it, I wouldn't have made it. I've heard stories of inebriated actors giving stunning performances; I was not among that number. From that experience to this day, I have never puffed anything nor sipped anything while working. Some of our most highly successful actors were/are drunkards or some other form of addict: Anthony Hopkins, Bradley Cooper, Carrie Fisher, Richard Burton. Writers, too. Ernest Hemingway and F. Scott Fitzgerald come to mind and there are scads more. I'm a writer now—and still a drinker—but I couldn't find the keys on this keyboard if I kept a lovely Baccarat glass full of wine at hand to sip from while trying to work. It's strictly coffee, water, or lemon water within reach.

We toured *Three Boards and a Passion* to New Jersey, Pennsylvania, and Ohio, performing in university theaters. A few of my family members came to Cleveland from Detroit to see me in the play. One of the pieces I performed with Ms. Lindfors was Strindberg's *The Stronger*. To reprise the play: Two actresses meet at a café. The older actress has married and, seemingly retired, now has a child and a home, the usual circumstance for a woman of the early 1900s. It's Christmas Eve and the younger actress is alone, circumstances that amounted to a sure sign of profound loneliness in that era. She does not speak during the brief play. She responds to the older woman in verbal silences, responding emotionally nonetheless. The older actress bares her anger and grief at nearly losing her husband to the younger actress. She's fearful that the younger woman may be still on the prowl for her husband. She verbally attacks the younger woman, accusing her of being a conniving bitch. Interestingly, the older woman has learned much from the younger woman and uses those wiles to reinvest in her own marriage. Dated but surely interesting.

Being the silent one, to me, was infinitely more challenging. But there I was, a very young, barely professional actress sitting opposite a pro, trying to stay afloat. She basically wiped me off the stage. My grandma in the audience didn't understand the structure of the play, that only one character speaks. My dad told me after the performance that he had to contain her because she wanted me to speak, to fight back.

"Why doesn't Denise answer her?" According to my dad, she asked that question three or four times during the performance of the short piece, getting more exasperated and louder each time. He tried to explain to her that only one character speaks. She couldn't grasp the concept and was raring to storm the stage. If I have any spunk at all, that's where it comes from.

I arrived back in the city at the tour's end anxious to begin my New York life. Working with Ms. Lindfors and the others had upped my game. I was no longer in the novice artist category, but there was still a distance to go. I'd picked up an accent from bouncing around the Deep South and I worked hard to not allow that accent to creep into *Three Boards and a Passion.* But I liked how that Southern accent rolled off my tongue—little bits of it, a word here, a word there. The Creole accent, unlike the Southern accent, to me, is sexy, rich, and beautiful. Some years later I spent time trying to reintegrate it into my speech. But in New York, at that particular time, I had to drop any hint of Southernisms. Each character places different demands on the actor.

My next stop was with Joe Chaiken's Open Theatre, working in improvisations. During my Free Southern Theater years, Gil Moses had tapped the brilliant improviser Severn Darden from Second City in Chicago to come to New Orleans to run an improvisation workshop with us. Severn demonstrated the possibilities of improv by doing his *A Mouse in a Cello.* It was magical, and I relished expanding on what I'd learned from him

From the Open Theater workshop, I was cast as a replacement in their production of *Viet Rock* at the Martinique Theatre, off-Broadway. That was right up my alley as I was passionately against that war. Too soon, I experienced my first New York theatre closing night on New Year's Eve, 1966. I walked out of the theatre into the cold night air without a job. In the back of my mind, a sneaky thought refused to sleep: *I'm not sure I can take this road I'm on. I'm out here on this cold dark street with not two nickels and nowhere to go to celebrate the New Year. I'm not liking this.*

I was forced to do what artists of all types are forced to do at varied points in a career—get a job doing anything that offered a payday to help stay afloat. My extra outside skill set was office work. In high school, back in the days of typewriters, my stepfather insisted I take typing so I wouldn't have to ask others to type my papers when I got to college. Best advice ever.

Soon after, the Judson Poets Theater offered me an acting job in a poetry show. Two of the people who came to see that show were Robert Hooks and Douglas Turner Ward who were setting up the Negro Ensemble Company. Based on my work in *Viet Rock*, my performance with the Judson Poets Theater, and my two years with the Free Southern Theater, I was accepted into what would become the original company of the NEC. That is the true beginning of my professional career, and it changed the trajectory of my life. In the meantime, though, I was penniless and begged for an office job in the original NEC offices above the Victoria Theater on Broadway. That saved my derriere.

The NEC was the brainchild of Hooks, who was already enjoying a busy career as a Broadway actor and film and television star. He'd previously founded the Group Theater Workshop in 1964. Now, along with playwright/actor/director Ward and Gerald Krone on the business side of things, he set out to establish a theater company at the St. Marks Playhouse at 133 Second Avenue on the Lower East Side. I still get butterflies remembering the electricity in the air surrounding this momentous happening. When the news hit the street that the NEC had been awarded a Ford Foundation grant, all of the Black actors in New York City turned their attention to the St. Mark's Playhouse.

We began with an intensive training program. The goals included knitting the 13 original actors into a unit that could carry a season of varied plays: William Jaye, Hattie Winston, Rosalind Cash, Norman Bush, Francis Foster, Arthur French, Moses Gunn, Clarice Taylor, Allie Woods, Esther Rolle, Judyann Johnson, David Downing, and yours truly. We trained in movement for actors with dancer Louis Johnson, affectionately called *Thunder Buns*. When he moved across the floor demonstrating what we should do, his elegant heft gracefully owned the space. We loved watching him move. Our acting teacher was the late Paul Mann, with whom we did scene work. The brilliant Kristin Linklater contributed her expertise on the actor's voice. Her exercises helped especially the younger ones to get on top of our nerves, which do restrict the voice.

The hard work was the gift. This was no *come when you feel like it* course of training. It was the first phase of the job. To say it was fabulously demanding says it all. It was also, at times, frightening. It asked us to push against our individual limitations and insecurities. The intensity challenged us and aimed us in a direction—the direction of ensemble.

The Song of the Lusitanian Bogey by German writer Peter Weiss (author of *The Aesthetics of Resistance*) was our first production, directed by Michael Schultz. We opened the NEC's first season on January 2, 1968. This production laid out a dedication to the truths of history, and a translation of those truths that could be told from the stage. Preparing this show was like going to university. We did graduate level research on the European rape of Africa, from natural resources to human beings. We studied the history that informs the play before putting one foot on the stage for rehearsals, focusing on the Portuguese in Africa: *Lusitania* is an ancient name for Portugal.

Coleridge-Taylor Perkinson's score lit up the St. Mark's Playhouse, and we all put our very best work onto that stage.

The reviews were spectacular. We came out of the gate a winner.

The remaining productions in that first season were Nigerian playwright Wole Soyinka's *Kongi's Harvest*, Richard Wright's and French writer Louis Sapin's *Daddy Goodness* (*Papa Bon Dieu*), and Australian playwright Ray Lawler's *Summer of the 17th Doll*. We were on the theater map of New York in our very first season, blazing with the glory of exceptional talent popping out all over the place.

Walking down Third Avenue one bright sunny day, coming toward me I recognized the same tall, handsome, regal Rudy Lombard whom I'd first met a few years earlier in Mississippi. That chance meeting on a warm day on the Lower East Side began a friendship that teetered back and forth between a profound love and my inability to consistently inhabit the space where profound love lives. I was an actress in a business that has more than a bit of slime attached to it. Women are treated better now in this industry than when I came through the tunnel. Rudy, on the other hand, was a Civil Rights Movement honcho. His self-confidence and lack of fear during his time in Mississippi and Louisiana tell the story. He was dedicated to the fight for the vote for Black people and for the lives of Black people in places where death loomed around every corner. He was unrelenting in his dedication to the Movement and to humanity in general. I was drawn to him, I think now, because he sensed my fragility, my lack of a good foundation in ways beyond books and movies. I was a very insecure person who managed to sell herself as anything but in an industry that demands selfishness and hardness. We never had that conversation, but we lived it. He was the first person beyond my father who seemed to be trying to bolster my inner self, my spirit, my heart. I was the girl with the pretty face and smile that hid the terror I felt most of the time (these realizations came much later). I believed him to be as close to sainthood as humanly possible. I was not that. Nor did I want to be that.

I never felt worthy of him until many years later, after much therapy, and by then it was too late. I felt deep inside that I would disappear. To my fragile emotional self, he seemed beyond me. His independence and inner strength frightened me, I think. I put him on a pedestal that precluded any possibility for a healthy long-term relationship.

Rudy became a fan of the NEC, coming to all of our shows over the time that I was in the company and beyond. He remained connected to my life either closely or at a distance, but always there, until his death in 2014. For a brief time, we had a profound love relationship. He spent time in Los Angeles. I spent time in New Orleans. We drifted apart. He wasn't a fan of Hollywood, and I was running from ghosts trying to find a safe place to land. I think now, too, that I was terrified of poverty. I wanted to have my own money, my own property, my own everything. I wanted to be successful, I wanted to live well, I wanted to travel. And that's what I aimed for. I did better at work than I did at love. No doubt.

This brief time was also when I felt most tossed away by my mother. She emotionally disowned me when I went South. She was excellent at very basic things but I did not know—yet—the reason she never ever gave me the emotional support that I needed.

Even in her dementia, she said to me recently, "You didn't think I loved you. But I did and do." Maybe she did. She didn't show it beyond the basics. I needed more. I felt I was out of place in my family and in my life. She did nothing to assuage those anxieties. Her own guilt about my birth shut her down where I was concerned.

In the 2020s, this time of book banning, historical erasures, and pretense that recorded horrors didn't actually happen, *Song of the Lusitanian Bogey* would be denied or picketed, or slammed by critics, as it was in London during the NEC's first European tour. Ripping the scab off colonialism definitely brings out the defenders and sympathizers of that nightmare. Defenses of colonialism's horrors do nearly as much damage as its original sins, prolonging the darkness, the anger, the pain, the feeling of being invisible.

For the run of *Bogey*, we were charged individually with learning one other actor's pieces in case of sickness. I was given a significant piece to learn in addition to "my" parts. I rehearsed my standby piece a thousand times. I knew it. But I'd never performed it before an audience. And when I did, I went up on the lines. Everyone on the stage was struck dumb. The terror in the theater was stunning. It took years to put that nightmare into a lockbox of no regret.

That night, there were a couple of major talent agency reps in the audience. We on stage had no idea of who was out there in the dark. As it happened, that living nightmare excited the interest of one of them. I found out later those agency reps were there specifically to find actresses to test for the role of guidance counselor Liz McIntyre, on the new ABC series, *Room 222*.

The agency rep reached out to me and set up a first reading at ABC headquarters in New York City. It was hard to fathom why they reached out to me after I went up on the lines and nearly tanked the show. When I think about it, I believe it was the fact that I was doing well before the line fiasco, but more importantly, I had to stay the course, finish the performance as if the horror never happened. I recovered in front of their faces. That terrifying incident led, eventually, to my television career. Sometimes our failures or missteps push us to a greater understanding, to a different and better track for ourselves.

There were other actresses in the company who read for the role. ABC and 20th Century Fox, I found out later, read actresses all over the country. From that in-person audition, I was selected to fly to Los Angeles for a screen test. I wanted that job, so I basically put cotton in my ears for anything else and went for it.

From that moment, my position in the company changed. It wasn't easy. Jealousy is real and actors are great carriers of the jealousy genes, me included. Because I never felt that I deserved one fabulous thing that happened to me until years later, I nearly tried to apologize for winning. I see, looking back, that as weak-kneed as I was about some things, I must've had steel in my veins because I never stopped trying.

Billy Dee Williams got a screen test for the role of Pete Dixon, the high school history teacher and series lead. We tested together. I was so sure he'd get the role and I wouldn't, because he had had so much more experience. The late Lloyd Haynes won the role of Pete Dixon.

Imagine: I'm flown to Los Angeles, first class, my first trip to the West Coast. I'm picked up at LAX by a liveried driver who grabbed my bags and escorted me to a long black limo. Inside the elegantly scented limo, there was space for at least five more people. I was pretty thin in those days so I barely took up space for one. He delivered me to the Beverly Hillcrest Hotel on Pico and Beverwil Drive, a few blocks from then 20th Century Fox studios. A representative of the agency I was signed to at that time waited for me at the hotel to give me my marching orders for the next day's screen test.

He was so good looking I thought he was a movie star. All of this before my 25th birthday.

Not long ago, I was driving back from the ocean down Pico Boulevard, and sat staring at what used to be the Beverly Hillcrest Hotel. It's still a hotel, now called Cameo Beverly Hills. Back in the day when I stayed there, the bar and the restaurant felt very old-school Hollywood. I drank at the bar and ate at the restaurant, which was excellent then, and the entire wait staff had been notably tall, thin Black men wearing black uniforms, as elegant as you'd ever want to experience. I asked the bartender on my second trip there who were the men waiting on tables. He told me they were all retired Pullman porters. My jaw dropped.

On screen test morning, my instructions were to be ready for pick up at six. I hammered that scene into my brain seven ways to Sunday, and I struggled to get any sleep the night before. In my young days, skipping sleep (I loved to dance so I missed quite a bit of sleep) didn't show on my face the way it does now. I need to sleep 10 hours to even remember what I used to look like. In the mirror the next morning, I looked fine.

I got the job on *Room 222,* but only after being flown out to Hollywood for a second time to film a personality test. This required that I stand looking directly into camera and talk up a breeze about anything and everything. Over the years, I've thought of various reasons for that test. I think it revealed one's potential ability to yammer on and on at press briefings on promo tours for the television series, and on nationally broadcast talk shows, which was an important part of the job. I could talk fine. But this was 1968, so there may have been another issue in play here: the network wanted to be sure I presented as a well-educated, middle-class young Black woman.

In those days, I was out and about every time I could manage it. I loved hanging out, loved dancing, loved being admired by too many men. But, for the most part, I behaved within wide margins of good behavior. Let's put it where it needs to be. I had a good time during those early years. And, thank God for birth control pills.

For the two years I'd worked with the Free Southern Theater in the Deep South, I did not even think about television. I had not a clue what that world was or could be. While in New York, working in theater, I did not own a television. All of a sudden, I'm in the world of television in a big way. As a young person, my brother and I watched television at our grandparents' home. But I arrived in Hollywood not owning a television, not understanding really how pervasive its influence had become.

For my personality test, I did a comedic presentation, a "fish out of water" telling of my sojourn in the Deep South. There were howls of laughter on the sound stage as I somehow found uproarious humor in being chased around by the Klan. Producer Gene Reynold's jaw dropped. All these years later, I doubt I could even approach what I did that day. I don't even know where that approach to the story came from.

After *the personality test*, I remained in Hollywood doing guest appearances on a few shows—*The FBI*, *Marcus Welby M.D.*, *To Catch a Thief*, and a small role on *Night Gallery*—before being shipped back to New York City to face a major decision about my place with the Negro Ensemble Company. My dream at this juncture was to go back and forth working in television in LA and in New York continuing at the NEC during my breaks from filming.

Doug Ward had a different idea, one derived from his idea of building an ensemble and in time a repertory theatre. He basically sent me packing. I didn't get everything

I wanted, but *Room 222* assuaged my sad feeling about not getting it all.

Hollywood beckoned and I answered that call. Rudy and I stayed in touch wherever I was, wherever he was. Each of us had other relationships going and not going. There would come a time when his presence in my rickety life meant everything. I only wish all the therapy I managed to get later had been done earlier. He was way beyond me. Maybe he should've been the man of my life, but I wasn't anywhere near ready for that. He became my never-ending dream and always remained a friend. I began working on myself during this time, edging toward therapy, but I was wallowing in the dark, a second-guessing bundle of insecurities. I never felt I was good enough for Rudy because he seemed to me to be almost god-like. As a younger woman, I read a ton of romantic fiction. *Wuthering Heights* haunted me. I tended at times to see my own life through the characters in these books and the films of these books.

I packed up everything I owned and moved to Los Angeles to do a television show. I did the work well. I traveled over this entire country doing promotions for the show, as did the other main cast members. But in my heart of hearts, I truly thought my talent and my looks would lead me to film, which I loved. As time passed, the racism in the country and in the industry began to eat at me. I was in a box. I wanted to work in high-quality film projects. Increasingly, I wanted to write. But it was too soon for me. It's still a struggle for a Black actress to have a full career, but it does happen now. There are Black actresses starring in television series as the leads, and in films as well, and Black women writing and producing television, film, and theater.

I rented a television for the lovely studio I found at the French Hill Apartments on Olive Drive just south of Sunset with patio and pool—a far cry from the hole I lived in on the

Lower East Side, with the tin "bathtub" in the kitchen and rodents behind the walls scratching all night long. Was I in heaven or what? Sometimes leaving is the most excellent thing.

I also rented a car and my first big drive alone in Los Angeles was to a dentist in the valley to deal with an impacted wisdom tooth. I'm chuckling at the metaphor. Wisdom? Really? I will never forget driving on the 405 freeway for the first time. To this day I do not know how I made it out there and back without incident.

In working on this book, I decided to drive over to see the old French Hill Apartments. Not what it used to be. Back in the day, actors working on long term film projects cycled in and out of the French Hill Apartments. It was a friendly place for celebs— I remember meeting Jon Voight and Donald Sutherland in the parking garage.

Once I was moved in, my dad came out to LA to check on me and stayed at my French Hill apartment, which I'd swiftly upgraded from a studio to a two-bedroom with a full kitchen. That was over a Thanksgiving holiday in 1970. I'd been charged with cooking my first turkey which he and I planned to carry over to my studio hairdresser's house for dinner. Ann Wadlington became a close friend and years later came to Georgia to work on *In the Heat of the Night*. Her heart gave out and she died there while we were working.

Well, I cooked that turkey with the little bag of giblets still in the cavity. Dad chuckled at my culinary ineptitude. That night, I was more interested in the dressing up part, wearing the item everyone was wearing who could wear them—*hot pants*. I had an elegant pin-striped hot-pants suit. My dad, being my dad, invited me to change clothes and calm down my makeup before he'd let us walk out the door. Just like he'd done years before when I went on a first date: "Go upstairs and clean your face before you walk out this door."

9.

I BECAME A TELEVISION CELEBRITY PRACTICALLY OVERNIGHT. There was no handbook. It was learn as you go and try not to make a fool of yourself. As much as I wanted to win the job on *Room 222*, I had deep anxieties about disengaging from the theater. I wanted to hold on to it, and I tried. That part of my desired journey didn't work. For that time, it was television and only television. As I mentioned earlier, I didn't own a television in New York City, so I was a newbie—with an attitude. After all, I was coming from a hugely successful theater company in New York, that had received wonderful reviews during its first full year of production, from *The New Yorker,* the *New York Times,* and other big-time outlets. I already had something to be extremely proud of when I landed in Hollywood. I was on the map. But the theater map did not compare to the television map. Not even close. If you lived outside the immediate environs of New York's theater world, you were as unknown as you were when you first stepped off the bus. Television changed all of that, quickly.

With *Room 222,* James L. Brooks created the most ethnically diverse series ever to hit America's television screens to that point. We premiered on ABC in September 1969, with the roaring, turmoil-laden '60s nipping at our heels.

Martin Luther King Jr. and Robert F. Kennedy had been killed the year before. In the South, whites fumed in response to the Voting Rights Act and other results of the Civil Rights Movement. The Vietnam War picked up steam and protest against it raged right along with it.

I believed, briefly, that our show reflected profound changes in American society, changes that augured a new era. I hazard that *Room 222* wouldn't have happened at all if not for the Civil Rights Movement and the fight to integrate the schools in this country. But in the years that followed, the issue of integrating public schools tore cities apart and, in the end, that conflict has diminished the brilliance of our public education system. Over the decades, too many people have turned to homeschooling, private schools, charter schools, or any other kind of schools rather than integrated public schools, filled with children of varying ethnicities learning and being together even when they disagree. Racism killed public education, more so in some states than in others. Every school I ever attended was mixed—maybe not to the degree that would have re-educated the entire population about ethnicity, but I can and have worked with all kinds of people. I consider myself richer for the experience.

Room 222 was the first show Brooks created himself, while still in his late 20s, the year before *The Mary Tyler Moore Show* made him one of the most successful producers in TV, and a decade before he launched his career as a movie director. On our set, Stage 10 at 20th Century Fox Studios on Pico Blvd., there was camaraderie all day every day. We lived in a kind of benign bubble. My co-stars Lloyd Haynes, Karen Valentine, and Michael Constantine, and all the actors playing the students on the show, were all dreams to work with, each from a different place in this country, each excited to have been chosen for this new venture. We felt we were the hope for the future in many ways—young, good looking, hanging out, working hard, living the Hollywood dream so many coveted.

It mattered that this particular show's diverse cast featured rarely seen (at that time) educated Black people in positions of authority. The history teacher played by Lloyd Haynes and my guidance counselor character were respected members of the academic and social communities of the show. The students of varying ethnicities, each with their own personal challenges—growing up being key among them—provided a rich platform for stories. We touched on current events—poverty, politics, parental mismanagement, death of loved ones—and spoke to the realities of life in big-city high schools at that time, often with a light touch and with much compassion.

The show as Brooks created it challenged the staff writers to deal with the issues of the day in light-hearted but often revelatory ways. Give people an answer, maybe not a universal answer but an answer that would calm the soul and mind. Give them chuckles to grease the skids, and give consolation to support them. If there's a comedic way to get into and out of an issue, by all means use it, but please don't laugh away the depth of the issues and the needs of the audience to understand while they're being entertained. It was a tall order and most of the time, I believe, we hit the marks. The show was thoughtful and wistful; it sought truth, but never skimmed over the difficulties of young life. And as I said, all of it with not just a light touch, but a *kind* touch.

Room 222 at its premier and immediately after felt like a rocket into space. We had youthful energy and when you do a series, that energy is a requirement. I felt that some of my theater friends believed I'd *sold out*. There's a wonderful haughtiness about serious theater people. I'd wanted to get to that point in New York, but television conquered me. In truth, I didn't think I was a strong enough actress for a big career in theater. I always had a little lump of fear in me. I think in my heart of hearts, I wanted there to be another option. I wanted to do film. I knew that my looks and my skill level would work in film.

My little face on ABC blew the roof off my home life. I think my mother was elated and also a tad jealous. And probably very fearful. There I was, chatting with Johnny Carson for all the world to see: her bastard-illegitimate child making a mark on the landscape in spite of my embarrassing beginnings. She may have been terrified that all of the attention I was receiving would reveal the big secret. At this time, I still did not know the truth myself.

My dad was over the moon. I remember a trip home to Detroit during a later year of *Room 222* when Dad and I went bar hopping. We entered one of his places just as Elton John's "Benny and the Jets" played. Dad's joy was never diluted by old facts. He'd let that go years before, and it never entered our world until I got the news from my mother and asked him about it. In his mind and the minds of his cronies, I was Miss *Room 222* and nothing else mattered.

By the end of season one, I began noticing that there were no Black writers at the writer's table. That was a real head-scratcher. There were a number of Black characters on the show, which translated to me that there should be one or two Black writers involved somehow.

I began a soft campaign to get at least one Black writer on staff. I pushed enough that Gene ultimately set up a trip to New York City so I could introduce him to every Black writer I knew in New York at that time. Lloyd Haynes had other issues with the writing staff. There was one female writer at the table that he had an issue with. He fussed about her—but not about the lack of Black writers.

This was a kind and gracious move on Gene's part. We gathered at the Fox offices in New York City. There were about eight Black writers assembled, most of whom have passed on now. However, not one of the writers was given a shot. Though good writing is good writing, the tools and training needed to master the technical aspects of writing for camera were not as accessible as today. That was another hill yet to be crested. I was deeply disappointed. Soon after, I began submitting story ideas for *Room 222* myself, but could not get in that door.

Many years later, Gene called to congratulate me for the great reviews he'd read of my novel *Freshwater Road*. He told me he knew then that I'd been serious about writing all those years ago. I appreciated the call. Gene Reynolds, like Jim Brooks, had a skyrocket career in TV after *Room 222;* his next project was the legendary *M.A.S.H.*

Doing a series will make you very strong or it will bring you to your knees, or both. The hours are long and the work can be tedious. On one scene Karen and I were doing, the clock had ticked past the normal end of the day. We weren't struggling with the scene because of emotional difficulty but because we kept giggling while the camera was rolling. We did take after take trying to get a handle on our silliness. I think that evening we did close to 20 takes for a very short scene. I have not a clue in my memory bank as to what that scene was about. Whatever it was, we keyed into each other's funny bones and giggled our way into overtime.

I did talk shows promoting *Room 222* and myself, of course. I even had the temerity to sing on the Johnny Carson show in New York while on a break from filming the series. My play sister, Marcia Stevenson, went to the Carson show with me and sat in the audience having a heart attack because she knew what I knew. *I was not a singer.* I can laugh about it now, but that day, I was a wreck. However, I looked good, thankfully, and that took some of the heat off my middling performance. What possessed me to think I could sing on national television? I hit all the notes but my terror had to be on my face or at least in my eyes.

I wanted to do film, and with my toehold on television with *Room 222* and a couple of earlier guest shots on the *The FBI* and *It Takes a Thief,* I became anxious to push forward with movie work while on hiatus from *Room 222.* I looked around and what I saw wasn't exactly what I had in mind for myself. Having said that, I was ready to push for film. The Black Exploitation period of American cinema was rolling. For Black women, there were roles opening up. Most of them required some level of nudity, so that wasn't going to happen for me. Strict instructions from Dad: "Do not let me walk into a movie theater and see your naked ass up on that screen." End of story. Really, though—I was appalled by the product. I had somehow convinced myself that we as a people had graduated from the old-timey disparagements often seen with us in film. I guess my head was full of the wonderment of the Civil Rights Movement. I had conned myself into believing that we had arrived. This period in film history provided work for many fine actors. But the material being done, for the most part, left much to be desired. One movie about drug dealers is plenty. One movie about violence in the "'hood" is enough. How about a movie about violence in Mississippi?

I did get hired on *Blacula.* Years later, I was working on a film project in Toronto, Canada and the crew guys recognized me from *Blacula,* telling me it was a classic hit in Canada. I appreciated that. Back to television.

Each project added to my confidence even if the material was lowbrow. Actors want to work, so we withhold judgement until after we get paid. There really wasn't much to go on for "leading lady" Black women. Over the years, my looks seemed much more important to what was happening in my personal life than in my professional life. Men certainly let me know how they felt about my looks. Women sometimes shied away from me because of them, back in the early days before I began the slow fade that we all experience. Perhaps I'm delusional on this.

People have said to me that with my looks, I should've been this or I should have been that. Sure. If I'd been white. My looks meant little or nothing in this industry because of race. Period. I wanted something more but I couldn't get it at that time.

From the time I was a tiny tot, people have remarked on my looks. I learned as I grew to maturity that my looks seemed to fascinate people. I'm mixed. From DNA analysis, I know now that I'm more than half Northern European (Irish) and the remainder Nigerian. In the 1970s, being told I was beautiful had a strange knot in it. In this country, to be Black was to *never* be beautiful. That was reserved for the Nordics. Certainly, Lena Horne, Dorothy Dandridge, and others were recognized beauties. But they struggled in a business that didn't allow too much Black to be beautiful. Hollywood has always kept a tight grip on who's beautiful and who's not.

Even as I became famous, I receded into the private part of myself that is my writing self. I will find a way to be that self no matter what else is going on. When I'd tried to wiggle myself into the writing room on *Room 222*, and it hadn't worked, that still did not stop my passion for writing. I began to see that writing gave me so much more satisfaction than many of the roles I was able to snatch. I began writing ideas for series and ideas for episodes of various series, and I continued writing rather dreadful poetry. Every once in a while, though, I'd hit something wonderful with a poem or a story idea. It was during this period that I first began thinking about writing something that reflected the experiences I'd had in the South during the Civil Rights Movement.

We on the cast and crew of *Room 222* worked our fannies off. We fussed, we laughed, and we cried together. Did we agree on everything? Absolutely not. But we stayed in a team-like frame of mind even when the going got tough, and gradually got to know each other better.

The 20th Century Fox lot was right next door to the Century City Mall. In fact, the mall was built on what had been Fox studio land. Karen Valentine and I escaped the sound stage on occasion to traipse around the mall. We wore our costumes and makeup and roamed in and out of stores spotting possible wardrobe "likes" that we'd tell the wardrobe people about. Early on people began recognizing us and doing double-takes when they saw us on our wanderings.

One of our big shared responsibilities to the show and the network was to do promotional tours. Karen and I did a promotional trip to Seattle, and after our talk shows and racing around the city doing press, our hosts took us to dinner at the Space Needle restaurant. Karen and I ran our mouths, imbibing too much wine, having a swell time. Then we had to use the restroom. Off we went to find it as the Space Needle turned the restaurant ever so gently around, giving us spectacular views of the city and the port. We came out of the Ladies Room and our wine-soaked brains couldn't locate our table. We scurried around the restaurant first in one direction and then in the other. We really didn't know our companion-hosts, so it could be that we got close to them, didn't recognize them, and went off in a different direction. When we finally found them, we were laughing hysterically

I traveled all over this country promoting *Room 222*, often with a 20th Century Fox chaperone. In New Bedford, Massachusetts, I learned the history of the Cape Verdean people and their journey to America. New Bedford, a town of Quakers, had been an Underground Railroad destination, a more or less free place for people of color to live and work. It had been the center of whaling, the city of Herman Melville's *Moby-Dick,* and Frederick Douglass's home for a few years. And there I was with a gold shovel surrounded by cameras as I made the first dig on a site that would be a community center and also home for the NAACP. I traveled to Detroit, Chicago, New York, St. Louis, Oklahoma City, Kansas City, Pittsburgh, Boston, and on and on to promote *Room 222.* I enjoyed the travel and mostly I loved promoting our show.

In some places we were treated with good manners, but we often had the distinct feeling that we were on shaky ground—that people were *struggling* to deal with us—a discomfort that could only be due to our mixed ethnicity. So many local media people had never dealt with Black folks on equal footing before. They'd never had to book, interview, and watch Black television celebrities on talk shows; they'd never had to come out to welcome us as we stepped out of long black limos with liveried drivers who'd wait for us out front. To be clear, there were many folks on those city-a-day promotion tours who grinned in happiness to see us coming in the door. And we loved our show and that kept us going regardless of the oddball things that were said to us from time to time, and the uncomfortable anxiety some people exhibited.

Over the five-year run of the series, we had to fight to get our Black hairdresser, Ann Wadlington, into the union so she could work on *Room 222*. We knew it wasn't her skill level keeping her out of the union. She was a brilliant hair dresser, a professional woman who owned her own business. We eventually got her in but it was a struggle. We did have a Black man on sound crew, Will Yarbrough. And there were only two Black directors—Ivan Dixon (at the time still fresh off his acting role on *Hogan's Heroes*) and Sid McCoy. Lloyd Haynes and I knew that Ivan Dixon wanted to bring his show in on time and slightly under budget, with the hope that he'd be invited back. We decided to test him. To help him feel at home on our set, Lloyd and I staged a fake argument. Filming stopped as we began fussing, but the clock kept ticking. We ran around the set hollering at each other, banging doors, throwing things. Ivan was mortified. When we thought he might have a nervous breakdown because he couldn't control us, we let him know we were playing. I'm sitting here writing this and laughing all over again. What a look of relief lifted his downcast face!

During my early *Room 222* days, a group of engineers at Boeing reached out offering me a speaking platform for a company luncheon event they'd scheduled. The honorarium wasn't to be ignored, and I agreed to participate as the main event. My manager at the time, Sal Bonafede, and I loaded into a limo and off we went to Boeing's offices in El Segundo. I'd worked on my talk, opening with a bit of Hollywood chit-chat and quickly segueing to the more serious issues of the day. I was ardently against the war in Vietnam and when they offered me the speaking gig, they didn't mention that they didn't want to hear anything about that. My talk was *all* about the war: Why were we there at all? What was this war really about? Why were Boeing's B-52s being used for carpet bombing? My anti-war stance wasn't a new thing with me. But apparently Boeing hadn't done enough research on me to understand who I really was. To them, I was the co-star of a popular new series, a well-spoken Black woman who more than likely was an empty vessel.

The tension in the huge event room mushroomed as I went on railing against the Vietnam War. There were a couple of negative yells from the attendees, but I had cut my teeth in Mississippi performing in small towns. These Boeing engineers did not scare me.

However, after one fairly loud threat whistled through the air—"Go back where you came from!"—Sal beckoned to me with an intense head nod that said, *we need to get the hell out of here.* I got it and wrapped up the talk and practically ran to our table, where Sal grabbed my arm and yanked me out of there and into the limo as the negative cat calls strafed our backs. Sal told the driver to step on it. There I was in Hollywood having an experience that mimicked my experiences in Mississippi and Louisiana a few short years before, ducking the Klan.

In a real sense, racism forces the response it gets. Racism is threatening. It's not simply the scraggy words of some old-school white person sitting on the porch watching life march by. Racism is a threat. Sometimes racism changes the air in the room because of the implied violence. Other times racism is the act of violence itself. It forces us recipients of racist threats—in your face or implied—to deal nonstop with an issue that we'd rather put to rest. But I've come to believe that will never happen in America, because so much of the skeletal structure of our country is based in racism. It's a sadness I carry with me every single day and think of nearly every single night. After all this time, after all these incredible people have died in this struggle, we're still fighting the same old tired battles.

These realities were never far from mind, even as our show was such a sign of progress. One day, I was in the restroom right after completing a scene, which was situated in an alcove just beyond one of the exterior doors to the sound stage. I was scrubbing my hands, and I remember I was checking my full makeup in the scratched, slightly rusted mirror. Men's voices in the alcove outside the bathroom door were just audible. The voices belonged to a few of the teamsters who drove us to and from locations or even around the studio plant itself. It was much easier for the assistant director to keep track of us if we rode with the teamsters to locations. For my part, I loved driving my car to 20th Century Fox, parking by my dressing room trailer or as close to Stage 10 as I could get.

"Monkeys taking over the business," one voice said.

"We need to throw them out of the cars on the freeway. Watch them get run over," a second voice spoke, chuckling.

"Niggers everywhere now," a third voice muttered.

I froze. Had I somehow ended up back in Mississippi? I was five years away from the time I spent there. Had I dreamed the entire thing? No—but perhaps I had dreamed that Hollywood was farther along in its journey away from its own racism, away from feeding stereotypes and blatant lies about Black people, Native American people, and Latin people to the entire world. That's what I prayed for and wanted to experience.

I returned to the set shaken. I shared my experience of that incident with Bill D'Angelo, one of our newer producers, and with Lloyd Haynes and Anne Wadlington. The Teamsters were at that time a huge and powerful union. Their racism goes back a couple of generations, if not more. At any rate, I shelved some of my relaxation after that incident. It does something to you to hear that coming from the mouths of people who hold your life in their hands. They drive you around. They are capable of opening a door and shoving you out of the vehicle.

By 1970, Hollywood had hoodwinked many of us into believing that it was a liberal place often supporting liberal causes—some from the heart and some for the camera. Black people have spent the decades since then searching far and wide in this country for any *liberal* doors to bang on. But what had been put on screens in this country ever since *Birth of a Nation* and up till quite recently had hardly ever been liberal. Films that succeeded with the American public often mirrored the existing racism by pretending we were not even here, or—even when we were seen and heard—at best depicted as something less than a white person.

That's pretty much what Hollywood did for many years. Black people would read tiny blurbs about Black entertainers in *Jet* or *Ebony* magazines, or in Black papers like the *Michigan Chronicle*, the *Chicago Defender,* or the *Amsterdam News,* or even sometimes in the bigger publications, which might include a little about Sidney Poitier in a photo with an article announcing his latest project, or there might be a photo of Sammy Davis Jr. with Frank Sinatra, or maybe Harry Belafonte, or Lena Horne, or someone from Motown.

Our crossing over from success in popular music to film and television had been fraught. Getting Black folks on nightly television doing anything beyond performing a stereotype took a good while. Nat King Cole's landmark show lasted less than one season. Regardless, we found hope, believing we were conquering Hollywood, however slowly.

And it was slow. Imagine this: in the late 1950s, when there was heated discussion about bringing *Porgy and Bess* to the screen, the producer Harry Cohn argued that one way to ensure the film's success would be to use all white actors in

Black face. When I read that I slid right off my chair onto the floor. At nearly the same exact time, Sidney Poitier and Tony Curtis starred in Stanley Kramer's *The Defiant Ones*. How could the same points of view be at large in the industry at the same time?

All along, we Black people were so anxious to see ourselves onscreen, so euphoric every time we saw any Black person at all, that we hugged the Black performer who made it to the screen regardless of what the imagery meant for us as a people. I love *Casablanca*. But when Ingrid Bergman's character refers to Sam, the performer played by Dooley Wilson, as a "boy," my heart sinks—over and over, every time I watch this film. Imagine every Black man in America seeing this wonderful film, hearing seeing an obviously grown man referred to as a "boy," internalizing that, knowing that in truth, no matter his age, he is seen as a "boy."

Of course, race and Hollywood weren't always simple and uncomplicated. On *Room 222*, our makeup man was Layne "Shotgun" Britton, a character from the old days of Hollywood who'd done make up on the 1959 *Porgy and Bess* film. He was a wild and crazy recovered alcoholic, and we all adored him. I had the thought in the back of mind that Shotgun might have been brought on board because he'd worked with Black actors before. He was a Southerner, with all the baggage that comes with that, but also something else.

Shotgun and his family took a liking to the entire cast. He became my protector, especially during the difficult period of my marriage to Bill Withers. I was invited to visit Shotgun's home, which I did. Shotgun and his wife and family had two live caged monkeys, one named Rap and one named Stokely. Of course, these names were borrowed from the Movement leaders H. Rap Brown and Kwame Ture, who at the time still used his given name, Stokely Carmichael. When I heard these names, I didn't know whether to laugh, cry, or burn the joint down. I had a hard time trying to put the warm and playful personality of Shotgun on the set together with finding this outrage in his home.

There's a lesson in this. What you see *ain't* always what you get. And, the reverse: What you get *ain't* always what you thought you saw.

I spoke to Shotgun about the implications of his pet names. I can't know what he felt in his heart when I chastised him about the insult to me and all Black people, whether they were involved in the Civil Rights Movement or not. I let him know I'd never enter his home again. But by the end of the series, he was as devoted to us as we were to each other. He would always speak the same admonition into my ears over and over when I was in his makeup chair: *Be good to yourself.* He knew that I needed work in that area. He knew well that I was in a situation that was dangerous and debilitating with my marriage to Bill Withers. He knew because there were times when I came to work a hot mess, exhausted from the arguing and carrying on at home.

Shotgun never stopped talking about my looks. He would cheerfully take a powder puff, put a tiny amount of power on it, and airily—without actually touching my face—wave the puff near my face then say, "You're ready, get out of my chair." Shotgun had worked with Frank Sinatra and adored him. That in itself gave me hope that Shotgun could grow. Sinatra was no mollycoddler when it came to racism, or at least that's what was reported from time to time.

During my early years in Hollywood, I felt it my duty to try to talk white people down from their racism if I detected it. My relationship with Shotgun lived on a more profound, complex level than might have been expected. I knew this man adored me, was protective of me. We talked deeply at times. He supported and encouraged me in leaving my marriage. I did push him on his old-school racist nonsense. *And he responded.* He did. But what does it really take to change people who've been living in their own ignorance for so long? They're comfortable; it's what they know and cling to. Then here comes a Denise trying to educate, to open the mind vault. I never stopped trying with Shotgun because somewhere in there, I knew there was a good heart. He showed it to me. That was tough.

We never know what folks have "at home," in terms of their upbringing. Shotgun was an older man who'd been born in Texas. You'd expect some of his gnarly beliefs.

Many years later, when I was working on *In the Heat of the Night* in Georgia, Shotgun passed. I flew home to LA for his funeral. He became so dear to me over the years because I could see that he cared about me, in a place where genuine caring is often scarce. I believe in my heart that the cast of *Room 222* opened his heart a bit more. It was obvious that he beamed with pride about being with us. That was the public face. I don't really know what the private face did after his experience with us.

Back in the day, before the entire travel experience became so onerous, I was rolling. I won a trip to Japan on *The Dating Game* TV show in 1970. The idea was that I'd be joined by my winning date on the trip. My date seemed to be a nice fellow, but I didn't do the show to find a date—I did it to get the trip. In fact, I only agreed to do the show in the first place after the producers agreed to send me on an *overseas* trip. I didn't care which sea—whether to the east or to the west. Sadly, my travel bug is no more. If I get myself to Santa Monica and sit there staring at the ocean for a while, I'm good. There are places in this world I'd love to experience. I just don't want to have to travel to get there.

The Dating Game trip was organized for cultural exchange and probably also for business interests of which I have no knowledge. I remember walking through the hotel lobby upon arrival in Tokyo. A Japanese photographer working in the lobby thought I was a model. I was nearly bone thin in those days and never was I caught without my three-inch heels. I'm not particularly tall, but I wore heels that put me into the tall-for-a-woman range of about 5 feet 9 or 5 feet 10 inches. I'd slipped on my heels in the car ride from the airport, understanding the value of making an entrance. I assured the photographer that I was not a model. I noticed then how tall I was compared to the indigenous folks. That height issue came home sharply when I attempted to use the very low-to-the-ground toilet in my hotel room. I had to grab the counter to hold on.

On the days we toured, I released my heels for something that could get me through the day upright. With the chaperone and the date, I roamed the Ginza shopping area and attended a Kabuki performance—in which the women are portrayed by the male actors called *onnagata*. I couldn't tell they were men—and I worked at trying to tell.

The next day, we took the train to Nikko to see the Toshogu and Futarasan-jinja shrines built in the 17th century. What struck me most from the brief wait at the train station and on the ride north was that there was no shoving, no pushing. We were in close contact but you never felt the body of another person. At that time (and, I hope, to this day), the Japanese were the most well-mannered people on the planet.

My heart was opened to the beauty and rigor of Japanese culture. The beauty of it made me dizzy—I suffered a touch of aesthetic overload. The rigor of it, I learned, would take years of study to fully understand.

Back in Tokyo, I had a cross-cultural experience that

delighted me and the other person involved, a waitress at a lovely shabu-shabu restaurant. We looked at each other and almost immediately began giggling and nodding at each other, which continued through the meal. The other lunch guests at the table probably thought we'd lost our minds, grinning and trying to connect, as though we were long-lost girlfriends. It was as if across the language barrier, the cultural barriers, the miles and the extraordinary history that our two countries shared, and whatever else separates people from such different places, we knew each other, had known each other for quite a while. It was a dear moment.

This trip to Japan was, in fact, my first "big" trip. I'd traveled to Puerto Rico, Jamaica, and the Bahamas to that point. Going to Japan opened the world to me, which is exactly what I wanted it to do.

Years after *Room 222,* I attended one of the big network soirees. I was working at the time on a short-lived, half-hour comedy called *Baby, I'm Back,* opposite Demond Wilson, who'd become famous on *Sanford and Son* not long after I was on *Room 222.* With my champagne glass held carefully, my fur coat around my shoulders on a very cool Los Angeles evening, and my size-small diamonds sparkling, I said hello to one of the network executives. We began the usual cocktail party chit-chat about work. When I mentioned that I was aiming myself in the direction of producing and writing, he turned on his heel and walked away from me while the words were still exiting my mouth. I remember clarity slamming into place in my mind: *The last thing he wanted to hear was some Black actress talking about writing and producing.* It's still a rough road, but there's been great and beautiful progress: Ava DuVernay, Lena Waithe, Gina Prince-Bythewood, Stephanie Allain, Debra Martin Chase, Kasi Lemmons, Neema Barnette, and more.

Yes.

10.

When my friend Clarence Avant died in 2023, it had been only four months since my brother Otto's passing and three months since Mildred Stevenson—my dad's significant other for too many years to count—passed. Memories flooded in.

Clarence passed at 92 years old. He'd lost his wife, Jacquie, two years earlier when she was shot during a home invasion robbery. We hadn't recovered our balance from that travesty. As a community, few of us managed to wrap our minds around this madness. Jacquie was a quintessential lady—elegant, kind, calm, and lovely. How could this happen? But happen it did. A hard-driving businessman, a husband, a father, Clarence was an innately conscious human being who understood our need as a community to be represented at the tables of power. He was a friend to many, admired, adored. Clarence used the word "motherfucker" so often, a pal who called soon after his death to discuss the news asked if Clarence had created the word. He didn't create it but he sure as heck owned it and relished releasing its rhythmic assonance with over-the-top finality. Clarence was an original with no copies in the works.

Back in the day, meaning the early 1970s, Clarence

donned his matchmaker hat and invited me to the Troubadour Club on Santa Monica Boulevard to meet and hear his new client Bill Withers. Clarence that evening was as happy as I ever saw him over many years. I saw early on that in some respects, he was like a father figure to Withers, or so it seemed. Clarence wanted a star recording artist and he put his energy into Withers as the found one. Their relationship went through its own travails as time passed.

I was in my second year on *Room 222* and even though I'd gained something like nationwide celebrity status, my understanding of the power of same was still limited at best. The invitation from Clarence had a tinge of matchmaking behind it, but even I realized that as a young, new celebrity, my presence there would add a bit of Hollywood sparkle to the moment. I wasn't a frequenter of that club, but I'd certainly been there before. Plus, I lived nearby. Off I went.

Bill Withers's music conquered me before our relationship actually blossomed. One might say, I think, that the music drew me in first. Folksy music with the guitar as the lead instrument reminded me of the music of the early 1960s. I loved Bob Dylan and other artists of the period. In Withers, I loved the mournful quality of his voice. "Grandma's Hands" brought tears to my eyes because I loved my own grandmas so much. "Ain't No Sunshine" may well be one of the sweetest songs ever written. Its lyrical simplicity sinks into your soul and hits the depths of a human experience.

Shortly thereafter, Bill and I began dating. He was tall, somewhat thin, and had an air of seriousness about him. I of course took all of that to mean he was deep, a poet of song. He was as close to a 19th-century bard as you could find. His spiritual home had to be Mount Parnassus. I was very good at creating my own backstory that had snippets of reality attached but not many. He was all of those things, but there were other things there that I could not see early on. I'm sure, if we could sit and talk about our time, he would have similar things to say about me. And, in his defense, behind this face, he could not see my own issues, my stumbles and my searches. I was an actor and had learned how to hide my truths.

We two were working people who could only see each other when we managed two minutes in the same space. He was on the road, and I was working at 20th Century Fox. On a hiatus from *Room 222*, I was able to go on the road with him—to New England in winter, the small city of Bangor, Maine. It became clear early on that what I imagined about him missed some important things—his sorrows, his dreams, his deeper needs, his fears. And, as is often the case, I think he assumed that my looks and my success meant I was agony-free. We were souls lost in the blizzard of our growing relationship, both wanting and needing an island of warmth, of understanding. But also, we wanted success. Thinking back, we terrified each other, I think.

We couldn't have come from more dissimilar backgrounds. Detroit, Ann Arbor, New York City, the Civil Rights Movement were my shapers. I knew nothing about the mind-set of country or small-town life. I'd run from it while in high school. Perhaps we both harbored a fear of the *big bad wolf* of Hollywood. Truly, I believe we both had a lot of fear, a cascading fear of being consumed by the industry, and not in a good way. One had to be smart and quick to stay on an even keel.

I traveled to London with him when Bill was performing with The Spinners. On that trip, Bill had an artistic melt-down during a rehearsal. Not sure what caused the explosion, but I'm sure my wanting to go sightseeing rather than sitting there listening to the same songs over and over in a rehearsal may have been a part of it. I was independently dependent, as I still am. I didn't see it as his work trip. I saw it as my chance to go to London for the first time and I was ready to hit the streets and the museums.

I got out of there to go shopping for the Wedgewood china that to this day sits in its lovely antique cabinet in my home. Artists exploding over many things at different times wasn't strange to me. I'd been around actors and writers practically my entire adult life at that point. I'd seen explosions from artists quite a few times before I met Withers. There was plenty to explode about during my journey with the Free Southern Theater, not the least of which was the constant pressure from white supremacists who'd rather see us dead. The pressure built up and it had to go someplace. Often the thing that precipitates the explosion is not the *raison d'etre* of the explosion. With artists, it's usually a lot deeper than what ends up in the air—as I'm sure it was with Withers and has often been with me. We are the odd mixture of boldness and frailty.

We returned to Los Angeles and things were mostly smooth for a brief time. I returned to my own work and he to his—performing, touring, promoting.

There's a magazine cover photo of Bill and me from the early days of our relationship. I stare at the photo's sweetness, the love in it. It is stunningly beautiful. Looking at it I'm to this day flummoxed by where it all went. I understand intellectually, but often there's not a ton of coherence in life.

Early on in our relationship, Bill and I made a quick trip to Detroit. I wanted and needed my dad's take on Withers. My dad had a sincere fondness for the man, though my dad was not a folksy kind of guy. Remember, Gil Moses arrived in my life with a guitar, wearing blue jeans. Dad befriended him—though he also took him out to buy him some *grown folks'* clothes. This was not my dad's milieu but he also loved show business and Withers's success fed my dad's ego a bit, though he was polar opposite. Even before the stop in Detroit, I had talked to my dad honestly about what appeared to me to be serious problems brewing in my relationship with Withers early on. He seemed to put it off to two young people trying to find the best field of play for our relationship.

We were two people who needed the security of a relationship but some element of our success as individual artists seemed to demand we be free. The push and pull in opposing directions yanked the joy out of it all for both of us. The tears (as in torn fabric) began to pile up.

In short order, Bill and I married, quickly, in Vegas. Clarence and Jacquie Avant hosted a small reception for us at their Trousdale home. Dad came out from Detroit to support me and to remind Bill that I was not alone in the world. He knew well that I needed familial support. I have a great photo of me and my dad from that day—smiles wide. Dad was more Hollywood than I've ever been. And the thought of having two stars in the family? Otto Nicholas, Sr., was over the moon.

Neither of us had other family members with us. Strange. Things were moving too fast for the normalcy of gathering family to celebrate a coupling.

So what went wrong?

When Bill and I married, we purchased a sprawling ranch-style house up Benedict Canyon, complete with a tennis court and a pool, but the construction was flimsy. The kitchen and family room were huge, but the dining room was the size of child's playroom. You needed track shoes on to get from one end of the structure to the other. My work schedule was demanding enough to preclude enjoying the pool and the tennis court beyond periodic uninspired moments of relaxation and play. Bill was able to put a recording studio in what had been a garage, if memory serves. But now I had to make my way down Benedict Canyon to get to work, often well before daylight, in my Mercedes 280 SE.

The house overwhelmed me. My work obligations did not change with the marriage, and getting my arms around that house, which I ultimately found uniquely uninteresting, was more than I could handle. There was no walking into ABC-TV and 20th Century Fox announcing that I'd be taking a few days/weeks/months off to get the house up and running. There were no personal days off. If you had a fever or ended up in a hospital? That qualified for an OK absence. Not much else did. As importantly as anything, our relationship was in tatters.

At Hollywood events, Bill seemed to want to hold me back, put me behind him, be seen less. That was sort of typical for Southern men or conservative men of whatever place at that time. But we were also in the uproar of women's rights, abortion rights, the right and privilege to not be married and be just fine. I had one foot going forward, raring to get into the new, while pretty much dragging the other, which seemed to find some comfort in the old ways. It was a confusing time of change for men and women both.

My wifely chops were not great, admittedly. My earlier marriage had as much to do with the work of the Free Southern Theater as it did anything else—I barely knew I was married then because so little changed in my day-to-day life. In the Free Southern Theater, we worked seven days a week. During *Room 222*, we worked five days a week for hours that ranged from five or six in the morning to past midnight. When I began work on *In the Heat of the Night* years later, it was the same—only harder because it was on location and that meant you could be called to work on Saturdays.

I'm basically a worker bee and always have been. I liked it and was proud of it. I had the all-consuming experience of the Free Southern Theater behind me as a template of sorts, because a television series becomes your life for the run of the show. It owns you. You basically have two homes: the home where your stuff is and the home where you work, and you spend more time at your work home than the other one. My nose was basically to the grindstone.

I was a liberated woman, at a time when that was becoming a bigger issue among women across the country. I was in my twenties and successful. As part of that, I loved dancing, hanging out, and having fun on weekends. By that time, quite a few of my New York pals had either migrated to Hollywood or were traveling back and forth between Los Angeles and New York City so often, they began getting apartments out here or buying property, Robert Hooks, Rosalind Cash, Glynn Turman, Hattie Winston among many others. I was doing exactly what most young people in my position would also be doing—working hard all week and playing hard on the weekends. It was disco time and I loved to dance.

I absolutely didn't understand the full power of my celebrity at that time—the power of my little face being on millions of television screens every single week, in the living rooms of people I'd never met and never would meet. I had that face, and a warm personality that translated through the camera; at that time, neither film nor television offered audiences a plethora of images of Black women for public consumption. There'd been precious few of us for fans to swoon over in the decades of the entertainment industry to that point. Diahann Carroll, Nichelle Nichols, and I were pretty much it when it came to the Black women materializing in American living rooms every week. To an extent I didn't appreciate, we became the fantasies of many, many men—of all ethnicities.

Working in television meant people, strangers, *men,* came at you, *all the time*—men who want to conquer you or just be near you because they dream of you on the screen. Fan love can be quite powerful. Fan love can kill. Nothing seared that into my brain more than an incident that happened while I was still living in a high rise on La Cienega. A crazed fan with a large knife got by the doorman and managed to get all the way to my apartment door before the police arrived. He yammered through the door on and on about me being selected as one of *Allah's chosen* to come to Heaven—sooner than I at least had in mind. After repeatedly saying that I was not Muslim, I shook in my shoes behind my apartment door until the police arrived.

Hollywood is a stone-cold business, not a therapy camp. My problems were my own to deal with. I began to feel like a stuffed rabbit in a shooting gallery. I realized that I had believed success meant some kind of nirvana, but that isn't how it happened. Truth be known, success tends to appear much more benign than it is. I was doing very well in some respects, but Hollywood can be a lonely town—much like New York. Having a like-minded mate may very well save you or, as happens too often, do you in. Bill and I may have thought we were like-minded, may have wanted to be like-minded, but sadly, we were not, not even close.

Here's how all of this worked out in the moment. None of it had been easy. A lovely beginning, mutual respect for his music, my TV show and work in the theater, but from the beginning there was tension. Before too long, I realized I was most definitely in the wrong place with the wrong man. I was what I was when I met him. But Bill seemed in the grip of the past in his wish for a stay-at-home wife to cook three meals a day and have his children—basically, for someone *not* to be the independent, career-oriented young woman that I had made myself into before we became a couple. He saw my career and success as competitive with his, though we were in two completely different areas of performance. I sensed that he needed to be the only star in the family. I was not absolutely clear initially in our marriage regarding my desire to have or not to have children. But as my career advanced, I wasn't stopping to have children. I believed parenthood would snuff out my career. It began to eat at my soul that I was tied to a man who had some pretty old-fashioned ideas about what a woman is supposed to be. I'd been working my entire adult life so that I wouldn't have to do housework unless I felt like it. It's a small luxury but for women, an important one. Men in that vein of thinking want built-in mothers, house cleaners, nannies; I wanted none of it. But what I can articulate and write about now is not what I could articulate back then. Neither of us had a solid understanding of the things that were moving us, confusing us.

At first, we argued. Soon items were flying through the air. Our relationship became an accumulation of many nightmares followed by make-ups, then more fussing. Things smoothed out with a little counseling. But not long after, all hell broke loose. The beginning of the hell had two foundations.

Bill was on the road doing concerts all over the place. On one trip home, he brought an STD, which sent me scrambling to the doctor, stunned and embarrassed. That was a first *and* a last. He never wrote a song about the effects of that circumstance on a relationship. He certainly never contracted an STD from me. That presaged many arguments and brawls as well it should've. We fought as if our lives depended on it. We threw things at each other and stormed around slamming doors, huffing and puffing. It was our very own *Who's*

Afraid of Virginia Woolf?

Adding fuel to the flames, I had switched from birth control pills to using an IUD, thinking this new pregnancy preventer would have less of a negative impact on my body. Unfortunately, the IUD I was prescribed was the notorious Dalkon Shield which, as it turned out, caused many women grief. The research on the Dalkon Shield and its connection to bacterial septic infections even at the time should've been enough to remove it from the market. That finally did happen but not until 1974.

Even wearing the IUD, I became pregnant. There was no way on God's earth I was going to carry that pregnancy to term. Bill wanted that pregnancy to proceed, even understanding that the presence of the Dalkon Shield could possibly mean bearing a child with disabilities. More importantly, to me at least, many women died as a result of complications from using the Dalkon Shield. That information was leaking out even in the early '70s.

My decision to have an abortion, combined with his discomfort with the steady stream of men hitting on me due to the power of my little face on television, was way more than Bill could stand. In truth, some of it was more than I could stand as well. I wanted safety and I couldn't find it. His anger deepened. My fear of drowning in the pit of that marriage occupied my mind.

Not long after that go-round, my then-husband put his hands around my neck and tried to choke me because he didn't like a dinner I'd prepared for him—this after I'd worked a 15-hour day. Of course, it wasn't about the dinner. It was about who I was and remain. It was about me terminating the pregnancy against his wishes. It was about my little bit of stardom. It was about men coming at me without regard or respect for my marital status—me, who never once slept around as a married woman. Not ever. It was about my inability to subsume who I was into his idea of the structure of a marriage.

That day in our kitchen, with his hands around my neck, I was losing consciousness. I was going to die in my own kitchen because my husband didn't like the soup-and-sandwich dinner I'd made when I was bone tired. He threw the food around the kitchen. My anger mushroomed up out of me like an atomic bomb exploding. I raced around the kitchen picking up debris, fussing as I went. He wanted a *real wife*. I didn't qualify. I screamed back at him. *You don't qualify to have a real wife.* By that last brawl, I knew if I didn't get out of there, I'd be dead. That fight nearly killed me, and certainly ended the marriage. Clearly, I was too much for him, and he was way too much for me.

That night, I packed up and left. I tossed my suitcase of odds, ends and nightmares into the back of my Benz. I drove down Benedict Canyon in such a dangerous state of mind, I was in almost as much peril as I'd been in our kitchen. By that point, the leaving was an act of self-preservation. Ann Wadlington invited me to stay in her swanky home in Baldwin Hills. That's where I hid. Bill came over there and stood in the middle of the street yelling my name, begging me to come home. I had the covers over my head, hiding in Ann's guest bedroom in the basement. Picture that.

We divorced. I was forced to pay him alimony because he didn't work for at least one year of our time together.

I bought my very first home of my own in that same Baldwin Hills area, a great little house with open-beamed ceilings in the living room, a fireplace, a pool that was bigger than the house, and fruit trees in back up a hill.

I've just flung out that sentence as if that process was an easy one. It was not. A single woman trying to get a loan to purchase a home in the early 1970s was fighting a kind of war. Being a Black woman attempting this made that struggle worse. Fact was, I had enough money to pay cash for that house. That meant nothing at all to the various banks and savings institutions I visited in my search for a loan. Finally, I found a smallish Black savings and loan that would give me a mortgage loan. That sweet house was a little bit of heaven, and it was mine. My life settled down after a period of healing from the emotional disaster I had been embroiled in. Two new things helped: I went to therapy and I began writing seriously. I even took singing lessons and wrote a couple of songs.

Bill recorded my first attempt at songwriting—*Can We Pretend*—only after his musicians encouraged him, maybe even subtly shamed him. When I listened to his recording of it later, I could hear the resistance in his voice. The song reflected a feeling I had as things between us unraveled completely. It was a plea for a better time. I couldn't really hear the song fully until years later when Nicolas Bearde recorded it. It came on when I was listening to the jazz station here in LA, which is no more. The disc jockey credited Withers with writing the song. I called the station to make the correction. The guitar solo by Jose Feliciano is stunning on the original recording.

Before his death, Withers and I had a couple of opportunities to speak briefly and respectfully. We ran into each other at a few events. One was a huge party in Malibu given for AC Cowlings—OJ's best friend. Withers walked up to me as I was leaving the party.

"Hey, Miss *Freshwater Road*," was how he greeted me. He mumbled a congratulations on the book. I thanked him and headed on to the valet to get my car and get gone. My date that evening was aware of the history and was kind on the ride home.

At another event, a Christmas party at the Bel Air Hotel, Withers walked up to me and accused me of trying to turn my father against him. Where that came from, I do not know. My dad passed in 1990. It was 2014. I responded that I did no such thing, that he in fact had turned my father against him all by himself. I walked away. These words were not spoken in anger, just a kind of sadness.

Was he trying to at least connect in a positive way, a way that leaves the past in the past? I can only hope that was in his mind. From those early good days to the days of our ill-fated marriage to this precise moment, I've never spoken publicly of him in any way. I had moved on with my life and he seemingly was still trying to turn me into the Wicked Witch of the West.

Over all these intervening years, the too-public nature of our dreadful time together has haunted me. We were both celebrities, so our troubles were acted out in front of the world to a degree. That's painful for a person as private as I am. Over the years, strangers and even a friend or two have asked me about the lyrics to songs he recorded that seem to speak of me. I suppose he wanted to have the last word, put his take on things out there, to tear me down and paint a scarlet letter on my breast even as I was walking out the door.

I took my lumps, my failures, zipped my lips, and went on my way. I know that having the last word can be therapeutic.

During this healing time, I traveled to New Orleans frequently. Rudy Lombard took me under his wing to help me back to sanity. Rudy also was a Southern man, but he hadn't absorbed the whole Southern zeitgeist in most areas of life. He was, in short, liberated.

11.

It was 1974, late summer. *Room 222* had ended in January after a five-year run. My divorce from Bill Withers closed that book, or so I believed in that moment. I had moved into my new home in July. All was well. What follows was an anecdote from that time that stands out as one of my clearest memories.

My Grandma Ethel, my mother's mother, and I sat in my kitchen at a small oak table I'd snared at a warehouse sale in Culver City, and she told me a story. The nearby window looked out to the pool with its narrow concrete coping. The pool was nearly as big as the house and had a diving board. It was deep. The other kitchen window, over the sink, framed a view of downtown LA's meager early '70s skyscraper profile, hugged by urban sprawl that bled up the foothills of the San Gabriel mountains. On a clear day, from my little house on the hill, you could see it all.

On a train between Cincinnati and Detroit in 1938, my petite, smooth-brown grandma had locked eyes with a dashing Pullman Car porter in his dark uniform with bright shiny buttons.

"I could see my face in those buttons." She paused. "After we married, I'd watch how he'd sit up at night with a rag and

113

some polish working on 'em. Made 'em like tiny mirrors. He was a proud man." She turned her face away from me. "Tall, dark, and handsome. Avery Collins."

Grandma half-smiled, perhaps seeing a memory of her younger self in those shiny buttons. Her life reawakening. At the time, she'd been alone since John Jones, my grandfather and the father of her two girls, had passed during the early days of the Great Depression. Family lore says he had been able to pass for something other than Black to secure employment much of the time. He too was a handsome man. At any rate, he died leaving her a single mother with two growing daughters to raise.

Grandma struggled to feed and clothe her girls during the Depression and was forced for a time to place them in foster care in Cincinnati while she moved from place to place trying to secure any kind of work. That clarified for me the contentious relationship I'd always observed between my mom and her mother. Finally, she was able to move my mom and my Aunt Ruby, to Detroit from Ohio in the late 1930s.

Grandma picked up a delicate Wedgewood Turquoise cup using two fingers and a thumb to sip her coffee. Her missing middle finger fascinated me as a child. I felt close to her, concerned for her. I was missing something, too, but had no notion then what it was. I held my breath praying the cup didn't fall to the tabletop and shatter into a small pile of irreparable pieces.

I'd purchased the china in London when I traveled there with Bill Withers. Unfortunately, it had been shipped to my old address, his home at that time. A round of fussing ensued. Finally, I got my very formal and very beautiful bone china. It was precious to me because it reflected the instruction of my other grandma, Waddy B., who'd passed in 1970.

She was the lady of the fine china, silver, crystal, flowers, and always a gorgeous dining room table.

"Now, child, they give all the Porters the name *George*, after that Pullman man, to make it easier for the white people to call them over." She put her cup down with a soft clink. "It was '*George*, bring me the paper.' '*George*, bring me a sandwich.' Never was a please or a thank you in it."

I was half up out of my chair heading for the coffee pot on the counter trying to visualize what she'd just said. It shocked me, this dehumanizing name business. I truly couldn't wrap my head around the disregard in every man being called George to make it easier for whites to boss them around.

"Grandma, you want more coffee?"

"You got any whiskey?" There was not the slightest bit of mirth in her eyes.

"Uh, let me see what I've got." I happened to know that she kept a small bottle of bourbon under her kitchen sink in Detroit. Why a grown woman felt the need to hide her nipping bottle, I didn't know. Nor did I know about drinking hard liquor at nine o'clock in the morning. Champagne? Absolutely yes. Bourbon? Not so much.

I hustled into the dining room to check my stock. It'd been pretty much depleted during my recent house warming party. Of the bottles nestled on the tray, only the Johnny Walker Black had enough in it to even take into the kitchen. Grandma was on the first vacation of her life, visiting me in Los Angeles, and I was determined to treat her to anything she wanted. I grabbed the bottle and went straight to the kitchen cabinet to get her a glass.

"Put mine in this cup, Denise."

"Okay." I didn't let her see my laid-back surprise. As I poured the whiskey gently into her cup, she told me that during Prohibition, women had opened "tearooms" backed by bootleggers and served bathtub booze poured into beautiful china cups, just like mine.

"Grandma, did you ever go in one of those places?" I poured a taste for myself, capped the bottle, and sat down feeling like me and Grandma were in a Prohibition speakeasy.

"That's for me to know and you to find out." Grandma knocked that drink back fast, like she knew exactly what she was doing and where she was going. Her eyes twinkled.

We were quiet for a moment, she again staring out the window. That hard liquor hit my throat and cascaded to my stomach with a burn.

"I called him Mr. Collins every day. Didn't sound right calling a man 'Avery.'"

I poured Grandma another shot and another one for myself. She was in the mood to story-talk, and I loved nothing more than listening to the sound of her voice, her way of extending and curving syllables. It was a mid-South accent that periodically slipped into a Deep South parlance on some words. It wandered in tone. When she got going, her stories meandered like nomadic wagon trains lost to the shifts of time.

She continued schooling me on the real lives of the Pullman porters, who live in our imaginations in the Hollywood version. Happy Black men in spiffy uniforms strolling up and down the aisles of rolling trains, serving dressed-to-the-nines white people whatever they wanted. Grandma said the segregated trains were nothing more than the Old South on wheels. She had that *don't get it twisted* look on her face when she said it. The Porters were treated like property, worked half to death, berated, attacked physically, sworn at, and God only knows what else. Maybe there'd be a tip but most often, not. Serving the segregated Black passengers got you fired. The Porters did it anyway, every chance they got.

I bounced up next to my chair thinking it was time to lighten things up a bit.

"Was Mr. Collins taller than I am?" I had on my clogs, which added at least two inches to my five-feet-seven inch height.

Grandma was a smallish woman. I wondered if he had really been a tall man or if she'd enhanced his height in her memory. She'd never shown me a photograph of the two of them together, or any photo of him at all.

Grandma glanced up at me standing where Mr. Collins stood on the train that day. "Yes, he was tall like that."

She turned away from me and pushed the kitchen curtain aside.

I glanced into my small living room. The fireplace, the open beams in the ceiling, the orange leather wingback chairs, and the oatmeal-colored sofa seemed so calm, so quiet. I'd gotten into meditation during my healing time.

A soft pain crossed Grandma's face.

"You all right, Grandma?" I raised my voice, remembering that she often turned her hearing aid down early in the day.

"I'm fine, child. I'm fine. Very nice what you have here."

"Thank you, Grandma. I'm so glad you're here." I needed family, lost in Hollywood as I was.

We were quiet for a moment. She focused on the pool. Maybe the sight of water calmed her insides down. It certainly did that for me.

"He told me why he came to Detroit in the first place. Mr. Collins."

I was hoping for a back and forth, a girl chat with her, but something told me to be quiet and let her say what she had to say.

"He graduated from one of the Negro colleges down there in Texas and planned to live in the town of his birth, teach school there. He wanted to be a citizen in the town where he was born."

The yearning, the directness and simplicity of this statement, stunned me.

"There was a man." Grandma spoke slowly. "Mr. Collins said the man's name was Zekiel something or other, and he was accused of raping a white woman. But the colored people in the town knew it was not that. She'd come to the colored part of town seeking him. She found him. The poor woman stayed too long a time or two and word got out. The town's white folks went crazy, burning and destroying everything in the colored part of town—all the businesses and many of the homes. Don't know if they ever asked her what her business was in the colored part of town, or if she had accused him."

Negroes had evidently made good progress there before that point, so the losses went deep. Grandma Ethel said they kept Zekiel under guard in the courthouse, but the white townspeople burned the building down to get him. He died in the fire. They went into the ashes and got his dead body, dragged it behind a truck through the town, then hung it near where the courthouse had been and set it on fire again. Mr. Collins boarded a train for Detroit.

My head throbbed. What could I say or do to release her from that memory? A lynching drove Mr. Collins away from his home. An old story from my dad's side flitted through my mind. One of his cousins had to escape from Kentucky when a white woman became more interested in him than in her own husband. He escaped to Chicago, and she went with him. They'd stopped in Detroit on their way to Chicago. I had no idea of the backstory at the time.

Grandma rarely spoke of the racism she and others in our family faced in Ohio and later in Detroit, too. Her mother, my great grandma, Etta Hines, and the fearless women of that time took life's meager offerings and twisted them into ropes for climbing out of nightmares. They raised their children, educated them, and never rested until the day they died. They didn't do a ton of moaning and groaning about racism because they were too busy trying to survive it.

"Were things better for Mr. Collins in Detroit?" Perhaps a little positivity on Mr. Collins would help Grandma let it rest.

"The Detroit Board of Education wouldn't hire a colored man who'd been educated at a small Negro college; said he wasn't qualified. He found work on the railroads as a Pullman porter, and lucky he was to find it."

I'm sitting there wondering whether there were any Black teachers in Detroit schools in those days and playing tag team with that thought was my gratitude to A. Philip Randolph.

Grandma went back to staring out the kitchen window at the pool. She'd already told me the story of how Mr. Collins stopped at her seat a few seconds before the train entered a curve, forcing him to sway over her right shoulder. She said he actually touched her shoulder, and she stopped breathing for a moment. He apologized and slipped her an orange wrapped in one of the dining car's signature cloth napkins, and whispered to her to hide it. Sometime later, she realized Mr. Collins knew that curve was coming, knew exactly how far his body would hover over hers and for how long.

They married soon after meeting and settled into a two-bedroom apartment on Detroit's West Side. Grandma continued her work, now part of the war preparation, sewing Army uniforms at a plant on the East Side, and Mr. Collins rode the trains. My mom and my aunt attended the newly integrated Northwestern High School and were on their way to adulthood.

Grandma told me this part of her story over time, in bits and pieces. She knew how to tell a story.

At the time of these events, Mr. Collins worked the Detroit–Chicago–St. Louis–Kansas City route. Grandma noticed that Mr. Collins seemed to be growing away from her. He quarreled over small things. When he wasn't fussing, he sheltered himself from the goings on of the house. He slept more and more when home. And he periodically stayed a day or a night longer than she figured his job required. He'd say he slept at the bunkhouse the men used when their schedules didn't allow them time to go home.

At first, Grandma accepted his reasons, chalked his distance up to the rigorous, backbreaking work schedules of the porters. I tried to picture her handsome, shiny-buttoned man bowing and scraping to white people who at that time wrote the book on rudeness when dealing with Black people in whatever situation—trains, shops, shoeshine stands. The list is short, because at that time Black folks couldn't just wander into some establishment and expect to be treated like a human being.

The growing distance between Mr. Collins and Grandma gnawed at her. There was something else about it that she couldn't put her finger on, a feeling that the air between them had changed.

One spring morning, lilacs blooming and the grand trees of Michigan sprouting green pearls, Mr. Collins, in his uniform, eased out the front door. Grandma said once he was out, he picked up speed. She laughed and without a thought initially, hummed "My Wandering Man," by Helen Humes. *I've got a man, but he's the wandering kind.* As she hummed and softly sang her imitation of Helen's voice, anxiety crept in. *He goes to all kind of places, to find his peace of mind.*

By this point, I had rested my head on my folded arms

on the table. When she said that line of the song, my heart began racing. I sat up straight waiting for the rest.

Grandma said she was sweeping the kitchen when that clarity-of-thought made her drop the broom. Her instincts stabbed her in her heart and woke her singing mind. It was time to dig a little deeper.

Early the next morning, she packed a small overnight bag and grabbed her lightweight wool coat. She ran to get the bus to the Michigan Central Station and boarded the train to Chicago. She concocted a story to explain her presence on the train in the event she ran into any of Mr. Collins's pals: she'd been called to Chicago to care for an ailing aunt. She settled into her seat on the train, napping off and on, dark dreams flitting and precluding any real rest.

Grandma blended into the exodus from her train until she was able to separate herself from the pack. She was in no hurry. She figured by now Mr. Collins was in Kansas City. But, Chicago was his favorite town. He never tired of talking about Chicago, how the fast pace gave him energy. Even that small thought of him gave her stomach a shudder. *What was her plan?* She stopped mid-step as doubts began to squirm in her mind. What was she doing? What did she hope to find? What did she *not* hope to find? She walked around the station, lingered in front of shop windows, inhaled aromas from the coffee shops and hot dog stands. She moved on until her legs and feet began to ache from walking on the unforgiving floor.

In an alcove over by the darkish sidewall, Grandma spotted the "Travelers Aid for the Colored" kiosk. With her feet crying out for any kind of reprieve, she headed toward the tiny booth. As she arrived, a young man slammed a stack of the weekly *Chicago Defender* newspapers on the countertop. Grandma knew from Mr. Collins that the porters on the southern routes handed bundles of the newspapers to local delivery captains at big-city stops like Memphis, Jackson, Atlanta. The headlines all had to do with the war in Europe. Grandma felt like she was managing her own war with herself and that was enough of war for her.

"May I help you, ma'am?" Miss Constance "Connie" Long, as printed on her nametag, stepped to greet Grandma at the counter. Miss Long might've been in her late twenties, with perfect makeup, glistening red nails, and smooth shoulder-length hair.

"I'm not sure." Grandma needed to make a decision. "Can you tell me what time the next train to Detroit leaves?" She didn't have a molecule of surety about this gambit or about going back home so quickly. Helen Humes's voice sang softly in her ear. *Since I met that man . . .* She shook off the song and listened instead to the station noise echoing off the stone floors and walls. Grandma snapped herself back into the moment in front of her.

Miss Long checked her paper copy of the schedule. "There's a train to Detroit at 5:15 p.m. and then the very last train tonight departs at 9:30, arriving Michigan Central Station at 2:30 a.m. tomorrow. Have you enjoyed your visit to Chicago?"

"I have, thank you."

Grandma said she conjured up another tale, one a young woman would certainly accept. "My youngest daughter is pregnant, and her husband works long hours. She's terrified she'll go into labor and be there alone. I'd better get back. My name's Mrs. Ethel Jones."

Grandma sold me on her ability to spin a yarn.

"Very nice to meet you, Mrs. Jones."

"I'll take the 5:15." Grandma relaxed. She glanced around the station. "Can you tell me which of the restaurants in here serves the colored, without insult?"

"Only one place has a separate section for us where they treat us decent. That's Fergie's. The rest may accept you walking in the door, but you'll wait and wait some more."

"I see." . . . *why he comes so quick, then he's gone with the wind.* Humes's voice spoke to her.

"You know what? If you want, I can certainly take you to my place, and we can have lunch there. Fergie's is thick with cigarette smoke and too much country stench for me. I'll get my second in charge, and we can go."

"That's very kind of you but certainly much too much trouble. Fergie's can't be as bad as all that."

"No trouble. I was just ending my shift. The colored-owned restaurants are a ways south of here. My place is south too, but not quite so far. The Clinton bus will get us there in just a few minutes."

My grandma was sitting in my kitchen telling me she hooked up with a strange woman and agreed to go to the woman's house for lunch. It was all I could do to not glance one of those *did you really do that* looks at her. But I pushed my chair back a bit, crossed my legs, and focused on her as she continued.

Grandma said she'd taken that trip with trepidation, feeling foolish as soon as she got off the train, but she appreciated that this young woman was offering her a kindness. And she was drawn to Miss Long—she liked her style, her ease with strangers. She was a big-city young lady, with the kind of sophistication Grandma wanted for her own daughters. She felt welcomed.

The two walked to Clinton Street to catch the bus. Out the bus window, Grandma marveled at the size of Union Station. After getting off, they walked half a block to the woman's two-story apartment building. On the top floor,

Grandma entered a small but nicely furnished apartment with enticing bay windows across the front.

Grandma sat in the woman's window seat, the perfect spot to enjoy the street below and, with a slight turn of her head, the apartment's décor. Miss Long's place had elegant upholstery, crystal vases with silk flowers, a newspaper holder, and somber paintings of woods and dark stormy oceans. Grandma's place in Detroit had none of this. Her work schedule and her determination to save money to buy a home took the air out of decorating. Maybe she could do a few things, she told me she remembered thinking, just to bring it up a little.

Miss Long served Grandma a hot lunch of smothered cabbage with white potatoes and tiny pieces of bacon, as well as cornbread and rice. The afternoon sunlight spread a soft hue on the surroundings. Grandma relaxed, feeling comfortable, safe.

Miss Long dabbed her mouth with her napkin. "My father had his own restaurant in New Orleans. His gumbo sold out every time he made it. Thought he could eventually have a restaurant here serving his favorite New Orleans dishes. But he found work in meat packing on the killing floor and it was too much for him. He died not long after they came here. My mother lives with her sister a few blocks from here. My brother stayed in New Orleans with family."

Grandma said she loved Miss Long's accent, the soft elegance of it; she didn't want the other woman to stop talking. Grandma folded her napkin beside her plate.

Miss Long began collecting the dishes to take to the kitchen. "I mean no rudeness, but may I ask what happened to your hand?"

Grandma didn't want to talk about her meager working-class life. "I work on industrial sewing machines making uniforms. For the Army. It's steady." She didn't go on about her aspirations. She had two almost-grown daughters and a second husband who was mosly gone, traveling for work. She wanted her daughters to thrive, to be elegant, like this young woman. She was calm, not rough like so many coming up from the south. The bay windows, the elegant dishes, cloth napkins—Grandma wanted these for her daughters, too. But she also realized she wanted them for herself. There was still time to take her life up a few notches.

"I'm relieved to know that you have family close by. I'm sure your mother is very proud of you. Do you plan on having a family of your own?"

Miss Long stepped away toward the small hallway leading to the bathroom and a bedroom. She returned carrying a framed photograph close to her heart. Grandma smiled seeing the coyness blended in with the passion in Miss Long's face. This woman was in love.

She placed the framed photo on the table, turning it so my grandma could see it with no effort at all. And there stood Mr. Avery Collins in his uniform, buttons blazing in a shaft of sunlight, and his arm gently around Miss Long, whose smile was so huge it seemed to jump right out of the frame. Mr. Collins wasn't old but he looked old enough to be Connie Long's father.

Grandma told me it took all the energy in her small body to not scream. She said her face froze in a limp smile but her forehead became a knot of stress. She felt as if she had cotton in her ears, and not a drop of moisture in her mouth. She searched the photo for the wedding band Mr. Collins wore at home. It was nowhere to be seen.

The meal turned to mud in Grandma's stomach. She quietly excused herself to use the restroom, tears releasing from her eyes as soon as she passed Miss Long. In the bathroom, she turned on the water to hide her heaving pain, still on the verge of screaming. She flushed the toilet, then tried to gather enough strength to get out of that apartment. She refreshed her makeup and balled her hurt into a fierce root of anger—not at poor unsuspecting Connie Long but at that double-dealing, shiny-button-wearing, too-dark-for-her-anyway man who was getting blacker by the minute in her churning mind. *Tall, dark and handsome* became *black as the ace of spades,* and *nice colored gentleman* segued to *low-down nigger with a wasted college education and too much charm for his own damned good.*

My grandma took the bus back to Union Station alone. Of course she never let on anything about her husband. Had this happened because she wasn't sophisticated enough? Was she too working class, not far enough away from southern Ohio? What would this do to her house-buying plan? What would this do to her life?

On the train back to Detroit, she stared out the window at the tenements and smoke of Chicago's south side, her mind going blank for a while as she waited for some kind of solution to present itself. She had to go home. She had to deal with it. She caught a glimpse of the Indiana dunes just as night eased in. *What if she'd never taken this trip? How long would it have taken for things to combust?* On that train ride home, she reexamined every word he'd ever spoken to her, every mood, every exit from their home. She'd been blinded by those shiny buttons just like that poor young lady in Chicago.

At home, she dragged herself over the deep canyon of her hurt and anger. What if she hadn't been so nosey? What if she'd not gone? She went to bed but didn't sleep, and heard the door open the next morning when Mr. Collins tipped in. She threw on her robe and met him in the living room, hands gripping her hips. If she let go of herself, she'd fly into him with fists balled up and insanity in her eyes. All of her admonishments to herself about remaining calm, quiet, and reasonable were shot to hell as soon as she looked at him. But just as quickly she pushed it all back down, deep down into her soul.

"I met the woman you gonna marry. In Chicago. Miss Long. Saw a fine photograph of you two." She delivered it without cracking, moving her hands from her hips to fold her arms across her chest.

Mr. Collins seemed to sigh inside himself. He was trapped between Grandma and the front door. She felt only one creaky notion of a good outcome from this: her girls were old enough now to handle this breach. They might learn something from it—if she could ever bring herself to tell them the truth. But as it turned out, she would be holding this story in for many years.

Mr. Collins put his overnight bag down but didn't move forward or backward. Grandma noticed he had his wedding ring on. "When'd you put your ring on? Sure wasn't on when you took that photo."

He glanced at his ring finger, cleared his throat. "I didn't mean for it to go so far. I wasn't really going to marry her."

"Not faithful here and lying like a rug there? That's more than even I can stomach." *I'm gonna get a new man who never wanders from my door* hopscotched through her mind but exited quickly.

Grandma told me that by this point she suddenly felt worn out from it all. Revelations. Thinking back through the times he'd been very late or didn't show up until the next day, the irritable Mr. Collins ducking out on the life of his home, his mood swings and lack of interest in whatever she offered him. She wanted to sit in that moment but knew she could not. That would be like caving, throwing in the towel, forgiving him. She could not. She felt a longing for the good thing, but her heart skipped over it.

She'd loved this man. She didn't know at that moment if she had any love left, but she decided to separate her heart from him and figure out the rest later.

"I'm sorry." He made the smallest move toward Grandma.

"You probably need to not talk. There's nothing more to say."

Grandma told him to sleep on the floor, on a chair, or anywhere not with her. She went back to bed. They lived in silence from that day forward. Soon after, Mr. Collins was diagnosed with tuberculosis and went into a sanitarium for treatment. When he was released, my grandma took him in as a kind of boarder. They never slept together again, but she took care of him until he died. She never said another word about Miss Connie Long and neither did he. When he died, she buried him and stood at his grave for a good while. She would not marry again.

By the end of it, I simply didn't know what to believe. I certainly knew then why she had no photographs of my step-grandfather. I didn't question her story—but I believed she may have enhanced it in her memory. It was a hell of a story, and by then I'd learned she was a yarn-spinner by nature.

Grandma Ethel stayed with me that summer for two weeks. I prayed that my small offerings to her on that trip made a difference in her life. I'd done my best to let her know in no uncertain terms that she was loved.

Meanwhile, I was in a pickle career-wise. I wanted desperately to break into film. But when ready to make the leap from television to film I ran into a brick wall laced with concrete. The craze for "Black exploitation" films was sweeping through Hollywood like wildfire.

What I got was *Blacula* and *The Soul of Nigger Charley,* one of the worst films ever made.

I got depressed. Hollywood doesn't give you a ton of time to make these leaps. And in those years, Hollywood truly didn't know what to do with Black women. There were breakthroughs—Cicely Tyson in *Sounder,* Diahann Carroll in *Claudine,* Rosalind Cash in *Cornbread, Earl and Me,* but they came few and far between.

If not for Sidney Poitier, I wouldn't have had a film career at all. I had looks enough, talent enough, brains enough. But Hollywood was largely closed to Black women in the *leading lady* category. Those roles were reserved almost entirely for white actresses. I do see a tiny bit of progress in that category since that time. Tiny being the operative word. My passion for acting began fading after crashing into too many barricaded doors. I didn't fit preconceived, or possibly stereotypical, notions of what a Black woman was, is or wants to be, I guess. *What is she? She doesn't look Black. She doesn't sound Black.*

In that mid-'70s period, thankfully, Sidney Poitier's team decided to take Richard Wesley's fun-filled romp of a script called *Let's Do It Again* to the screen. *Let's Do It Again,* a sort of follow up to *Uptown Saturday Night,* became my personal hill I was prepared to die on. Sidney wanted a female with a more *character* look rather than a glamour face. Whereas I had a glamour face. We went at it, me fussing at him, trying to convince him to let me read and test for the role. He resisted. Finally, he allowed me to read. After a solidly good reading, I felt confident that I had the part. He said, "No, your look is too glamorous." I continued whining and fussing, begging him to test me to see if my acting chops would slay his notion of me being too glamorous. In my personal life, then and now, I'm much more that girl who wears ginormous T-shirts, clogs, and head scarves than a glamour puss.

Mr. P. finally agreed to test me. I prepared for that test like it was the last job on planet earth. I found a size-huge bra and stuffed it with padding, wore a tight red dress, and went at it. Sidney sat on the camera, and when I began cracking that chewing gum and pretending to be a hard street girl, he nearly fell off his seat laughing.

I got the part and loved every silly minute of it.

I played Bill Cosby's wife and Lee Chamberlin played Sidney's wife. What a fun time we had. The film also starred Calvin Lockhart, Jimmie Walker, and Ossie Davis among many others. Curtis Mayfield, with whom I'd been in fan love since I was in college, did the film's music and the fabulous Staple Singers sang on the soundtrack. At the Los Angeles screening, my scenes provoked uproars of laughter. I'm thinking, this is the beginning of my film career!

Soon after came Sidney's *A Piece of the Action.* That was light, fun. But there were NO auditions being offered for what I'll call Class A films for me. Just more exploitation product.

The decade wound down. I kept my writing going— now a secret passion that I rarely shared with anyone. I sold my house on the hill and moved into an apartment for a brief while. Eventually, I used the profit to buy an apartment building and began learning how to be a landlord. It certainly consumed me. I enjoyed the feeling of property ownership as I always had, only now it was a four-unit building that needed work and that I didn't live in. It certainly took my attention off the Hollywood dream for a good while.

12.

It was 1980.

For a few days before the call, I couldn't shake off a premonition that a cataclysm approached. It was an inkling, not a hard lead that sends you racing to call the emergency hot lines of salvation or smacks you upside your head as it tells you in plain English not to misinterpret, not to sideline or secrete in soft boxes of old photographs and letters.

When I worried a close pal with my distinct feeling of foreboding, he told me to stop worrying, that I was luckier than most, *out there in California living in high cotton.* In his mind, I was lolling in the blinding California sun, waiting on a good acting job, a new house to buy, a better man to love and to be loved by. Of course, the literal image of *high cotton* with its shadows of violence for those who had to pick it sneaked into my mind.

I'd spoken with my sister Michele before a weekend trip I was taking. She was heading from Chicago, where she lived and worked for Johnson Publishing Company, to New York for a meeting. After that, her plan was to come to LA to search for on-camera work as a journalist. She deserved the screen—a beautiful face with eyes straight out of North Africa, a great mind, a sense of adventure. She'd graduated from Michigan State with honors.

Her subdued voice on the phone, though, fed my anxiety.

"Is he there?" I did my best to get a handle on my nerves. I knew she was in the midst of a break-up.

"Yes."

"Stay calm and focused. No fighting. See you Monday." My last words.

She was trying to untangle herself from a situation—one that in my judgment asked too much of her. It sounded to me like she was helping the guy she was breaking off from, that his needs had become burdensome. While trying to end that relationship, she'd met a new person, another journalist at Johnson Publishing Company with whom she had scads more in common.

I'd met the guy she was moving away from when she brought him to Los Angeles a couple of years earlier. I wasn't impressed. I was concerned that if I spoke out against the guy, it more than likely would've created a wedge between us. He was older than she by nearly a decade. I remained quiet about my true feelings. Regret.

Michele and I were nine years apart. She was well aware of my Withers nightmare, but I didn't discuss the details with her. Nor did I have any reason to think that the guy she was leaving was physically abusive. She never said he was violent. I worried she was naïve. She had been sheltered in ways my brother and I were not, as she was born into relative comfort—not wealth, but comfort. Mom was not running around trying to keep a roof over our heads as she had been when my brother and I were very young.

Michele grew up in an all-white town that was peaceful, though it may not have been universally happy that a Black family had entered its fold. She attended good schools and was an excellent student, a high achiever. She played piano and flute. She loved flying and became a pilot and a member of the Bessie Coleman Flying Club. Now, because of this bad relationship, she was on shaky ground. She was trying to move forward. Had brought the new guy she'd started seeing home to Detroit to meet family only months before at Christmas. He was also well educated, a journalist with a bright future.

I went off to Oakland unable to stop thinking about the sound of her voice.

Scads of Hollywood's Black artists made the weekend trip to Oakland each winter to attend the Black Filmmakers Hall of Fame. The weekend was a grand party with a very serious purpose. The celebration provided an excellent antidote to our feeling unwanted, underknown, misunderstood, and devalued in Hollywood—even when we worked. In those days, we were Hollywood's unending sidebar, still trying to get into the race.

The ceremony at Oakland's Paramount Theatre honored Black performing artists from years gone. Each year, they honored so many deserving artists that the show went on for hours, with all of us worn down to the marrow by the end. We loved every minute of it even as we groaned. At times during that weekend, I felt duplicitous, smiling at friends, fans, able to chat but all the while pushing myself to stay on top of the very bad feelings taking shape in my soul.

By the time I got back to Los Angeles to begin the new week, that unease had congealed into near dread. But my anxiety had a nearly blank face until the call. I'm definitely a card-carrying member of the Worry-Wart Club, a direct emotional descendent of my mother, who wears the crown of silent worrying. My worry self is rarely silent. I speak or write my dread.

I got the call at my small production company offices, Masai Films, on Hollywood Boulevard. Fritz Goode, one of my partners, yelled for me to pick up the phone. There was a call from Johnson Publishing Company's New York office. I picked up the phone fully expecting to hear Michele's voice telling me she was taking a later flight. Instead, it was a voice I didn't know, a man who said his name which went in one ear and out the other.

"The NYPD found a body in a parked car in the Hertz lot at LaGuardia Airport." The stranger on the phone struggled to speak. "It's not Michele, but we need someone to verify that." He paused. "Just in case it is. Please come to New York as soon as possible, and bring your mom and stepfather."

Verify that it's *not* her? What was he saying? *Just in case it is*? He'd put Michele in the possibility-of-death column? The hint that death was in the small print reached into my existing anxiety and got a firm grip. I tried to focus on the particulars, the structures, the exteriors. Who was this man? Why was her place of employment calling with this? Do I need to call my mother and my stepfather? He said to bring them—how did I do that without revealing the issue at hand?

Blood swooshed through my body trying to find the place to protect me. In those days, I jogged in Hancock Park, a beautiful old section of the city with large houses, many of them full-scale mansions, including the mayor's residence. It was and is full of old-growth trees—California sycamores, Asian elms, jacarandas, olive trees—and a lot of broken pavements. I'd periodically break into short wind sprints at top speed. One day, I tripped on some of that broken pavement and hit the concrete hard. My brain was able to put a wrap on that pain for a few seconds as I collected myself. I needed that *pain wrap* in the moment of the phone call, but it wasn't there. The Johnson Publishing guy hung up, and I sat there holding that empty phone.

I was free-floating, my ears full of cotton, my heart racing as I flew out the door and drove home like a maniac to pack. The strange tension I heard in her voice on that last phone call rolled around in my head. The monosyllabic way she answered my questions. And now this? *Dead in a car? Bring Mom and Bob?* A steel vise closed around my head, pressing against the stress roiling my brain.

Mom and Bob had settled into Los Angeles a couple of years before this nightmare. They had found a huge two-bedroom, two-bath apartment in a complex called Park La Brea, which was lovely at the time; during the period between selling my house on the hill and trying to figure my own way forward, I'd also taken an apartment there. Bob had retired from the Bureau of Prisons, and then they'd spent a couple of years living in New York City while he worked for Medgar Evers College in security.

I hustled Mom and Bob to LAX, and bought tickets. I screamed at the baggage handler that day for dawdling over our luggage. I was rude. There was an abundance of confusion, agony, guilt, a nightmare creeping into place, and I had no power whatsoever to stop it. I don't remember what I said to my mother and stepfather. They'd gotten the same call. An even more profound horror had to be shuffling into place in their minds and hearts. Losing a child. Losing the youngest?

On the five-hour plane ride to New York, my mind jockeyed back and forth between sweet memories and dark foreboding. In between those thoughts, I chastised myself for all this foreboding before I actually knew what had happened. Then there were the thoughts of my own years of neglecting Michele. I'm nine years older. Siblings separated by that many years have a harder time bonding. It often comes later when everyone's grown. That's precisely the way it rolled out. As a child, she drove me nuts playing with my stuff! Michele and I bonded as adult young women. I visited her in Chicago. She took me to the Sears Tower, where we had drinks and bonded even more so. I visited her apartment which was modern and lovely. I met some of her friends.

In the mid-'70s, Michele and two other visiting Detroiters, my stepmother, Mildred Stevenson, and her close pal, Becky Royster (the sister of *my* close pal, journalist Ed Boyer), visited me in my home on the hill in LA after my divorce from Bill Withers.

Michele had recently graduated from Michigan State. We piled into my new Benz and drove up to San Francisco on Highway One. That road trip became the subject of my first published story, appearing in *Essence* magazine. When I read it now, it's rough, beginning-writer work—but the soul of that trip, the experience of it, is still there and still beautiful. In the *Essence* story, I renamed my road dogs to protect the innocent, and titled the story as "Augustine, Myrtle Marty and Me." That little trip was the only travel my sister and I ever did together. Today, I'm the only one still living.

Michele traveled to Europe before I did. She knew of my passion for Spain and my particular interest in Morocco, and she encouraged me to take the trip to Tangiers that I eventually made a couple of years before her death. In Tangiers, I saw her beautiful dark eyes everywhere.

We landed at Kennedy Airport. My sister-friend Marcia Stevenson, as close to me as a real sister, had transplanted from Detroit to New York City years before, and she met us. Mom and Bob went by cab immediately to the 114th Precinct, and Marcia and I went to the morgue. Not long after, my brother Otto's flight from Detroit landed and he too went straight to the precinct.

Marcia and I huddled in the viewing room at the morgue, in a nondescript building not far from LaGuardia Airport. An attendant behind a glass partition pulled the curtain back as another attendant wheeled a gurney into place. He pulled the sheet from the body. Marcia and I stood there staring through the glass. There was nothing about the body that resembled Michele. I started laughing. *It was a mistake! Hallelujah!!*

Marcia didn't recognize the gurney body, either. We laughed. As we laughed, we peeked again at the body. Maybe? No. My head pounded. I went closer to the glass this time, my laughter quelled and quivered between tears. *Michele?*

You're supposed to be on your way to California to stay with me and Mom and Bob. Remember? A new life in California? You cannot be dead. Get up!

I laughed. Stop playing around! I laughed and cried and Marcia did, too. There was no transition between our laughter and our tears. But Michele did not open her beautiful brown eyes.

The attendant closed the drapes and came out with a paper for me to sign. "Is that person Michele Darlene Burgen?"

"Yes."

"Your relation to the deceased?"

"I'm her sister."

He pushed the paper in front of me and handed me a pen.

Certificate of Death: Michele Darlene Burgen, No. 156-80-403089

Date Filed: February 28, 1980, 2:32 PM

Place of Death: LaGuardia Airport

Date and Hour of Death: Found February 25, 1980, Hour unknown. Female 26 years old.

Queens Borough Mortuary, 26 February 1980. Homicide.

Gunshot wound to head and brain.
   ME: Case No. 1133
   Name of Informant: Denise Nicholas
   I signed and a grim memory came rushing in:
   A small plane crashed into the old administration building on the 20th Century Fox lot in 1970. On the Stage 10
set where we filmed *Room 222*, we heard the impact and ran
into the street in our makeup and character costumes. We
trotted to the crash site, aghast at what remained. Broken
plane parts, a small fire. Distinct human brain matter strewn
amongst the plane's wreckage on the pavement.
   It's an image you never forget. You can't unsee horror. It
will always find a way back to your conscious mind.
   Michele was murdered by gunshot to the brain. The
images of that 20th Century Fox crash flashed through my
mind when I saw her body. There was no actual connection
between the two events, but my mind never let go of the
visual of destroyed brain matter.
   Later, in the precinct, I was on guard. Police *earn* their
crusty behavior, their cynicism, but not their racism. So
many seem to be born with it, though. In America, we think
in racial/racist terms first and last.
   Detective Harvey Goodhart got Michele's case. In the
precinct, I was lost. My entire family was lost. He seemed to
know. He seemed sensitive to our need to find any dollop of
understanding, to find any crumbs of the why and wherefore.
Knowing the subtext, understanding that people rarely give
Black folks the good parts of anything, Detective Goodhart
affirmed the last molecule of faith I had in humanity just
by being decent to us in our hour of extraordinary pain and
confusion. Whatever he was in his inner life or his personal
life, I do not know. I am grateful that what he showed us that
day, and after, was compassion.

At the 114th Precinct Detective Goodhart led us with our travel-weary, cried-out eyes through a blur of fluorescent lights, scarred desks, metal chairs, and clouds of cigarette smoke into a room of men who seemed to want to be helpful. Could they see our pain? Did they care? My mother, my stepfather, my brother, my sister-friend, and I were all lost sheep being led through a process that we only knew from television shows and films.

Michele, they told us, had registered at a hotel at LaGuardia Airport. In her room, they found a suitcase of clothes. I stared at the clothes, picked through them. They didn't look like hers. There was a haphazard selection to them that made no sense. She would've packed for her trip to Los Angeles. These clothes were not right. She was a meticulous girl.

The police tried to tell us delicately that this kind of killing is a "hit." A bullet to the temple is a hit. *What the hell is going on?* Michele never once even mentioned the word drugs to me. And how had they found the guy she'd been living with in Chicago so fast, the guy she was separating herself from, the guy she'd brought to my home a year or so earlier? He was *already* at the precinct. *Who is this man? The NYPD say he's an informant for the Chicago Police Department? Really? Informing on what?* Perhaps he'd gotten in trouble earlier and made a deal to keep himself out of jail. Had this guy, her soon-to-be ex, or someone, talked Michele into being a drug courier as a way to make money? She was not afraid of risks. My mind was a swirling mess of conflicting information that I could not make clear.

I tried to peep through the door when the detectives went in and out, trying to see this man who earlier in their relationship she had said she loved. When Michele brought him to my home in Los Angeles, something about him startled me, made me anxious, but I didn't say anything to her.

After the grueling, devastating meetings with the NYPD in Queens, which netted more questions with barely an answer to be had, we dragged our worn-down selves to Detroit to plan the funeral of this 26-year-old young woman we all loved so much. Feeling helpless encourages me to busyness. In that moment, we didn't have the luxury of mourning. Out of my mind, I tend to take over. It's better than drinking, another move I make in those circumstances, to try to numb myself. But now a body had to be shipped, a funeral arranged, an obit written, a repast organized. You do these things through a mist of terror, as if the world is suffocating you.

We arranged shipment of Michele's body to McFall Brothers Funeral Home in Detroit. Detective Goodhart became the voice of the NYPD in our ears and hearts. He stayed in touch with us for more than a year as he attempted to solve the case. I'm grateful, because to be in that situation surrounded by men who hate your guts on a good day would've broken what was left of my heart.

The New York Times ran a quietly uplifting obit with a photo of Michele. A life in an obit.

At Michele's funeral, we filed past the casket afraid to look in, heard the words spoken to help us accept this death, harangued a photographer who took a picture of our girl in the casket as we told him he could not do. Otto and the other men were aggressive with this photographer. It made no matter. There was her photo in *Jet* magazine in her casket. It was a portent of things to come. No privacy, no standard of public behavior. All of that has slid into the past.

We inhaled subtle whiffs of rot from mountains of flowers. This death was not yet real, though we put the casket in the ground, roamed the cemetery like wolves, heard clomps of half-frozen dirt hit the lid. Old people died, not people younger than we were.

Much time would pass before we turned to ourselves for explanations, before we looked in the mirror. For now, it was all about the world outside, the violence in America, the violence between women and men. I knew about that. Had she only seen the worst part of my life and not the best? We can never know how our words and behaviors affect the younger people who love us. At 26, she shouldn't have been bound to anything or anyone beyond her own heart's promise. She had the world in her hands. Michele had fast-tracked her life in the direction of accomplishment. Was she moving too fast, making risky deals with whatever devil offered help? She'd already spun a web of study, of travel, of doing. Was she threatening to someone? Was a frail ego involved here? I knew about that, too.

My brother and his wife, Kay, hosted us all at their home after the funeral. Otto and Kay had a comfortable basement party room complete with full bar, seating, music, television. We told stories, as many as you can when the deceased is barely 26. We laughed, talked, made it a party, as mourners are wont to do. I spoke of our car trip to San Francisco less than five years earlier. Michele's new friend, Chris Benson, was there with us the whole day. He was as stunned as we were. They hadn't even really begun any sort of life together and now she was gone.

"On her last trip to California, Michele rented a plane at one of the small airports and wanted to take me up for a 'spin.'"

As I was telling my little story, a voice called out from the thicket of the party.

"Did you go?"

I laughed and shook my head with regret. "Are you crazy?" I was terrified of small planes. Michele had laughed at my fear when I declined.

Poor Bob seemed lost in this celebration of her short life. He wouldn't let her go. His pain seemed disjointed, strange. At first, we thought he'd consumed too much alcohol; he was not a drinker. We know now that he probably didn't grasp that Michele wasn't coming back. Or maybe he did. We know her death hastened the onset of his full-blown Alzheimer's and eventual demise. It took some time to thread all of these needles.

My poor mother. She had lost her youngest child and, it eventually became clear, her husband on the same day. He was never the same and neither was she, and neither were the rest of us. Murder is like a burn that never quite heals.

The next day, me, my dad, his common-law wife Mildred, my brother, and my friend Rudy Lombard, who'd come to Detroit to share the load of our grief and with whom Michele had bonded on a trip to New Orleans, hunched over the kitchen table at Dad's old house in Detroit, drinking hard liquor, trying to sound like we knew more than we actually did about murder and mayhem. Chris Benson had already gone back to Chicago after the funeral and repast.

I'd been sitting at that kitchen table since I was a wee child. My brother Otto and I spent a lot of time in this house even after our mom's life stabilized. The feel, the smell, the memories of that place have never left me. All these years later, I remember that we couldn't sit down to a meal before Grandad took his place. Otto Jr. ate fast and his knee did a small bounce, as if his engine was about to propel him into a run as soon as he finished eating. He'd been doing that since we were little children.

The smallish pantry—an alcove off the main kitchen—had always been packed when we were small, with shelves of food items on one side and dishes and glasses on the other. Pies, cookies, and cakes were covered and always sat on the narrow counter under the shelves. A small stack of dessert plates were close by. The window looked out to the backyard.

The kitchen was much the same as it had been when my grandmother, Waddy B., ruled the room. The only comfort I felt in that moment came because it hadn't changed one bit. That room felt unbothered by life's never-ending vicissitudes, like the sanctuary of an old church.

Otto Nicholas, Sr., was a gambler. We children, of course, fantasized that he ran the Italian mafia out of the Detroit numbers racket single-handedly. Dad was a cool guy who rarely showed anger. He was definitely a race man, and that's where I get it. We know in his younger days, he was tough. He hit the streets during the Detroit Race Riot of 1943. In truth, we didn't really know if he ever had occasion to blow someone to smithereens in his younger, more aggressive street days. Not that he'd ever tell us that. We do know he was in the numbers racket for a long, long time. He was very good at it. He was loved all over the west side of Detroit. We saw it when he took us with him to do his *runs*—to the cleaners, to the shoeshine stand, to restaurants, and eventually to New York. He showed us off to his pals, beaming with pride. We saw how people reacted to him. Always glad to see him coming. Always sorry when he left.

How much love the community felt for this man was on full display when he passed years later. It seemed the entire west side of Detroit showed up at Otto and Kay's home for Daddy's memorial soiree, held outdoors on Otto's beautiful double-lot yard. Dad did not want a funeral. He wanted a party and we gave him one.

"Where's that boyfriend, the one she was getting away from?" Dad broke the quiet in the kitchen and cut to the chase. He gave me a quick glance to let me know he was tipping into quicksand territory. None of us felt any fondness for the old boyfriend. We drifted in his direction as the culprit, though there was no proof. We knew the NYPD had accepted his alibi and that was that. But we also knew that men kill women they're intimate with all day long in this country and in a few others. It's the oldest news there is.

"Detective Goodhart said the old boyfriend had an alibi, wasn't anywhere near New York. He was in the precinct when we were there. I saw him." Otto Jr. paused. "He didn't have to pull the trigger to be in on it." He tapped a ballpoint pen on the tabletop.

"Now you're talking." Dad nodded his head in the affirmative.

There was an overlap with her relationship with these two men. She'd begun seeing Chris before she completed her departure from the old relationship. That happens every day and twice on Sunday. Did that matter? My inner voice said for sure it matters. It matters.

"She told me she was breaking up with him." My head sank to the table on my folded arms as I said that. Remembering, I thought I felt Rudy's hand on my back. Comfort. But that was my imagination. Rudy was standing his 6-feet-4 frame against the wall next to the door to the basement. He was quiet.

Otto, Rudy, and I announced to the rest of the family that we were going to clean out Michele's apartment in Chicago and look for clues as to what went wrong. There had to be answers somewhere. Surely a young woman who graduates college with honors, is a card-carrying member of the Bessie Coleman Flying Club by age 24, has traveled in Europe, has been hired as an editor at a national magazine by the same age—surely this girl was on the fast track to success, not the cemetery.

Michele's apartment in Chicago was part of the investigation. We could only enter with a police escort. We'd have to leave Detroit very early to give us time to get with the Chicago Police Department to arrange the walk through.

When we told my dad we were going to Chicago to clean out Michele's apartment, he offered us his gun. We were definitely in a gun mood—though again, this was fantasy. We knew nothing about guns. Rudy was an intellectual. He was flawlessly educated, counting among his close friends the Marsalis family in New Orleans, James Baldwin and his family, Toni Morrison, David Driskell, Bob Moses, and so many others. My brother loved architecture and model trains. I was a reasonably successful actress who dreamed of writing. That's who we were, not gun-toting justice seekers. No.

My dad's gun had been my grandfather Sam's gun, a slender-barreled handgun with wiggling, clanking parts, something from the days of *Bonnie and Clyde*. It clanked loudly enough for us to hear it in the kitchen when Dad was bringing it down the stairs to give it to us. He put the gun in a bag on the table.

"How old is this thing?" I gently, carefully pulled the gun out of the paper bag. It clanked like its parts needed tightening. "Does it need oil?"

"Don't make no difference how old it is. It shoots. There's a few extra bullets in the bag. I'm not giving you this thing for you to go starting nothing. It's for your protection. You don't know what's going on over there. Do you hear me?"

His muscular tone threatened us to behave or face his consequences. We mumbled that we heard and understood his warning.

"You need to sit there and handle that gun so you're comfortable. Shoulda taken you out to the country to shoot the damned thing. Too late now. You leavin' so early."

I sat there handling that gun. "You sure we won't blow our own hands off if we shoot it?"

My brother gave me the *girls know nothing about guns and retribution* face. He knew as much about guns as I did. *Nothing.* We huddled around the gun as if it had some mystical value to offer relief from our madness. We put our confusion and ruminations on the table, our broke-down gun now wrapped in a soft cloth in a brown paper bag, as if it were a precious family heirloom from a lost time. We thought we were ready.

The sun had set while our heads swiped back and forth in confusion. The house was lit up as if we were having a social gathering on a weeknight. Mildred cooked us steak and eggs at 8 p.m., as we drank shot after shot of Crown Royal. We yanked at any shards of hope that we could find, any little molecules of reason in the madness we felt and faced.

Rudy furrowed his brow, then backed away to stand in the corner of the kitchen. What was he thinking now? I imagined it was about black people hurting each other, doing the white man's work for him. Rudy was unrelenting in that area of our lives. He had put his body on the line in Mississippi and Louisiana for black folks. He was a very serious human being.

The next morning, we three well-educated, well-dressed, crazed thirtysomethings hit the road with Lou Rawls singing, *Goin' to Chicago, sorry but I can't take you.* Crimson-eyed, hungover, sleepless, we rode high above the true devastation that we felt. We slid our silly gun under the front seat of my brother's big Chrysler. We wanted to confront our enemy, our devastator, put a bullet in *his* brain. But in truth, we didn't know who our enemy was. We talked big. *An eye for an eye.* Our voices rose up octaves, talking as much in falsetto as David Ruffin on the car radio singing, *Before love breaks my heart.* You can feel the approach of pain in Ruffin's rising falsetto.

Rudy, my long and forever lost love, sitting next to me,

must have been thinking, *so that's the way you felt about us when you walked away, because I know it wasn't from lack of love. Doesn't matter. You walked. We both suffered. Case closed.* Thank God, the song finally ended. The biggest mistake of my life was behaving badly and losing him. He was not fond of Hollywood. That was a problem for me back then. Add to that my drive to do exactly what I do now: drive around in a Benz, live in a beautiful home with a pool, travel all over the place first-class.

My brother had his foot firmly on the accelerator as the March Michigan landscape blurred by. Leafless trees anchored by dirty piles of crusty old snow, branches black against a low sky, gray and ominous, an overly washed Army blanket. Dying sky. No great ball of fire with rays in bands of warmth. I missed California. Nothing soft here to remember. Just the cold Michigan winter, and Chicago promising to be even colder.

We blew by the turn-off to Ann Arbor, where my adult life actually began all those years ago. Ann Arbor, I reflected as we drove, was my stepping-stone to New York City. My escape to the city of my dreams began with a Spring Break trip. But I was sold on New York when I was a small child, and my dad took my brother and me to the city to educate us. Didn't we arrive in the city in Daddy's long sleek white convertible Cadillac? Didn't he take us to Harlem to the Hotel Theresa, to the Red Rooster, to Sardi's? Didn't he take us on the Circle Line cruise around Manhattan? My childhood excitement at being in New York with my father and brother never left.

We arrived near Michele's apartment in the afternoon, spotted a payphone, and called the CPD to let them know we'd arrived. We lurked around in the cold like lunatics with our ramshackle gun. We sat in the front seat of my brother's big Detroit car waiting, we hoped, for the villain of this story to appear. Of course, we were in a delusional frame of mind, fed by movies, fantasies, and total lack of any real knowledge about criminal violence. We waited for the police for our walk through.

I was confused. This wasn't the apartment I visited not that long ago, in a modern high-rise building, airy and bright. What was this dark and dingy place with things strewn about? When did this happen? She told me she had been helping the old boyfriend. Was he helping her at something beyond *going to the dogs,* as Grandma Ethel used to say? I was appalled. Had I given the example of living on the edge to my younger sister? I'd survived my own tightrope walk. I had the luck of early success so I could walk when the going got tougher, and it certainly did. And thank God I had my own money.

There were no answers for us there. It was time to go home.

13.

THE DECADE THAT FOLLOWED, THE '80S, STARTED WITH A
nightmare and didn't get much better until it was almost
over. One year after Michele's murder in New York City, I
married for a third time. I think at that moment in my life,
I would've married a tree if it had asked. Was I running for
cover? Yes. Was I completely undone, destabilized by her
murder? Yes. As was my entire family.

My sister was dead and there was not a murderer in sight
to be held accountable. My mother receded into the extreme
pain, the near insanity of losing her youngest child. My stepfather sank into the horror of Alzheimer's disease. Michele
was his only child, and his heart would not heal even a tiny
bit before Alzheimer's claimed total victory. He was gone.

My dad, suffering from severe heart disease, began having a succession of heart attacks, the last of which took him
from us in 1990. He lived to see me in my first *In the Heat of
the Night* episode, but not to see my "Written by" credits on
the episodes of that show that I eventually wrote. He didn't
live to see how I honored him in my first book, *Freshwater
Road*. He was the template for the father character, Shuck
Tyree. If I felt alone before his death, I felt a kind of emotional destitution when he passed.

Then there was the acting career, or the lack of one. At the opening of the decade, there was nothing in film or television. I mean nothing. I was walking around devastated. I continued dabbling in writing, my usual dismal poetry, story ideas.

My one superior experience during this time was when I did a deep dive into the life of the 19th century San Francisco power broker, Mary Ellen Pleasant. A pal had handed me the book of her life, at that time, the most complete examination of her story. The image of her, the things I read about her, fascinated me and never left my mind. Why had I never heard of her before? Why had there been no film or series about her extraordinary life? I traveled to San Francisco to research her: the San Francisco Historical Society, the Bancroft Library at Berkeley, and beyond to Sacramento and the California State Library. I began trying to find a way into the story of her life. I collected everything I could find on her journey.

I formally met my third husband, Jim Hill, in Sacramento when a group I helped to create, The Media Forum, toured a poetry show up and down California. Jim had a friend, an educator there, who helped The Media Forum set up the reading in the Sacramento area. She was the go-between, the hook-up lady. She informed me that Jim wanted to take me to dinner back in Los Angeles.

Jim was a famous sportscaster in LA I'd watched him on television for years, perhaps nodded if I saw him at some event, but I did not know him. He was much admired around town, and also had a reputation as a *player* when it came to women. In my emotional doom and gloom at that time, I heard it but went ahead anyway. What's that line from Maya? *When people show you who they are, believe them the first time.* I rationalized. I also knew that sports guys pretty much all had that reputation. What else is new?

We had not one thing in common. But like I said, I was in so much trouble emotionally, I figured it couldn't be any worse than how it already was. I don't even know how we had even a tiny conversation. He was a man's man. He evidently had a woman on the side. Put it this way: it was not the lady at the television station where he worked who kept calling my home. He did a lot of disappearing. Then I started disappearing, and that's all she wrote. There was some arguing, for sure, but no real fighting.

Over the course of our nearly one year of dating, I was the beneficiary of his material generosity. There were beautiful gifts, diamonds, masses of roses, and life-sized stuffed animals. These last puzzled me. I truly did not know what to do with a near life-sized lion standing in the living room looking at me when I walked in the door. Was this some sort of metaphor of what life with Jim was to be? Being guarded by a stuffed lion?

One thing is for sure: taking into account my emotional state at that time, I should have been running for the exits. Instead, my stubbornness held me in place. I was going to die on another hill of my own making.

He gave me an exquisite white fox coat, calf length, that I had the audacity to wear in New York City on a blustery day. The coat was a stunner. I left my hotel heading to a luncheon, but the volume of catcalls, whistles, boisterous yelling, and gesturing at me by construction workers on Fifth Avenue motivated me to return right to my room to change into a less flashy covering. It was and is a beautiful coat. If I wore it in New York today, it more than likely would be the object of a different kind of violence—paint being thrown at the fur or worse. I no longer wear fur coats no matter where I am.

We married at Los Angeles's First A.M.E. Church a year or so after that first meeting. It all looked so good from the outside. *Showtime!* We hired a wedding planner who came in the door with a mountain of details. She brought decisions to be made on colors, napkins, cloths, flowers, name plates, table spacing, music, dancing, and on and on. Just the kind of activity I tended to duck. The entire time I wanted to shake her silly, tell her to just do it and leave me alone, which of course she couldn't do because it was my wedding.

At our humongous reception at the Los Angeles Music Center, I was a smiling, pretty bride in front of a mass of wonderful people so happy to be there to celebrate us both. There were a slew of sports celebrities, a slew of actor celebrities— Carroll O'Connor, Sidney Poitier, Magic Johnson, to name just a few. I remember in particular how a group of my gal pals flirted openly with the limo drivers, all of whom had big-screen good looks. Did I say they were *fine?*

There was palpable excitement over this coupling that had nothing to do with us as individuals. Jim's people didn't really know my people or me, and my people didn't really know his people or him.

We all admired each other because of the accumulated success. Hollywood loves success, loves big smiles and beautiful teeth. We had all of that in spades. That seeming richness of my life then, under the brilliant California sunshine, couldn't really break through the darkness troubling my soul, a sense of being lost as life swirled around me. I couldn't get a grip, but most of the people around me couldn't see what was really going on. There hasn't been a day since Michele's murder that her death has not bounced around in my head, tearing at the walls I set up to protect me. The outrage that no one has ever even been charged in her death tears away at my sense of justice, of fairness, of comfort even. I was drinking far too much. Struggling to reach any grab bars that I could see or feel. I'm an actress who'd learned how to present, to be suffering and not show it, to be drunk and not appear so even if I wobbled a bit on my heels, or laughed through a slight slurring of my words. I was a paper tiger.

Jim Hill couldn't have known that my heart and soul were unreachable under my actress façade. I have no idea what he saw or thought he saw in me beyond a pretty face who also happened to be Black. He lived in a white world but for the athletes. I lived in a mixed world and had done so for years—even during the Civil Rights Movement, we were an *integrated* group.

I don't even know if he cared that I was living during that time in a prison whose walls were grief and confusion. Looking back at it from this vantage point, I think he saw me more as an object, an acceptable complement for his career—not untypical for macho men of the 1980s and before. Whatever was going on in my mind and heart was of no or very little interest to him. That's the old way of being married. Sharply distinct roles, very little overlap.

We shopped for a home with our two very different emotional and physical makeups driving us. He was a hot celebrity in town here, so he wanted to live a kind of behind-the-gates life. I didn't want to live behind any gates. I want to be able to feel the people, different kinds of people. And I needed to live close to my mother because her husband, my stepfather, was in the throes of dementia. She'd lost her youngest child and her heart was broken.

We ended up buying this now 100-year-old pile that I've spent an eon in and a wad of money on and loved every minute of it. I knew when we walked in that it was my choice. The house spoke to me, calmed me down, helped me heal. He was not happy about that. In the end, he bought himself the kind of property he wanted, much more lavish, far up a hill, beautiful but (in my opinion) with not one bit of seasoning in the air of it. During this same time, I purchased a four-unit apartment building five minutes from this house and began what turned into an almost four-decade lady-landlord journey.

I can't say that I didn't sense the grave distance between us before the marriage. I can't say that I didn't suspect that he was in no way open to my sadness or anything else about me that wasn't made for some kind of marital advertisement. Something in me wanted to stay hiding in the jail of sorrow I'd erected. When I peeked out, there was no one there. I remained closed off and inside myself for the three-year sum total of our relationship.

Jim worked a massive number of hours, so there wasn't a ton of time to do what I considered fun stuff. He also had a never-ending trail of women basically following him around—right to our home, on more than one occasion. You heard me right. They called him at home. They parked in front of my home. One even *came up the driveway*. I'll say this: they were persistent. At the time, I dealt with it as best I could, but I knew deep inside that the situation was much more troubled than I could've guessed. I found a nearby escape place—a pal who was only a pal, who offered a bit of laughter and quite a bit of marijuana.

I still loved travel in those days, even when my heart was dragging me away from happiness. I'd imagined myself in the great cities of the world from the time I was in elementary school. We took a trip to England, the two of us, and then another trip to Europe with Jim's friend Kareem Abdul-Jabbar and his significant other (I won't name her here because I've not seen her since that time and have no idea of her situation). There was a corporate dinner at the Paris office of Adidas, a modest amount of sightseeing—the Louvre primarily to see the *Mona Lisa*, Versailles Palace.

Then on to Rome. We took photos by the Colosseum and Trevi Fountain.

Kareem and Jim took a prearranged side trip to Germany for a basketball camp, and Kareem's lady and I flew to Milan to shop and, of course, to eat. I took a side trip by train to Florence on my own, where I walked the center of the city, inhaled the opulence created by the Medici, had a drink at Harry's Bar and lunch at a sidewalk café. The train back to Milan was so crowded, we were practically hanging out of the windows, riding standing like on a city bus, swaying and bouncing. I arrived back in Milan in time for the street celebrations after Italy won the 1982 World Cup championship. That was a wild, crazy night, dancing and drinking and celebrating with the entire city emptied into the streets. That was a wow time! Everything I'd heard about how open Italian men are in their praise of good-looking women held true.

Jim and I never had profound conversations about life, love, or anything else. He was a wall of silence for the most part about emotional-life issues. My deeper self that I eventually let Jim begin to see was basically a wall of mourning.

My manner had to be offensive, to some degree, to such a macho guy. I could be Miss Weepy, clawing and scratching at life, but mostly I was hiding behind my veil of sadness and deep feeling of displacement. I see now that my baggage was dragging down my whole life— and why would anyone want to help haul that around? I don't blame Jim for this failure. There were occasional moments of real sharing, but they were moments that passed swiftly and if you blinked, you missed them. Jim began spending more and more time other places. Eventually he purchased that other home and moved out. Divorce quickly followed.

It was supposed to be that way. We should not have been

together. That's not a comment on him or me, really. We simply were very different people. There was no crying or mourning for the dead marriage. I have a quality that I'm sure must come from dealing with a lot of different kinds of difficult stuff starting with my birth. As a general rule, I don't do a lot of looking back. Maybe it terrifies me.

I began picking up the pieces of my life. My acting career was nearly dead in the water. I inched toward writing more, acting less. I could control my output. I didn't have to wait around for a production company to use my skills. I began using them myself as a writer. Writing has saved my life.

I began my internal rebuild by going back to school. And, thank God, I found an excellent therapist.

14.

I BEGAN MY *REBUILD DENISE PROJECT* AT UCLA SUMMER
school by picking up Astronomy and Microbiology. I'd lost
my science credits when I withdrew from the University of
Michigan. Beginning with science classes put the grit back in
me. A lot more difficult than learning lines for a sitcom. The
knowable structure of study helped me get back to sanity's
door. I needed that structure.

I began doing upgrades on my beautiful house, which
included first putting in a pool, then eventually a new
kitchen, new bathrooms, and new windows where needed.
The building I'd purchased was a dump, and I began the
rehabilitation on each unit—plumbing work, electrical
work, new appliances. I ripped out old moldy carpets to find
reasonably nice hardwood floors which, once redone, were
gorgeous. The apartments had great windows in the living
and dining rooms. I began plotting my own move to this
building in the event that became necessary. I wanted a place
I could run to when the going got tough. In truth, I had dug
myself so far in on my house, I would've committed murder
to stay here.

UCLA was my choice for summer school because it was
cheaper than USC. My home is equal distance from both

schools. Located in Westwood Village, UCLA can be a madhouse. Parking was a nightmare. It's a great school, no doubt, and more like Michigan than USC, as both are public institutions.

I went back and forth as to where I wanted to finish the undergraduate degree I'd begun all those years before. USC was more contained; it had a kind of *behind the gates* (it has actual gates) feel, like most everything in Southern California for the wealthy. At that time, I needed *behind the gates* to feel protected. School centers me and that's what I wanted. That's what I got. I took theater classes and writing classes primarily. In my theater history class, I learned that two theaters I'd been part of were featured in the textbook: the Negro Ensemble Company in NYC and the Free Southern Theater in Mississippi and Louisiana. Imagine the surprise when my fellow students heard me talk about those experiences in class discussions. I became a quiet student celebrity.

I graduated from USC in 1987 with a degree in Theater. At my undergrad graduation, Mom was right there, her pride like a waving flag on her beautiful face. I had finally fulfilled a dream she'd had my whole life.

I immediately registered for grad school. I was on a happiness roll. There, I was able to knead my Mary Ellen Pleasant research into a one-act play called *Buses,* which illuminated a fantasy meeting between Mary Ellen Pleasant of late 1800s San Francisco and Rosa Parks of the 1955 Montgomery Bus Boycott, the exquisitely organized event that changed Montgomery, the state of Alabama, and most of the South.

Both women were ejected from public transportation in their respective cities because they were Black. Mary Ellen Pleasant fought her battles in the California courts. Rosa Parks took it to the streets and doing so helped ignite the modern Civil Rights Movement. I wanted to put these two women from different centuries into the same context and let them go at it, because though their yearnings for equality were equal, not much else about them was even in the same ballpark. Mrs. Pleasant was a businesswoman, a sly fox, a brilliant survivor during the rough and tumble days of the Gold Rush and the Barbary Coast, right up to the turn of the century. She was bold, a sort of street brawler, with no fear of the powerful.

Mrs. Parks was soft-spoken but strong as a Florida gator, religious, determined but never showy. She presented as the height of calm, unchallenging in her way of being in the world. They were equally strong on the inside but presented so very differently to the world—Mrs. Parks was a paragon of moral virtue. Mrs. Pleasant was a woman who did what she wanted to do when she wanted to and basically told folks to deal with it. I am both these women and that's why I loved them so.

For my research on Mrs. Parks, I interviewed her a bit by phone and invited her to dinner in my home, which was lovely. She was a beautiful human being from the outside in and inside out.

I had begun regaining my productivity, my spunk and spirit, and others began to notice. *Buses* received great notices, and won the Phi Kappa Phi Student Recognition award in 1989. I felt myself coming back to life as the person I wanted to be. I remembered my early attempts to sell story ideas on *Room 222*. I remembered all the hours I'd spent in the libraries doing research in my drive to bring these two ladies to life on stage.

Eventually, Ricardo Khan of Crossroads Theatre in New Brunswick, New Jersey, picked up *Buses* and produced it, directed by the late Shirley Jo Finney, starring Iris Little and Petronia Paley. By then, 1991, I was *really* rolling. I could feel the blooming of a new part of me. I was a writer. I had done something unique and I was dizzy from the experience. Watching Little and Paley on the stage, saying words I'd written, nearly made me break out in a happy dance. The excitement I felt was palpable.

Later, I developed a film treatment based on the life of Mary Ellen Pleasant. Her story—what's known of it —swirls in my head to this day. I shopped the film treatment around town but found no takers. I could see it so clearly in my mind—this incredible Black woman walking the hills of San Francisco in the mist, running her boarding houses, making backroom deals for property and power, perhaps (so legend has it) even helping John Brown with finances. A remarkable woman who received as much press in San Francisco in the late 1800s as a big celebrity would today. There were full-page spreads on this mysterious woman who, as she accumulated wealth, was feared by powerful men in Sacramento because she knew how to gather and keep their secrets. She understood well the power of secrets as weapons. One day, I still believe, a good producer will grab this story and run with it.

This breakthrough for me as a fledging writer seasoned the pot, fed my drive to go forward as an actor-writer. I dreamed of being that hyphenate. In terms of my work life, nothing made me happier than being recognized for my ability to both act and write. Now I really was living in "high cotton."

In 1985, on a break from school, I took an acting job in New York City, at Woodie King Jr.'s New Federal Theatre. *Long Time Since Yesterday* by P. J. Gibson was directed by Bette Howard. I worked with the wonderful Loretta Devine, Starletta DuPois, Thelma Carter, Emily Yancy, Ayana Phillips, and Petronia Paley. The New Federal Theatre was a creation of Detroiter, Woodie King Jr. I'd known him for years but never worked for him until this piece. His theater did plays primarily but not exclusively by Black playwrights.

While back in New York, I lived with my great sister-friend Marcia Stevenson in Queens and took the train back to her place late at night after each show. That experience put hair on my chest, grit in my jaw and ferocity in my soul. Walking from the subway stop in Queens to her apartment graduated me into being a big-time city girl again. No cushy rides in limousines here! I had loved living in New York in the '60s, but here I was terrified every night and couldn't wait to get back to Los Angeles and my car.

At this point in the '80s, the roiling situation in South Africa and the fight against apartheid was of huge importance to me, and I became involved in some activist work. I became acquainted with Randall Robinson and Arthur Ashe and others involved in the cause. I was asked to produce an event at the Beverly Wilshire Hotel, a fundraiser for Artists and Athletes Against Apartheid. This involvement also led to what I think of as my salvation affair, with a man 18 years younger. This young man, who will be named Keith to protect whomever needs protecting, knocked on my door to volunteer to work on this event.

The Artists and Athletes Against Apartheid dinner raised over $50,000 with my old friend Sidney Poitier and many other celebrities in attendance. That sum today would equal close to $200,000. We filled the banquet room of the Beverly Wilshire Hotel. It was a very successful evening.

After the dinner, I retired to my suite at the hotel and Keith joined me. Joy is when you've made love with a good man and when he leaves, you watch him out of the window as he does a skip and a kick on his way to his car. The whole evening was so fine, so enriching—an event for a cause

I wanted to support and a man who shared the moment unselfishly. Praise the Lord.

On our first formal date, Keith picked me up in his car to go to a movie. Now, if it's not clear yet at this point in the story, I'm a luxury car girl—a walking cliché from Detroit who graduated from my dad's many Cadillacs to my own many Mercedes-Benzes. So, I walk out and get into his young man's car, which is very low to the ground. It's black and kind of rough looking, but not too bad. He's very well mannered, holding my elbow as I get in, closing my door. We chat and then he turns onto Olympic Boulevard and miraculously, there's little traffic. He took off in that little car, bouncing over potholes the size of craters, with the music blaring. He was deadly serious, driving like a maniac.

"Maybe you can slow down?"

The glint in his eyes belied the seriousness of his tone. "In this car, you really feel the road. You've been riding in luxury cars far too long. It's time for you to get down on the level the vast majority of humanity lives on."

"Get down? Now there's an expression I love." I yelled above the noise of the bouncing car and the radio.

"Get down!" He started singing. "Get down, baby, get down!"

I started laughing so hard tears were streaming down my face just as we hit a giant pothole and I nearly bounced out of the car.

"I'm not going to make it!" I yelled. My breasts hammered up and down, straining the light bra I wore.

Keith changed to an oldies station.

"Is that for me?" I yelled over the noise.

He smiled. "That's *my* music, Denise. It's what I love. See, we have a lot in common, don't you think?" It's true, we were both movie fans and music lovers.

Gladys Knight came on, singing, *LA proved too much for the man.* I was thinking LA proved too much for everyone, especially me.

We made it to the movies and as the fates would have it, we ran into people we knew. That gave rise to more silliness, as I refused to hold his hand while standing in the line for tickets. I was ducking and dodging, while his chest was out as big as the world. Of course, we were seeing the most romantic film of the decade, *Out of Africa.*

Our other shared passion was the beach. Since I'd first come out here, I'd loved to stand on the beach watching the sun fling diamond chips on the water's surface, joyous as a flower girl gleefully tossing petals with every step.

In Los Angeles, from the southern tip of Zuma Beach, the meandering coastline reels north, the calamity that is Los Angeles nipping at its heels. To its east, Los Angeles gobbles at the edges of the Mojave. In its turn away from that burning bareness, as it grew the calamity lumbered west, dynamiting mountain tops to appease the gods of avarice and greed, carving roads through sacred grounds, before it arrived at the water's edge, emptying its uncounted bowels in the wide blue Pacific. Before long, this sparkling wonder would be dung brown. Instead of diamond chips dancing on its surface, there would be used plastic diapers, cigarette butts, and food wrappers polluting the water, killing the marine life and decimating the fragile shore.

This is the kind of dreadful thought never far from my mind. Why do I always go to the wall? Every frigging thing a catastrophe. The sky is always falling, and I was perennially Chicken Little. And when had I become so possessive of this place? I wasn't from here. Truly, California had been and still is, in many of this state's exquisite places, a land of milk and honey. It's hard to grasp how huge, beautiful, how varied in climate and botany this state is. Still, I embraced a nostalgia for what had been before the Spanish, the settlers, the developers, the water monsters and the screen dreamers. The Pacific clear, clean, and full of life.

Zuma had been my beach of choice for years as the beaches nearer to the city became so crowded, filthy, and incapable of quiet. The run from Zuma—a county park and beach—to the strip of public land near the shore at Trancas (Broad Beach) counted as one of my life's pleasures. Little did I know that a few short years later, I'd be driving to Carroll and Nancy O'Connor's Moroccan beach house at Broad Beach practically every other weekend. For now, coming to Zuma felt like a tiny vacation trip away from the clogged, hot, and often dusty streets of the city.

As I ran on Zuma Beach one weekend, I stopped for a bit to walk and look around. I could just see in the distance the dark figure of Keith, my friend-lover, who I'd left behind spread out on our blanket. Beyond him and our small place of mercy on the clean sand, the beach mansions of Trancas shone like playhouses in the light of the sun. They seemed to be gorgeous renderings, magic fronts on a movie set with no real livable house behind the exterior. The beach mansions nestled into the soft curve of the shoreline all the way to an outcropping of boulders, impassable unless you jumped in the ocean and swam around to the other side. Soft low dunes formed a boundary that seemed to move between the private properties of the very rich and the strip of public land near the water's edge.

Solitary runners, stick figures in the distance, pounded along the sand. I began walking, then fast walking, preparing to jog again. I needed to run, to drum out my anxieties over what life had next in store for me. But I felt free in that period after the absolute failure of my third and final marriage.

That day I hauled past a small group of men who'd planted brilliant green umbrellas in the sand. When I slowed, I heard their laughter and gentle, pawing conversation in harmony with the soft slapping of the waves. It was a strange juxtaposition of sounds, resonant laughter followed by sentence parts, whispered, confided, even screeched in two-toned falsettos. They were sleek and tan, gym rats for sure. They'd spread their blankets, opened their picnic baskets, and fallen into a circle around a small fire in a sand pit. The smell of grilled chicken floated over the beach. They made me smile and they made my stomach growl.

I picked up speed again, a cool breeze from the ocean pushing me, the packed sand at the water's edge a relief after I'd done the first part of my run through loose sand, the most difficult surface on earth to run on. I pounded to my finish near Keith, breathing in shallow gasps, the salt spray choking my hair into tighter curls. He didn't acknowledge my arrival, just lay there on the blanket, one perfectly muscled arm sheltering his eyes against the now slanting sunlight. He was fine, lying there like a smooth brown dream, a perfect sports body, strong enough to throw a football yards and yards and agile enough to take off running like a gazelle. Close afro haircut. College boy good looks. Before long he was heading to law school. He had time to careen around in life, make mistakes, and recover again in his press forward.

I was 18 years older and didn't have a minute to spare.

I stretched out parallel to the never resting, never weary sea. I put my head on the most comfortable part of his chest, knowing even this benign contact would shock us both with an electrical charge of sexual energy. He turned toward me, making my position impossible to maintain, then sat up to pull me down on top of him. What I felt for Keith was as close to a need as anything I'd ever felt, a thirst for fresh water after drinking vinegar for two years, a grumbling for good food after starving in my locked closet.

We rolled over and I spread my legs then wrapped them around his muscled body. He was a comfortable feeling man who didn't have to use his arms to hold you. His entire body held you.

"I'm hungry." I wiggled from under him and tried to point toward the guys with the grilled chicken.

"You've got that 'I'm almost old enough to be your mother' look." He held my chin and stared into me, past my anxieties.

"Yeah, if I'd had you when I was a sophomore in high school. And that wouldn't have happened, because it was all 'keep your panties up and your dress down, young lady.'"

My fear of being 18 years older tightened my mind. Things worked fine when the man was older; it didn't even matter how much older. But this being-older thing was a thornier path for women and came with toll. I'd already heard the sly comments from a few friends who knew about Keith, felt the askance looks. I'd never been with a younger man nor had I been with a man significantly older. I spent some time trying to figure this age thing between men and women out. No doubt, I did not look my age. Nor did I behave my age, I guess one could say. Truly, I was free spirit, with boundaries—but not enough boundaries to hem me in too too much.

"Life is short and love is scarce." I heard his words that day and thought maybe he'd aged 20 years as we sat there in the waning sunlight. He sounded like an old codger. But that was one of the charming things about him: he was young but had a spirit like he'd been here before. His emotional intelligence went well beyond the men I'd known who were age-appropriate. Keith arrived at his adult life with this quality. Some folks have it and most folks don't.

"You're as much a wonder to me as you think I am to you. So, where's the harm?" He laughed. "Masters and Johnson were right, you know."

I grabbed his lifeline and relaxed. "Did they really say something about this kind of relationship configuration?"

"I don't know, but if they didn't, they sure as hell should've."

"I never read them."

"I'll teach you everything you need to know about it." He said it like a boy hustler, a gigolo with brains and a body worth remembering. It crashed my resolve, though I knew it was young man hyperbole.

"Never mind, Sonny Boy." I went deeper with the thought, though, and said what I really felt. "I bet you could."

"I *know* I could." He smiled sideways and spoke quietly, losing his young guy bravado, looking more like a kid in a candy store with too much money to spend. It was a delicious look.

"These are supposed to be the best years of my life." I grew serious but stopped myself from tipping into my favorite zone—catastrophic thinking. For once.

"And I'm here to make sure they are." Young guy bravado galloped back in.

"I believe you, Sonny Boy."

With Keith I remember a feeling of being conquered, and that wasn't entirely comfortable for me during those days, or any days really. I called him "Sonny Boy" to snatch away some of the power I'd given him. I knew I was in too deep to walk away, too deep to do anything but let it run its course. And that was the fear. That it would indeed run its course. Life would be sure that happened.

Who else would be so much fun to be around when he

was gone? Who would take a balloon ride with me in the wine country and laugh like a nut when the thing crashed into the vineyards instead of the landing area? Normal people would've been terrified. Who would help me study for my science classes as I struggled with an eye infection that I swear I picked up in handling slides in Microbiology class? He sat beside me reading the textbook, making notes so that I could keep up with the class work. I could see the future and it appeared a lonely road was ahead.

He took my "Sonny Boy" barbs with good humor. His youthful swagger, his kindness, his humor, his sensuality put him in the winner's circle already. He'd won. I was down for the count and loved every minute of it. My efforts to push him away were totally without heart. He allowed my own sensuality to express itself without any effort at all. I say "sensuality" as opposed to "sexuality" because there was so much kindness, warmth, generosity, and freedom in our time together. I'm grateful that it happened when it happened. It was the gift from the gods of love and happiness that I needed most of all.

15.

BACK IN 1967, WHEN I WAS STILL LIVING IN NEW YORK, I'D mentioned to my pal Robert Hooks how much I wanted to meet his close friend James Baldwin. Robert obliged and invited me to join him for a dinner date with Mr. Baldwin at El Faro, a Spanish restaurant in the West Village. Knees knocking, I met James Baldwin—and literally swooned, my little face nearly sinking into my paella. He listened politely to this almost-actress who already dreamed of becoming a writer at some nebulous point in the future. He encouraged me forward, though he'd not seen a single word I'd ever put on paper. His graciousness, his kindness won my heart for all time. What he stood for, what he wrote, what he'd endured? I already loved him for that.

People in the Civil Rights Movement, white and Black, knew James Baldwin as one of us because he stepped up. He died in 1987, yet another travesty of that terrible decade.

Not long after he passed, I flew to Paris to visit my friend Denia Hightower, who lived in an awesome apartment with balcony views of the Eiffel Tower. We went food shopping the day after my arrival, which meant buying individual items from various vendors rather than pushing a shopping cart through a gigantic supermarket. One sold rotisserie chicken

smothered and smoking in garlic, olive oil, and herbs de
Provence. We smelled it from a block away and our tummies
began to growl like wild beasts on the hunt. We bought the
chicken, the aroma of which nearly drives us insane. We stop
at a cheese vendor for cheese, the bread vendor for bread,
the flower vendor for flowers, the vegetable stand for salad
greens, and home we go.

Denia and I sat in the kitchen of her grand apartment
drinking a wonderful Sancerre, eating that chicken with little
grease dabs all over our faces and hands, laughing our asses
off. Her beautiful Baccarat wine goblets had greasy finger-
prints and lip prints all the way around. Denia was infinitely
more proper than me. Actors are known for eating *all* the
food. We know that unemployment is usually right around
the corner, so we prepare by eating other people's food whenever the opportunity presents itself.

On that trip, Denia ushered me through Paris, the museums, neighborhoods, restaurants. Long glorious walks. After
a few days of that joy, she took me to the Gare de Lyon to
catch the train for Nice where I visited my director pal Asaad
Kelada and his family in their home in Saint Vallier de Thiey,
north of Grasse, home of the flower cultivation that supports
the perfume industry. Asaad and his brother, Shaker, met me
at the train station in Nice and off we went to Saint Vallier,
up the winding roads of the Alpes Maritime. Wonderful
experiences like these are among the blessings of my life.

Asaad treated me and his late sister Nadia, also vaca-
tioning from Southern California, to lunch on the beach in
Cannes where, for the first time in my life, I saw women
bathers with their boobs bared to the world. Asaad, who I
thought was studying his menu, was in fact looking over the
top of his menu studying boobs. We had a good laugh.

We drove to Monaco and roamed around, peeked into

the Casino, took pictures of the giant corpulent sculptures by Botero. I felt thin. Going west and north from Cannes, we stopped in small villages, bought Aretha Franklin tapes. In Mougins we stopped for the most amazing *soupe de poisson* God ever allowed humans to enjoy. We visited the Commanderie de Peyrassol vineyard in the village of Flassans de Peyrassol, sat outside tasting their rosé wine in the summer heat, then headed back to Asaad's beautiful home in Saint Vallier to drink red wine while dancing to Aretha Franklin on his white carpet. Yes, we spilled the wine and yes, Asaad directed us to get down on hands and knees to spot that carpet.

The following day, Asaad took me to the *Colombe d'or* (The Golden Dove) restaurant in Saint Paul de Vence for lunch. As we sat on the patio in the glorious sunlight, the actor now turned writer Eriq La Salle walked in. Our massive smiles at running into each there spoke to not just the showbiz camaraderie on display, but also that we were two American Black folks enjoying the best life had to offer in that moment in the South of France.

Having taken more than one art history class while at the University of Michigan, I was thrilled to tour the restaurant's smaller rooms to see many famous paintings. As the story goes, struggling artists visiting or even living in the South of France often had to pay their tab at the restaurant with paintings. You sip the last of your wine and then walk through the many smaller rooms of the restaurant to see Matisse, Picasso, Leger, Braque, Calder. I was breathless with excitement to be there.

My excitement at being so close to where James Baldwin had lived was palpable. When I told the maître d' I'd met him and his brother David in New York City, her face lit up with delight as she reached for the phone to call David. He absolutely remembered me.

After our lunch, Asaad and I headed to James Baldwin's old villa to sit with David under the grape arbor, sipping wine and talking books and the writing life.

I felt at home—as if I was exactly where I was supposed to be. Even all these years later, I try hard to get the feeling of that place on my patio under the gazebo, surrounded by plants, flowers, trees, enjoying wine and the calm, which it seems is always too soon interrupted by helicopters buzzing over, horns honking, dogs barking, and too often, the news of yet another mass shooting. I keep trying.

My highly romantic dream of being a writer rose to the top of my *to be done* list as I crept slowly toward middle age. I'd done reasonably well as an actor. My career in television after *Room 222* was cancelled continued for years of guest-starring on many shows. These ranged from *The Flip Wilson Show* to *Benson* to *Magnum PI,* to *The Cosby Show, Police Story,* and more. And of course, I also did a short-lived comedy series, *Baby, I'm Back* opposite Desmond Wilson.

Looking at that list of television guest appearances, it's plain to see there was no or very little growth in the complexity of roles.

Then came my last Poitier/Cosby film, the misbegotten *Ghost Dad.* I have no idea what this film was supposed to be. Cosby dies and comes back as a ghost. Some people can see him and others cannot. I played the next-door neighbor he seduces. I'd wanted to play a part that showed I had sensuality in my chest of abilities, but this was dumb as a wooden nickel. I was on top of him sweating and trying to make the moment work and he was about to disappear into his ghost self. All I remember is too many takes and me sweating like I'd just run a marathon. I could hardly wait for the entire experience to be over. I had no idea what that film was about.

I began to feel like I was going backwards. The business wasn't allowing the progress I was seeking, at least not then. For me, after *Ghost Dad,* there was nearly nothing in the movie business.

By the end of the 1980s, my desire to segue from acting to writing had gained serious traction in my mind. I soon discovered that my fantasy of writing and the real, bare-knuckled work of writing had nothing to do with each other. I'd slipped into the delusion that my good reading habits would automatically translate into me writing well. The joy I felt turning the pages of great novels provided a dream-like place of peace. But for the longest time, I didn't have a clue as to turning that dream into a reality of actually writing.

As I was searching for a way to get going as a writer, my agent called to tell me that Carroll O'Connor—still one of the most famous men in America after starring as Archie Bunker on *All in the Family*—wanted me to audition for the part of Harriet DeLong on his series, based on the 1967 classic film, *In the Heat of the Night.* I was ready to hurl myself into the next good thing. But I knew the industry, and though I'd had some success, I knew how rough Hollywood could be, especially for Black folks. I'd tried and failed to move myself toward more complex characters. I fretted: What kind of character was this small Southern town lady, Harriet DeLong? And even if I did get this part, what would happen to my still nonexistent writing career? Magical thinking.

At least I was thinking forward for a change. In fact, getting that job turned into both my acting swan song and the true beginning of my life as a writer at the same time. And Harriet DeLong became the most complex character I'd ever played. This lady had an ex-husband in jail, a disobedient son who was disrespectful to her, and she served as a City

Council person. To top it all off, she was in a romantic relationship with Chief Gillespie, a white policeperson. That's a lot. She also had a younger sister who was murdered. Carroll was very aware of the murder of my sister Michele. It was not an easy day when we filmed a courtroom scene about it all.

Here's how it all came to be. Via my agents, Carroll requested a taped audition. The show was already two seasons into production on location, one season in Louisiana before the move to Georgia. There were to be no live auditions.

I taped a scene and my agent sent it to Carroll who called to tell me he liked the work. There was a problem, though: his plan was to develop a romantic relationship between his character, Chief Gillespie, and Harriet DeLong. Carroll thought I made him look too old.

I said, "Carroll, I'm an actress. I can do it."

In back of mind I was thinking, *I'm aging so fast, by the time I get to my first episode, I'll look ten years older. Not to worry!*

I began yammering about aging and the look of the character. I was hawking myself just as I'd done with Sidney Poitier for the role in *Let's Do It Again*.

I got the part—which meant I began flying back and forth from Los Angeles to Atlanta to do the job on *Heat*. That was great for the accumulation of miles . . . to do what? MORE FLYING! Somewhere along my life's way, however, after flying all over the place for years, I had developed an anxiety about flying. I had to squelch that anxiety and pretend that I still *loved* flying because I was about to do a ton of it.

16.

THE *HEAT* PRODUCTION COMPANY RENTED AN APARTMENT for me in Conyers, Georgia, and I got myself ready for cameras to roll once again. Welcome to Conyers and Covington, Georgia! Welcome back to the Deep South. I'd come full circle in a way, beginning in Mississippi and Louisiana with the Free Southern Theater and now 25 years later in Georgia filming *Heat*.

When I began working on *In the Heat of the Night*, Beverly Magid took me on as a PR client. I'd been fairly dormant during most of the '80s in terms of my Hollywood career and needed to boost my public profile for the opportunity to give me what I needed going forward. Beverly went about garnering positive press for me. It was good for the show and good for me. Beverly, I learned, was also an aspiring writer, and she became a friend as well as a colleague.

When I began work on *Heat*, my life's two trains—acting and writing—were still coupled in my mind. By the end of *Heat*, the trains had gone their separate ways. Acting disappeared down the tracks and writing stood there waiting for me to get on board. *Heat* was a life/work transition point for me, feeding my ability to be strong in a new area of creativity. But not for one minute was the transition from actor to writer easy. That's precisely what I wanted to happen, though, even if making that kind of change in midlife was scary.

Two years into my *Heat* journey, I pitched my first story idea to Carroll. My spiel: "Now Carroll, you have a ton of Black characters on this show, and *no Black writers!!*" The pitch was pretty much what it had been 20 years earlier in 1971 on *Room 222.* That's how much things had not changed over the years. I stood in front of his desk doing battle for myself and by extension, other Black folks. I was *in the room*, and I used myself to struggle against what had gone before. That's precisely what we're supposed to do—understand and use whatever power we have.

Carroll, it turned out, had the courage to take me on as a fledgling writer, and I needed his push. My first *Heat* script, "Odessa," told the story of the first Black woman who attempted to vote in Sparta, Mississippi back in the 1960s. Years later, the town is finally ready to honor this woman, who had been berated and spat upon when she tried to register back in the day. When I told Carroll the idea, I saw his bright blue eyes begin to sparkle. It would absolutely work for his show. He told me he was buying the idea, and that I would write the script. That shut me up fast. I admitted, honestly, that I didn't know the first thing about writing a television script for an hour-long dramatic show. He said, "I'm going to teach you."

His teaching was not like, *sit down and we'll do this work.*

He was extremely busy running that show and doing his own writing as "Matt Harris," his pseudonym. His instruction was hit or miss, write and rewrite, structure the story for action and the involvement of the main characters, the police people of Sparta, Mississippi—those are the people the audience checks in to see every week. I did a ton of rewriting.

In purely practical terms, acting in television can be

lucrative. Nothing like a limo pulling up in front of your house to take you to the airport to fly you first class to your acting job. Nothing like having people to help you handle your life because you're so busy working and earning excellent money. I'd had quite a few years of that kind of luxury. I was spoiled.

I was accustomed to a lifestyle that writing would require me to give up. Writing novels that may or may not sell can leave one with massive dips on the financial side of things. I wanted to write a novel. I had to get ready for that part of the transition to writing.

I managed to turn out six scripts for Carroll with him as my mentor. The subject matter of those *Heat* scripts all had to do with my interests. Years ago, I'd seen a *60 Minutes* segment on Black farmers in Alabama losing their land to all manner of chicanery and skullduggery by the powers-that-be in various small Southern towns. That story parked in the back of mind and evolved into "Legacy," a *Heat* script about an old Southern gentleman leaving land to the Black family who'd worked for him for years and years for a pittance or less. The granddaughter of the Black family comes south to retrieve the bequest, but the workers in the documents department of the Sparta Court of Chancery are dismissive and rude and refuse to give her the will. The gentleman's grandchildren then refuse to honor their grandfather's dictates. High drama ensues. It felt old school and true to Southern life to this day. The process of multigenerational Black farmers being ripped off goes on.

Another of my scripts was titled, "Your Own Kind." It told the story of two high school kids, a Black guy on the track team and a white female student, who are infatuated with one another in typical high school fashion. That information seeps out of the school into the surrounding areas and raises the ire of local racists. This was the last of my stories that dealt with ethnicity and racism.

For the most part, I didn't find people in Hollywood at that time even remotely interested in the subject matter that interested me. I used to ponder what Hollywood might have done to knit this multi-ethnic population into a shapelier unity. Perhaps if Hollywood had been more forward thinking back in the day, more Americans may have been encouraged out of hatred and misogyny. Film has always been an extremely powerful influencer of public opinion. Remember, *Birth of a Nation* set the tone not only for what Hollywood would do and be for years after, but also much of America. Remember, Hitler himself loved American and Hollywood racism and used many dreadful things from this American product. None of it was pretty.

I began writing scripts centered on female characters with issues. Carroll responded to that well. "Flowers from a Lady" focused on a white woman involved in a traffic accident. The *Bubba* character comes to the scene and is helpful and compassionate to her. She attaches to him obsessively.

Another, "Little Girl Lost," was about a young white girl with a substance abuse problem. Carroll and I wrote my final script, "Poor Relations," together. This episode was fun-silly and starred Pat Hingle as the *Parker* character's incorrigible stepfather who comes to town hawking stolen art with thugs on his tail.

Carroll O'Connor's work ethic beat everyone else's into the ground. He starred, he wrote, he produced, and he managed the writing staff, the crew, the townspeople in Georgia, and visitors from all over the place who adored him. While in Georgia, the local Klan once did a mini-rally at the town center in Conyers. Carroll got the film crew over there to photograph that madness. We cast members lurked at the edge of the smallish crowd, gnashing our teeth at the horror represented there. Carroll had no patience for racism. He was a man of the world with friends from practically every ethnic group represented in this country. He embraced people and he didn't stand for too much B.S. He loved good conversation about politics, art, music, and on and on.

Shooting on location starts out fun and soon becomes near drudgery. We worked six days a week, often under forced calls, which means you can be forced back to work before you've had 12 hours off. You're paid well for working under that rule, but you also get worn down. Your face begins to show every overtime minute you've ever worked in your life. Your diet goes nuts because you can't eat on a schedule. In short, nothing ages you faster than a forced-call schedule. Eye bags get bigger and the poor makeup person has to work like the dickens to keep you looking like you look in the opening credits.

Carroll and Nancy O'Connor did some serious hanging out everywhere they went—New York, Georgia, Los Angeles, Montana, Ireland, Italy, Mexico . . . They loved spreading the good life all around. And I was a willing recipient. They invited me to New York to stay at their Central Park West apartment, and off we'd go to the opera at Lincoln Center. In Los Angeles, I spent many a day at their beach home, walking (or being run) by their ginormous, drooling dog up and down the beach.

I'd get a call from Nancy inviting me out to their Moroccan-style beach house at Trancas, just north of Malibu. I'd ask her if she wanted me to stop and pick up seafood at a precious little restaurant and market we loved on the Pacific Coast Highway. I threw my overnight bag into my trunk and headed for the Pacific Coast Highway; I loved driving by the ocean, stopping at the little market, buying shrimp, crab, whatever Nancy wanted, then heading to the beach house. We'd spend hours lunching on the porch if the weather was warm or at the big dining room table with other guests talking and laughing and drinking and eating wonderful meals that Nancy's cook prepared. There were evening walks as the sun disappeared in a blaze of red glory behind the Pacific.

Carroll and the other producers of *Heat* didn't share with me the hate mail they received about the relationship between Carroll's Chief Gillespie and my Harriet DeLong until near the end of the show's run. I, of course, was not surprised, not after cutting my teeth in the cauldron of hatred that was the Deep South in the mid-'60s. I dream of the profound, unspeakable horrors that have gone on there and still go on all over this country. And I remember the sadness in the eyes of people pushed to the margins, struggling to survive in the richest country on the planet. The curious thing is that because of the tortured history, the complexity of it, the contradictions of it, I loved it and also hated it.

Three to four years into its run, *Heat* began getting a lot of negative press. A couple of the actors had developed drug problems. There were arrests and, from what Carroll told me, much pressure from the network to recast roles. In a very real sense, we actors are well-paid hired hands. If one of your main actors is sitting in a jail cell or in a courtroom, there's no filming. Budgets are blown, gone as originally configured. The good press slides off the pages of newspapers and websites, replaced by gossip and inuendo at the very least. The effect on the other cast and crew is real and not good, no matter how much sympathy you have for the troubled ones. Networks are business entities not treatment facilities. They want the work done on the schedule that the show's producers negotiated with the network.

Carroll withstood the pressure to release Howard Rollins, who played Detective Virgil Tibbs, because he loved Howard as an artist. He knew the power of Howard's acting. Finally, Howard's struggle with substance abuse worsened to the point where assistant directors were compelled to go to his living quarters in Georgia, get him showered and dressed, then basically bring him to work. No one was happy about it.

After fighting with the network for some time to keep Howard, Carroll had to let him go. He replaced Howard with Carl Weathers, and Howard was invited back to appear as a guest star after he completed rehab.

To this day, when I close my eyes and think of Howard, I see him lighting up the screen in the films *Ragtime* and *A Soldier's Story*. I recently rewatched *Ragtime* and was as stunned by Howard's screen presence as I was when I first saw the film in the 1980s. He had a kind of magic that has you sitting there hoping whatever scene is coming next has him in it. The entire cast of *Ragtime* is marvelous, but Howard is a standout even in the vaulting company of James Cagney, Elizabeth McGovern, Mandy Patinkin, Mary Steenburgen, Debbie Allen, and Moses Gunn. It is a remarkable American film to this day.

In the Heat of the Night would become my swan song to acting. All praises to the *Heat* cast—Carroll, Howard, Alan Autry, Carl Weathers, Ann-Marie Johnson, Crystal Fox, Hugh O'Connor, Geoffrey Thorne, David Hart, and all of the company.

Back in Los Angeles after the series came to an end, my pal Beverly Magid turned me on to a writing workshop in Los Angeles led by the writer Janet Fitch, later to be the author of *White Oleander*, which was anointed by Oprah and turned into a major film. I walked into one of the most challenging creative work experiences of my life and I loved every minute of it.

Of course, Hollywood wasn't quite done with me, or I with Hollywood. But my interactions with it were gradually becoming more about finding my voice as a writer.

In 1992, CBS produced a comedy pilot based on the play and film *Driving Miss Daisy*. Robert Guillaume was the lead as the chauffeur, Hoke. Here's a sample of the character's dialogue:

"Lawd, it's a good thing I got patience, cause disyeah woman sho' tryin' it!" It couldn't help but call to mind, Butterfly McQueen as Prissy in *Gone with the Wind*, "Lawzy we got to have a doctor. I don't know nothin' 'bout birthin' babies."

A small furor erupted over the network's decision to produce this show. There were protests, letters written, voices heard—all standing against the production of yet another show using tired old Southern tropes and clichés—in this case, that of a very nice Black man who speaks like he was still on some plantation and acts as if he needs a white woman to fight his battles for him.

In the character of Hoke, the same ways of being in the world that have nailed Black folks to the cross of ignorance and dependency were on display yet again. Yes, the story takes place in the 1950s, but that was a time in the Deep South that was still quite similar in many ways to the days of slavery. The lynching of Emmett Till happened in the 1950s, not the 1850s. But so much else of import happened in the 1950s: Rosa Parks and the Montgomery Bus Boycott, the rise of Martin Luther King, the fomenting of the modern Civil Rights Movement.

There was plenty else to focus on in that era in terms of story and energy and change. But Hollywood chose for far too many years to ignore us coming into our own after hundreds of years of being ground into the dirt of America. This universal obeisance to white people, the inability to speak the English language, this total dependency on white folks to speak for us and protect us or kill us—whichever worked for them on any particular day—was about to do its biggest fade since Reconstruction in the 1870s. But at that moment, in the 1990s, Hollywood came up with another tired representation of Black and white people in the tired dance of the past.

The *Los Angeles Times* writer Howard Rosenberg penned a support piece for this throwback-to-the-days-of-slavery-sounding bit of television. It was entitled, "Miss D Meets the PC Crowd."

I wrote a response to Howard Rosenberg which was printed in the *Times*'s Counterpunch column. Among other things, I wrote:

Perhaps Black Americans (and others!) have seen enough smiling, benign servants coming out of Hollywood—I mean from the 1930s right through TV. We really have been well represented in that department. Perhaps the solution would be TV shows about other African-Americans who have lived, struggled, fought on the front lines of hatred and oppression and made it. This isn't a new idea, of course, but neither are characters representing the servant "class" who are black.

The writer Fred Johnson, who'd contributed to numerous successful shows, also wrote a piece that was printed in Counterpunch.

CBS pulled the series. The numbers on the night the pilot aired were *soft*, it was reported.

Now, Robert Guillaume was a friend. May he continue to rest in peace. I'd done a guest shot on his show *Benson* and I adored him. I visited Robert when he was near his end, in hospice. He knew that I cared about him.

But I'm a product of the Civil Rights Movement. My job—as I've always seen it, though not in contrast to anyone else—is about more than aggrandizing myself with career opportunities, money, and riches. I'm far from rich. But I am and have always been deeply committed to doing whatever I can to lift the image, the perception of Black people in the world at large and especially on television, where most people get their information—as opposed to knowledge. I was interested in the knowledge side of the issue.

I have opinions about these matters that some younger people will consider old-fashioned. When I was growing up, my mother would not allow us to see films that denigrated Black people in any way. Where language usage was concerned, she was unrelenting. There could be no bad grammar, no drawling and using words incorrectly, none of the nonsense spread far and wide by Hollywood entertainment and its derision of Black folks. We could not see *Porgy and Bess* or *Carmen Jones*. But even in Hollywood, change was in the air. In 1958 came *The Defiant Ones* and *The World, the Flesh and the Devil*. As a squeaky door opened a crack in Hollywood films, burgeoning television reverted to type with *Amos 'n' Andy* and shows of that sorry ilk.

Every Black person around my age has a similar story to tell. It didn't matter if we'd mastered English usage, were career oriented, owned property and so on. In terms of Hollywood representation, we were too often tied to the deep dreadful past of slavery and its sorry derivatives. The lesson from Hollywood was that no matter how much time passed, no matter what growth and repair Black people had managed to attain since we were enslaved, we'd always be as we were—in chains on the body and chains on the mind.

It was dreadful enough when white writers wrote for Black characters using slavery diction and delivery. Then because of our anxiety and desperation to get into Hollywood, Black writers and actors caved to the desire of white producers to do to Black people what whites had been doing for years.

Of course, I'm not the only one who resisted this madness. And in recent years there are more signs of progress. I'm a big fan of *American Fiction*, and of its screenplay by Cord Jefferson (Black), based upon the novel *Erasure* by Percival Everett (Black), which won an Oscar in 2024 for Best Adapted Screenplay. *American Fiction* tells the story of a troubled Black writer, played by Jeffrey Wright (whose work over many years in film, television and on stage has been nothing short of magical), who's obviously educated and intelligent. It is his story and the story of his family, a family that lives well—the writer's father was a doctor. His sister is a doctor. His brother is a doctor. But they struggle as so many of us do with the vicissitudes of life—the father has died and the truth of his life is not pretty, the mother develops dementia, and the two brothers are at each other's throats. They speak the Queen's English just like I and millions of others do. They struggle just like the rest of us—all of us—Black, white, Hispanic . . .

American Fiction is funny, sad, endearing, and insightful in its grasp of aspects of our lives, in ways that kill the perception that we Black people are locked eternally in some box of ignorance and banality. It's now at the top of the list—a very short list—of Hollywood films with contemporary, well-educated, successful Black characters that do not diminish us in any way.

17.

To celebrate his 60th birthday in 2000, my friend, the director Asaad Kelada, organized a trip to Egypt for his friends and colleagues from the entertainment industry and members of his family. Asaad had been the primary director for hit shows in the '80s, *Who's the Boss?* and *The Facts of Life* among many others. I had met him when he directed an episode of *Baby, I'm Back*. The series lasted only one season but my friendship with Asaad has endured.

There were 20 of us on the trip. One of his sisters was an expert on Egyptian culture and organized the in-country tours. Another of his sisters and his brother helped inform us regarding what we were seeing.

At the time of the Egypt trip, I was deep into Janet Fitch's writing workshop and anxious about missing even one or two sessions. I was fully transitioning from actor to writer—professionally, not just as a hobby. I hemmed and hawed responding to the invitation from Asaad. My pal Denia Hightower, who had traveled the world two times over, told me to get my hips out of that workshop, pack my bags, and go. Thank God for Denia pushing me out of my nest.

Traveling internationally can be not just fun but also full of information on the quirks of different cultures. You'll definitely have a host of new kinds of experiences, not all of them pleasant. Tourists often leave their manners at home— there's no fear of future dues to pay because the rude person will be leaving.

On a trip to Paris, in the rarified air of the Hôtel de Crillon restaurant, an American guest in an over-the-top, louder-than-necessary, scornful voice upbraided a waiter for not getting his poached egg precisely as he wanted. His imperious tone identified him as an asshole.

On that same trip, I'd asked a waiter in another restaurant for hot sauce. His face and mood in an instant changed from charming to slightly scornful, as if I definitely had a missing plank in my gastronomy platform. He brought a tiny dish of a peppery sauce with a tiny spoon. It was quaint and pretty but not particularly hot. I wasn't rude, only disappointed. I was hankering for Tabasco.

Back in the day, when I visited Spain and Morocco, I took the Ibn Battuta Ferry across the Straits of Gibraltar from Algeciras to Tangiers, as my late sister Michele had encouraged me to do years before. The ship was packed. At the bar, we were three deep competing for the attention of the brown-skinned bartenders. A group of American tourists berated the bar staff, calling them monkeys and other despicable names because they weren't being waited on quickly enough. I left the bar and walked around the ship praying for better behavior from us, the Americans.

When we docked in Tangiers, my rental car was rolled off the ship and held by the police. They took the car apart in a search for drugs and weapons—or so I was told. I was looking very much like a local and they assumed, I guess, that I was up to some bad business. I argued that I was American and showed my passport, which they pooh-poohed as a dime-a-dozen purchase. Eventually, I dug out my traveler's checks from Union Bank in Beverly Hills. That did the trick.

They put the seats back into my car and sent me on my way. I was petrified with images filing through my mind of me scratching the walls in some North African hole in the wall prison for the remainder of my life.

In Cairo, I was served by golden-brown waiter with dark eyes and thick dark wavy hair. His teeth needed attention and his waiter's jacket ballooned out from his thin body.

"Would you like hot sauce in your coffee?" He feigned seriousness.

"I think not." I smiled.

We grinned at each other, enjoying our private silliness. Earlier, when I had asked for hot sauce for my lamb, I quipped that I used hot sauce on everything except lettuce. My attempt to break the ice. The only items remaining on the table now were my coffee and the hot sauce bottle. Aside from the stewardesses on our Air Egypt flight from NYC, who got a little cranky with me when I told them I didn't speak Arabic, speaking with this waiter was the real beginning of my "communication" with Egypt.

The clanking sounds of food service echoed through the splashing fountain on the patio of the Nile Hilton.

"I hope you enjoyed your dinner." His smooth English and young man's voice, kind and considerate, welcomed me to this incredible place.

"I did. Thank you."

I glanced around the patio with its faux Egyptian décor and a smattering of guests. "Am I really in Egypt or am I dreaming?"

A slight concern flitted across his face.

"You are indeed in Egypt. In Cairo, Miss."

"Thanks. Wanted to be sure." I nodded and smiled my most beatific smile, probably looking like I thought I'd arrived at the Pearly Gates.

He was visibly relieved and walked away.

I'd eaten my last meal of the day, but the locals wouldn't even begin dinner until nine at night. I felt a bubble of indigestion just thinking about my body struggling to digest a hunk of lamb at midnight.

I returned to my room, remembering my travels in Spain, where dinner was on a similar schedule, with me standing at the door of many a restaurant, my stomach growling like a hungry bear, as I impatiently waited for the doors to open.

I opened the sliding glass doors to step onto the balcony. The Nile was seven stories below. *The Nile. I'm really here.* The idea of really being in Egypt felt unreal, as if I were dreaming. I stared across at the city, the fading light of day. Things were moving. I felt still.

Like the ringing of soft bells in the distance revealing no place of origin, the call to prayer lifts, then floats over and through the city, down narrow streets, up dark stairwells, surrounding the great mosques, Muhammad Ali Pasha Mosque, Salah al-Din Mosque, a heavenly voice that reaches through your skin, has you wondering if God himself is calling. It's time to bow down and thank God for the universe. The city noise lessens as a smog-red sunset washes the clay gray buildings, ghost light streaming over modern Cairo to the City of the Dead, glossing the river as it goes. The Nile shines through the murkiness. Is it one sage voice amplified a thousand times or a thousand voices woven into one like the stones of a pyramid? The muezzin from Salah al-Din takes his place in the minaret. Stop and give praise to God. And, I did, saying these words which are not a formal prayer but a prayer that came from my heart, my memories, my needs, my hopes.

At sunrise, I pray for a Nile that overflows its banks leaving loamy soil from the deepest heart of Africa.

At noon, I pray your life to be smooth and rich like the best cream.

In late afternoon, I pray your child's face is an ode to beauty.

At sunset, I pray your heart is filled with love and compassion.

At night, I pray and dream that you live long and prosper with children, flowers, rivers flowing, laughter ringing and above all, God in your heart.

The next day, we board a Nile cruiser. There's a large group of English tourists on board as well. They hustle themselves into first place in every line we form. We call them *The English*.

The ship's lobby is faux ornate, the stairwell bannisters in iron scrolls like a New Orleans bordello during the days of Storyville. My stateroom has double doors with wrought iron railings that open onto the river. I throw my suitcases into my room and head to the top deck, which is wide open with a shady protected space in the center. Chaise lounges, chairs, and tables for games are spread out across the wood floor. I park my Western self on a chaise, as cool as Smokey Robinson singing one of his most subtle ballads, maybe "Special Occasion." Cruising the Nile. I see how the Sahara nestles so close to the strip of fertile land at the edge of the river. There is no life here without it. Not then. Not now.

A couple of hours later, we arrive at Luxor and hustle ourselves down the gangplank to our big cool bus and our guide, Osama.

The desert is flowered with giant monuments, temples and underground burial sites. Hatshepsut and Thutmose II were half brother and sister and also husband and wife. She called herself *King*, pushing her husband into the background. After his death, she became regent for

Thutmose II's son (by another queen) and ruled for twenty-two years. Her large mortuary temple sweeps across the rocky cliffs, a grand portico. Huffing and puffing, we hike up the walkway steps, long and ascending in the monster heat. There is anxiety about the horrendous carnage that took place here not so long ago. In 1997, upwards of 70 tourists—Swiss, Japanese, English, German, Egyptian, French, Bulgarian, Colombian—were slaughtered at Hatshepsut's tomb, their bodies mutilated with machetes. The massacre was carried out by the Sunni Islamist movement, Assembly of Islam. Both the United Kingdom and the European Union considered it a terrorist organization. We remember.

The Valley of the Kings is hot enough to roast a Thanksgiving turkey. We walk down the slanting walkways into the tombs of Ramesses III, then to Seti I, then to Setnakhte.

Osama talks endlessly through a face of perfection. The sun does not bother him. Talking pictures on the walls of cave-tombs tell stories of lives and lead down narrow passageways to the sarcophagus. Osama fills in the history and I am melting into the walls, the paintings, into the stones. Nothing he says is foreign to me because I need this world so much, even as I fight the good fight against my claustrophobia. At the entrance to the last tomb, I decline. Osama's eyes go so sad. I need to be out in the air, even if the air is like hell's furnace. I need to see the sky. I walk toward the small trolley pickup point. No air-conditioned Mercedes buses up this far. It looks like the moon, all gravel, rock, and sand. Guards with Uzi machine guns wear white uniforms that don't fit. Young men watch over the dead. I want to be back on the river.

I am in a foreign place that in an odd way feels like home.

I look into the faces of strangers who draw no lines between us. They speak Arabic to me. When I say, *ma fee araby*, I don't speak Arabic, they don't believe me, like the stewardesses on Egypt Air. I feel like a disjointed part of the Americans. A dangling limb.

I ride back to our river cruiser in a horse-drawn carriage with a wild driver. His relatives must drive cars in Cairo. I see a man, two children, and two chickens riding on a bike. I see poverty but no hunger. I see children's faces that need washing. No fear of strangers in their eyes. No drive-by shootings, no helicopters grinding the air above my head, no locked doors, no doors.

At sunset, the farmers work the strip of fertile land next to the river. The mother, father, children, mule, cow, a camel in the background, a man wrapped in old cotton, a call to the past, like a forgotten cowboy deep in the dusk. I wave to him, but he's too far away, his camel walking the dunes that buttress the thin strips of fertile land. Children run to the banks and wave at our river cruiser. A man slides down a muddy path to retrieve his two cows who've somehow gotten down to the edge of the Nile sucking in all the water they can get, eating the rich green grass at the banks.

At night, the millions of stars and the moon in a crescent are the only lights. It is enough. The most exquisite quiet I have ever experienced.

We dine, we rest, we hang out until the night breaks out in music. Osama says that he knows by the songs that it's an Egyptian wedding. He tells us the wedding party goes from place to place, dancing and singing along the riverfront. Osama and we American insomniac night owls stand on the top deck with a desert breeze blowing our hair back, rocking to the music.

We ride in small boats, feluccas, to the island of Agilka.

Philae. The Temple of Isis. Of course, I have to go to the ladies' room. Of course, that's going to be difficult as we're on the river heading for a tourist destination that has no facilities. There is however a hut thing with a hole in the ground and a hose of gently running water. So. Outhouses in Mississippi come to mind. I'm quite familiar with those from my days in the Free Southern Theater. This is more primitive. There's nothing to sit on. You somehow flank the hole in the ground, squat, hold your undies to the side. I spy the hose and wonder if it's a kind of bidet. Am I supposed to wash my privates with that hose? There was no toilet paper, and I had no Kleenex. A travel pickle to say the least. And where was that hose water coming from? Much to ponder. I grabbed the hose and gave myself one splash. My burning thighs began to speak to me: *You've got about one more minute of this squat, kid.* I stood for a moment to be sure I was all there, splashing some hose water on my grubby hands. I headed back to the felucca and the Nile. We push off into the current.

In Egypt, eroticism is everywhere, in the art and in the air, and there is no apology. I swoon into erotic dream thoughts . . .

. . . a woman lies in the bottom of the boat dreaming of making love in the felucca as the body of the oarsman is revealed in a wind that catches the felucca's sail and lifts his djellaba above the Nile, above his dark sex. Her bent legs wide, her breasts lifted to the sky, she sees the oarsman's resting sex. Back and forth he guides the boat as if hiking switchbacks on a steep trail. He glides in the wind, from one bank to the other, dipping low until a stream of water rushes in on the wood seat and drains down into the pit of the boat and it's cool on her back, the wind fills the sail again and the felucca races the stillness, then slows, the wind again, like the teasing lover who never will let the night end.

The oarsman ties a scarf around his djellaba at the hip. His woman does the same. She throws her head back and her arms into the air, bent at the elbow, her fingers like a flamenco dancer, her sparkling earrings swinging, her hips throwing out a hot slap. He responds. They dance without touching but they touched every part of the other's body. It was a thrust here, another there, and steps around each other.

I become a voyeur in my own dream, my lips dry, my eyes at half-mast because to open them fully would reveal how much I loved what I saw. I drowned in the color of his skin. Deep caramel. Liquid. Dark eyes. Born of the sun and the desert sand, as if he walked out of a wall painting in the Valley of the Kings. Everyone stares at him, all eyes saying, "If I could choose to be any color . . ."

A memory of Grenada and the Flamenco dancers in the Sacromonte Caves crosses through my dream. The next second, I imagine I'm Gabriel García Márquez's Fermina Daza on the riverboat that will never go to shore again. I'm sailing up and down the Nile for the rest of my life.

Until I got to Egypt and looked into a smile or a sunset over Abu Simbel, I didn't know myself. Here, I am mesmerized again and again. The new color, this tan, this red-brown skin with depth, gleaming white teeth. I'm thinking is it the sunrise or is it the smile? Who are these people? A girl in the bazaar, young, odd—I kept looking at her. Her eyes. They were Egyptian wall painting eyes, lined in kohl, the shape so strange, like Africa and Asia met somewhere in Mesopotamia and ran back to North Africa with slanted oval eyes, a gift for the hardness of travel. I stared openly at her. My sister Michele's eyes.

I'm hauled from my reverie by an American white woman in our group asking me strange questions. Why are the Egyptians always looking at you and talking to you? Where did you get that bag, that ring, that hat, that white cotton so fine, that necklace, your hair? Do you know where your ancestors are from? Ouch. You could be from here. Osama is smitten with you. He looks at you when he talks on the bus. He smiles at you all the time.

Anxious White Woman needs to know that I have magic, too. She struggles for visibility like I do at home. I learn that the Anxious White Woman's favorite book is *Gone with the Wind*. Hello. She does a horrible imitation of Butterfly McQueen's speech in the film version about not "knowin' nothin' 'bout birthin' no babies." What enslaved woman didn't birth her own babies, in the slave quarters, in between the endless rows of cotton, on beds of sugar cane? Poor used Butterfly. I am quiet.

I sidle away from the group and hide behind a giant column whose crown is carved open papyrus leaves. There are things I know. I see these faces on the walls. It feels as if they see me.

We fly to Abu Simbel and bus to the monument area. Walk over the rough ground to the river, rounding to the left, and there it is. I am stunned, again. I sit down on a bench and stare up at the colossal statues of the great Pharaoh Ramesses II, the entrance to his temple. I cannot speak. It is tattooed on my brain, there to stay for the remainder of my years. We gather our entire group in front of the huge Ramesses statues to take a group shot.

That night, we sail back to Luxor. In my stateroom, the windows open, I stand in the near darkness watching the moonlit night, the tops of trees and mud brick houses in shadow, dreaming of dancing with Osama.

Some ancient cylinder, deep in its own forest of giant redwoods, rises up out of the pale peach-tan sand, a colossus with papyrus leaves open, lotus flowers not carved but drawn in stone, pulling your hands to rub the surfaces that seem soft. I dream of playing hide and seek in the columns, the voice of the guide drumming history into my head. All I can think of is how the body can melt into stone and leave an imprint that beckons.

Back in Cairo, we tour the museum. Tut is there and many others. We are witness to a genius people who built stone structures that have lasted thousands of years. In the museum, there are beautiful objects—jewelry, personal care items, implements of living, artful objects made so long ago.

My travel group calls me to come down to the museum gift shop in a hurry. I rush down. They point out a photo of an Egyptian woman who is my physical twin. The similarities are uncanny. It was like looking at myself in a mirror. My travel partners encourage me to buy the photo. I decline. There are spiritual laws against this. Her spirit is in the photo, and I can't own that. I don't want to.

The night before our departure, we hang out, eat late, drink hard liquor, dance and beam like the stars in the desert sky.

18.

When *Heat* ended its run, I hadn't yet figured out how I was going to begin and feed a second career as a writer. That was uppermost in my mind by the end of the 1990s. The show boosted my acting chops and my public profile, but more importantly it opened a door into the writing life that I'd dreamed of for so many years.

I continued working on the first 20 pages of what would eventually become *Freshwater Road*. I did a reading of those pages at Book Soup up on Sunset Boulevard long before there was a book. Those pages, submitted to Janet Fitch, became my entrance exam for her Journeyman's workshop.

Of course, it helped that I had friends in my personal network who gave me powerful encouragement. Toni Morrison honored me by reading a few very early pages of the *Freshwater* story. This was before I wiggled myself into Janet Fitch's class.

"I've finished reading your [manuscript] now," she wrote, "and am impressed with a lot of very good writing. The first pages especially have great authority and expert craftmanship. On the writing itself, I've mentioned that a lot of it is first-rate: the metaphors are provocative and lucid and your style of understatement and keen attention to details is just right."

She particularly liked the character of the heroine's father, named Shuck Tyree. Her positive reaction to the Shuck character helped push me forward. The character is loosely based on my dad, which made her comments all the sweeter. Of course, her neatly typed notes were not all positive. They sent a firm message that I had much work to do. But I was so giddy with excitement that she took the time to read the pages and give me notes, that it all seemed like a bit of heaven to me, critique and all. The appeal of the Shuck character in *Freshwater Road* also helped me secure a New York literary agent years later when the book was completed. Being accepted into Janet Fitch's workshop was a gift from the God of all good things. I'd landed in high cotton one more time. But let me be clear, I had to chop a lot of that cotton to get to the finish line in that workshop.

The workshop took place every other Saturday in Janet's home. My writing style would develop as I reworked and expanded on the basic idea of the story. I had to retrain myself to do this new work, and as part of that, at the same time, I had to endure and grow from the critiques of six other very serious writers who all seemed as if they'd been writing seriously for much longer than me. I was a dreamer who had finally taken the bit between my teeth to become a doer. Janet's brilliance as a teacher pushed me through. I had something to prove—that my dream of writing was more than a mere fantasy. I became like a dog with a bone. I didn't want to do anything that would interrupt my journey. I closed myself off in my home, stopped socializing, stopped hanging out. Refused to take on anything that might even tangentially interfere with what I was trying to accomplish.

Freshwater Road, to my mind, had to be the very best that I could do it because it was my statement on the Civil Rights Movement and its heyday in the early 1960s, a movement that changed this country for the better. Black people, with the help of volunteers of all ethnicities, grabbed the reins of their own lives, nonviolently, and began moving forward. The goals: Freedom Schools, voter registration, and health clinics in the areas most neglected by the powers that were in a community. People needed help and we did our best to give them that help. More importantly, we helped them to begin helping themselves in ways that had been blocked to them for centuries.

Although it is fiction, *Freshwater Road* had to evoke the realities of that time. A reader needed to wonder if it was in fact fiction or reality—and it is most definitely both. Lives were lost. Violence was epidemic. But we *kept on pushing*. I wanted to honor that with a work of fiction that just might outlive me. I wanted to be a literary writer, not a historian.

After workshop on some Saturdays, I'd drive home, pull into my driveway, and sit in the car crying because it was all so difficult. As I labored over draft after draft, my skills improved. The earliest progress I made had to do with writing dialogue. That's to some degree the result of dealing with scripts as an actor for more than 25 years.

If I needed any proof that my creative life had shifted to writing, in 2000, I signed on to do a play at Harvard's Hasty Pudding Theatre during this transition period, a powerful work, *The Ohio State Murders* by Adrienne Kennedy. For a brief time, I believed in a tiny place in my brain that I could be a serious actor and write well at the same time. Hadn't I done both on *Heat?* But television series acting and acting in a difficult play are immeasurably different. My focus on writing shortchanged my acting in a huge way. I did what I'll call a lackluster performance. I loved the play but felt I could not open myself to the emotional drama of the piece because my head was locked into the work on my first novel.

Recently, my friend Charles Floyd Johnson (a producer of *NCIS*, among a long list of other shows) found the reviews of that *The Ohio State Murders* production, and they're pretty good. I am often the first to diminish my own worth and work. That constant self-diminishment is the part of me that most needed and still needs therapeutic help. I have to admit I loved reading those old reviews, which were not nearly as harsh on me as I had been on myself.

Writing television scripts for characters on a show that's already developed is not in the same ballpark as writing a novel and creating all the characters, the places, the themes, the descriptions, the sensory work. I put my heart and soul into *Freshwater Road*, all the best of my intelligence, my everything.

My novel was taking shape in the workshop. In the end, the novel would take five years to write with two breaks— doing the play at Harvard and of course, traveling to Egypt. Aside from those two events, I was beyond focused on *Freshwater*; I was maniacal in my dedication to it. My home was quiet and an exquisite writing space then. I would read poetry before each writing session to help amplify the imagery in the text. I accepted the critiques of the other writers in workshop with no attitude except saying *thank you* a lot.

My passion for this book is based in my belief in what I see as the brilliance of the modern Civil Rights Movement. What happened during that time deserves many more books, movies, television shows. Keep in mind, the participants were not only Black, but also white and Hispanic young people. When you looked around you saw young Americans literally dying to make America a better place. I have never forgotten James Chaney, Andrew Goodman, and Michael Schwerner, and I never will forget them.

There's one love/sex scene in the book which takes place in a car on the side of the road near the house where the main character, Celeste Tyree, is staying for the summer. I drafted the scene and took it into workshop to get the responses of the other writers. At that time, there were two males and four females in Janet Fitch's workshop. One of the guys gave me his notes: "That's not a love scene in a car. That's a love scene at The Four Seasons Hotel." It was too comfy, too lovely, not difficult enough. I went back to the drawing board and toughened it up a bit, made it less comfy. It's a hot scene.

After the five years it took me to complete the manuscript, I began searching for an agent, and after finding one, in time, the book was acquired by Agate, which published it in 2005.

To sell books, you have to hit the road, and hit the road I did. A book tour was an entirely new activity for me and though it was utterly exhausting, I loved every minute of it. It helped that the novel began to receive stunningly positive reviews.

When the *Washington Post Sunday Book World* front page review hit, I was in DC, staying in Denia and Dennis Hightower's exquisite home on the edge of Rock Creek Park, complete with indoor swimming pool. Denia and Dennis at that time lived large and enjoyed the fruits of Dennis's business career, which ultimately saw him become the head of Euro-Disney when they lived in Paris.

It was a Sunday, and we'd had a light breakfast. My publisher had alerted me that the *Post* review would hit that day. I was a nervous wreck. The paper hit the driveway, and Denia and I ran out into a warm DC morning to grab it. I opened the paper to the *Book World* section and *Freshwater Road* was on the cover, with a beautiful artful rendering of the main character, Celeste Tyree.

I was about as close to a heart attack as I'd ever been. Dennis grabbed champagne and his Baccarat champagne flutes and we drank and toasted and laughed and I cried and laughed. What a day that was! Forgive me for quoting Samuel G. Freedman's positive review of my own book, but it distilled everything I could have hoped for after all my years of work to bring *Freshwater Road* into being.

> While she comes to the book with her memories of having performed with the Free Southern Theater in Mississippi during the summer of 1964, she has delivered something infinitely richer and more artistically satisfying than a veiled memoir. She has found the human complexity within the overarching passion play. Rather than dividing her characters into dastardly whites and saintly blacks, she boldly explores the fault lines of class, pigment, geography and character within the African-American community.
>
> It is impossible to praise *Freshwater Road* too much, in part because it arrives without a large promotional campaign or much publishing-industry buzz. The credit, then, goes not only to the author but to Agate, the publishing house in suburban Chicago that has brought such a worthy book into print and, with any luck, given Denise Nicholas yet another career, this one as a novelist.

DC was the first stop on the book tour, and from there I went to Detroit, St. Louis, Atlanta, Chicago, Dallas, New Orleans, Miami, Milwaukee, San Francisco, Oakland, Boise, San Diego, Phoenix, Hampton Virginia, and Baltimore.

On the Miami stop, I was invited to do a book event for a Jewish women's organization. Present at the book event was none other than the late Massachusetts Senator Edward Brooke. Senator Brooke and his wife invited me to dinner that evening. Having dinner with a famous senator gave me butterflies—more because I knew he was a Republican and I'm as far from that as you can get within the boundaries of American politics. He was kind and gracious in our conversation. I was careful to not go into my woman-on-fire way of being in the world, calling out those who deserved to be called out, et cetera. I was leaving by train the next morning to head up to Savannah to meet Denia for a brief sightseeing adventure.

In Savannah, Denia and I walked until we were dragging and eventually decided to try one of the Greyline bus tours. That was comfortable. We were the only Black people on the tour bus, though, which put me on tenterhooks. I knew the South pretty well for a northern woman. After all of my experiences there, I knew better than to get too relaxed. The tour bus narrator, a heavyset white guy with a fairly profound Southern accent, began his spiel as we pulled away from the bus depot. He talked about the history of the south, the productivity of the south, rice crops, tobacco crops, and on and on. At no time did he mention slavery or the role of Black people in creating the riches of Georgia. I grew weary of his lies by omission, his absolute erasure of Black people in the development of the state of Georgia. Soon, smoke was trailing out of my ears where Denia and I were seated in the back of the bus.

I'd recently picked up a book entitled *Black Rice: The African Origins of Rice Cultivation in the Americas* by Judith A. Carney. Up went my hand. I posed a question about that rice and who'd brought it to America and who cultivated it. I spoke loudly enough for everyone to hear. That tour guide spoke highly of everyone including Native Americans but had not mentioned Black people and slavery's importance to not only the cultivation of rice but to the entire economy of Georgia. He mumbled and stumbled and couldn't speak on the issue. Denia was holding me back because I was about ready to storm up the aisle.

I miss Denia. She passed in 2024 after a long journey with Alzheimer's. She promoted travel to see the entire world if you could manage it. She'd certainly done that in her life.

Of course, I also did book events here in Los Angeles—in fact, I am still doing them now when asked, all these years later, on Zoom. My dream when writing *Freshwater Road* was to write something about the experience of working in the Civil Rights Movement that would live beyond its publishing moment. I wanted it to endure, and to a degree that has been accomplished. I most recently did a *Freshwater Road* book talk online with a group in Missouri.

I went to work on a screen version. So many readers of *Freshwater Road* opined that it was made for the screen. The book was optioned four times for screen development, but we never got a deal to take it to the next phase. Since then, a few stories that deal with that period of the '60s have made it to the screen, like Ava Duvernay's *Selma* and George C. Wolfe's *Rustin*. Neither of them highlights women in the movement.

After *Freshwater Road,* I had to find some way to slow down. Writing had concretized my quiet side, my more solitary side. In my heart of hearts, I wanted to not need anything or anyone. That's a fool's journey because we all need personal nurturing, closeness. I floundered in my relationships. Work gave me the structure that I couldn't seem to manage without it. But I had to put a modicum of a personal life together.

19.

After the publication of my book in 2005, and after doing book promotion for three years off and on, I traveled to Chicago to do research on the meatpacking industry for another novel I'm still planning to write. I reached out to Michele's close friend, Chris Benson, the man she'd begun a new relationship with not long before her death.

I'd never had a probing conversation with Michele about Chris. I just knew she'd found someone new, an infinitely better choice for her than the man she was attempting to get away from. Chris was her colleague at Johnson Publishing Company in Chicago, well educated, a writer who is now a professor at Northwestern University.

Chicago was Chris's hometown and Michele's adopted hometown. I met up with Chris on my last day in the Windy City.

A vestibule abutted the freezing sidewalks of the city, marking the entrance to the restaurant. Chicago can be so cold in winter you need two entrances. One to allow you to catch your breath from the whipping cold, to stamp your feet to be sure they're still down there and working well. You struggle to catch your breath, taking off your gloves, loosening your wool neck scarf, unbuttoning your winter coat. The second door is the actual entrance into the warm space of the restaurant.

Inside, the place chattered and clanked. To one side, a sports bar—raw, loud television and even louder patrons. The colors vibrated with California nostalgia—desert sand set against rosy taupe and the polished green-gray of fan palms and king palms and fake birds of paradise. Every place wants to be our California dream however we stumble at times.

Chris had arrived earlier and grabbed a table for us. We ordered wine and our hands wrapped around the thick goblets for security. My roaming brain snatched a thought out of my subconscious: *don't drink too much. You won't understand what he tells you about Michele and what happened to her.* I wanted his take. But it was hard to focus. When I'm away I'm always anxious to get back to California. I don't grasp how much I love my adopted home until I'm too long apart from it. I wanted the rugged mountains and the soft hills that sloped down to the sea. I wanted to know the Pacific was there, rolling and thundering, offering the cool respite of mist and fog in a place too close to the desert for comfort. I don't like the cold.

My stealth eyes surveyed Chris's body, his elegant long-fingered hands. He doesn't wear a wedding ring, but I know he's married. A handsome guy, tall, thin, dressed like the professor he is. My lips smiled but my heart stumbled around for an explanation for the confusion I felt. I don't know this man, really. I'm taking the train west. That's a good conversation starter.

"I love trains." I sipped the tart wine. "If we had better, modern trains I'd never fly except to go overseas." A sort of innocuous opener.

In the quiet between us my eyes strafe the restaurant,

then settle on Chris's face. Green hazel eyes. Kind. Nobody knows better than this man how hard it has been to close the door on Michele's death. My brother suffers quietly. For my mom, it's been stratospheric pain and guilt—losing your youngest child, not to a dreaded disease, not to a reckless car crash, but to murder. What a crater of quicksand your brain becomes.

"Your book is good. You should be proud of yourself. Great reviews."

I blushed a thank you. He's a writer, too. I've read his work. He's good.

He drinks, checks the menu. The place has gotten even noisier since we sat down. We order burgers and fries, split the fries. I douse my side of the fries with Tabasco and ketchup.

"Thanks. Took me long enough to get it done. I'm slow."

"But you did it." He's intense. I feel it. Calm exteriors throw one off. Why was my mind not on the words coming out of my mouth or his mouth either?

"Thanks." I sip with caution. "I loved your book on Mamie Till-Mobley."

I'm still not over the murder of Emmett Till. Is anyone who saw his mutilated body? It is a visual of how much we are hated by large segments of this society. It's an image that never dies nor should it.

He nods. Corner of mouth smiles and deep glances break out and then retreat, out of propriety and a contorted history too burdensome to embrace. Was this the same person I met with Michele, and after? Had it been more than 25 years?

It's so loud I can barely hear him, but it doesn't matter. Why do I feel so close to him? He's a kind of brother. I'm trying to find the playing field.

"Do you have children?" I tiptoe into this territory of family and pragmatics. He eats like a heavier man.

"We decided against it."

"I always thought my decision to not have kids would be OK because Michele, being younger, would have them. She'd take up the slack of my selfish, self-centered decision."

"You're hard on yourself." He looked through me for an instant.

I hear my mom asking me when is she going to have some grandbabies. That was a long time ago. I was terrified of having children, anxious about my own demons and how they would affect my parenting no matter what was in my heart. The constancy of parenthood was a terror to me. I'd lived in my solitude for so long, I couldn't risk that kind of profound disruption. Writing is a solitary undertaking—especially for those as easily distracted as I am. By the time I'd had enough therapy to feel I was OK, and that I had much to offer a child, it was too late.

"Did you know her ex?" I ask at last.

I'm praying he'll have some knowledge of this person who may have had some connection to her death. I know there was trouble when they were breaking up because she intimated that to me. It was Michele's interest in Chris that precipitated her ending the earlier relationship. But, it was also the ex's behavior toward her. She told me that much.

He drinks a big swallow of wine. "I met him. She wanted to get away from him. Things were confusing. I think she needed a friend more than a lover."

"That's an odd thing to say. Maybe she needed both." My appetite slid away. "I saw pitchforks in his eyes the day I met him."

He chuckles, continues eating.

What he doesn't get is that I was deadly serious about those pitchforks. I let it lay there.

"What do you know that we don't know? I figure someone like you asked all the right questions." I'm getting down to cases now. He's a journalist and a lawyer and a professor. He knows how to ask the right questions. I'm merely the sister, an actress turned writer messing with something way beyond my skill set. No real ability to source out that kind information.

"The FBI closed the file." He doesn't flinch or blink.

"*The FBI?*" I flinch, blink, and drink, quickly. I had zero knowledge that the FBI was involved in the case at all.

"Drug investigation across state lines, people Michele may have been socializing with. I don't know for sure." Darkness secretes itself like a shadowy veil over his face. That's his pain, his confusion. And it is mine.

My head is pounding again. "Is that why there's no file in the New York Police Department's Cold Case Archives?" I had called the Cold Case Archives many times trying to find Michele's case, trying to find again the detective who worked on her case. I got nothing. Beyond that first year of the investigation, things seemed to drag, then just disappear.

"Could be. If Devil Man was a low-level informant working for the FBI or the Chicago P.D." I can see his mind skipping wildly through his memory.

"You talked with the FBI?"

"I tried. I got nothing. It's as if she wasn't murdered in New York City."

"Hell, it's as if she wasn't murdered at all."

To say I'm stunned is beyond understatement. I never saw my sister even close to any drugs. I never heard her mention the word. I'm baffled. She wasn't a user. No. Thank God for that. So perhaps she ventured into some deal promising easy money? Nothing that rides that close to death is easy. Based on my habit of soft-pedaling everything, I probably would've voiced concern if she had said anything, but I doubt I would've put my foot down. Michele was young but she was grown. People in their 20s don't like listening to old- sters. Unfortunately. And on our end, we need to believe that we might have helped someone fashion a different outcome for their life. In truth, people will find a way to do what they believe they need to do, even if it means a closer walk with Thee.

Chris and I continue to warm to each other, but I've got a train to catch. He gets the check, pays it, and offers to drive me to Union Station. Palpable relief. I bundle myself against the elements, that brutal cold that slaps one in the face upon opening any door during the worst of a Chicago winter. *Why didn't he save her?* I think. He was close. I must mind my own guilt, my own self-absorption. I say some things and other things I merely think.

We pick up my suitcase at my hotel in Evanston. He has continued to chat comfortably, then mentions his thoughts of suicide.

"Suicide? You?" I almost give myself whiplash my head spun around so fast.

He nods in the affirmative.

Does that mean he loved her? Or was that his response to his helplessness? I can't ask that question. Did you love her? He already stated he felt she needed a friend not a lover. What had she felt?

"I thought that, too, in my cowardly fashion," I tell him. "For a while I tried to drink myself to death. But even the wine began to taste like sand." I turned away as tears filled my eyes. I gathered myself. "So did my mother. She threat- ened to put a gun to her own head." We were quiet. I watch the city go by. It's damp, cold but exciting, too. It's Chicago, grown up and roaring.

We approach Union Station on Canal Street, the wind

blustering and whipping people along. We say our goodbyes, promising to stay in touch. And we have—to this day, Chris and I check in with each other every few months or so.

I zoom into the station, happy to be alone again, exceedingly happy to be warm, anticipating the solitude of my train car, my books, my cell phone, my wine, the rough ride of our American train system.

I keep talking to Chris in my head as the train huffs and puffs out of the station. I'm older. We're all older. Death is real. There is no closure. No going back. *Where were you when I was suffering? Where was I when you were? We might've helped each other through the worst of it, mightn't we? Pain and loss jumped the narrow gorge. I got better. I got worse. Where were you? It doesn't matter. The thought of you brought thoughts of her and her death. I didn't want to know from you although you were the best thing that happened to her in the last years of her life. I didn't even want to hear your name because we were too much alike, and I knew it. You didn't save her and neither did I. What was there to say? That our self-absorption blinded us to a train wreck?*

A train ride from Paris to Nice popped into my memory. It was certainly comfortable, clean and the food was infinitely better than on Amtrak. Smooth tracks. I saw a kind of horror there. A North African-looking young man—a younger version of Chris physically—was dragged off the train and beaten on the platform outside my window. He had no ticket. I was stunned because I didn't understand then the position of immigrants in France. By the end of that trip, I had a very good understanding of that position. All of that violence over a missing ticket? Then I remembered the film *The Battle of Algiers*. I understood then the hatred on display just out of my train window. I knew it because we have lived that hatred here.

I'm on my way west and happy to be staring out of another dirty Amtrak window. I want to see the America I've never seen while soaring above it all on Delta or United or American.

The Black porters recognize me from *In the Heat of the Night* and bring me free wine, food, whatever they have that I think I might want. I tip them, grateful for their care and concern. I feel as if I'm closing a very old door and opening another to a lighter world.

20.

It was mid-afternoon. Late 1990s. In Beverly Hills, much of the time, folks appear to be on a vacation at Cap d'Antibes. The sun glares down as if a gaffer had turned on a massive old klieg and gone home, leaving us to our over-sized sunglasses, sun hats, baseball caps, visors, sun block and purses full of moisturizers in travel sized tubes.

The traffic on Canon Drive gave a vibrant picture of the entrenched wealth in this crazy mostly wonderful place. You'd think Mercedes-Benz handed out cars to anyone who wanted one. I'm talking the S-Class. You see a Lamborghini, a Ferrari or two to agitate your imagination. Bentleys and Rolls-Royces are fewer in number but definitely on display. I've been around this picture of wealth since arriving in LA to do *Room 222*. It continues to boggle my mind.

Once parked, the highly advantaged floated in and out of restaurants, doctors' offices, boutiques, cheese emporiums, and wine shops, air kissing and smiling their perfect teeth at one another. They owned the town and the street and didn't care if you knew it. I felt like a fly in the ointment every time I walked in Beverly Hills, and I was a fairly well-heeled girl myself. Next to this depth of wealth in Beverly Hills, Bel-Air, and places I've only seen in magazine photos, I was practically living in the receiving line of life's handouts.

I parked in the public lot between Santa Monica Boulevard and Little Santa Monica, then walked the two blocks to my therapist's office on Canon Drive. In barely those two blocks, with me walking as close as possible to building fronts with awnings or any kind of overhanging shade opportunity, my armpits sloshed in sweat and my top lip had a perspiration mustache. The only thing remaining about me that was even remotely Hollywood? My Bulgari sunglasses. A splurge purchase, for sure. I'd retired from the rest of it to begin my new career as a writer. But, in all truth, I missed the perks, the limousine rides, the first-class everything, the crew of makeup, hair and wardrobe folks all there to assist you at every turn. It's heady stuff that requires extreme discipline to relinquish. I'm still working on that part of it.

Somewhere in the tangle that my life had become, I realized that I'd probably benefit from spending time with a good therapist. I hesitated for longer than I should've because my earlier experience during the Bill Withers marriage debacle had poisoned my mind on therapy.

Many of us Black folks pooh-pooh therapy for a host of reasons. We're embarrassed if there's even a possibility of needing therapy:

"I can handle my own problems."

"Therapy is for white folks, sitting around crying while they own the world."

"I don't have time or money for that nonsense."

I'm not the first to say it, but I certainly see it and believe that we, as a people, suffer from post-traumatic stress that is never ending, so it's not "post" anything. The trauma keeps coming. We absorb constant and profound disregard every day of our lives.

My first therapy experience had been with a Freudian psychiatrist. His not-so-subtle message was that women should walk a few paces behind, marriage was immutable, bearing children a requirement for a good life, and outshining your husband a sin of near Biblical proportion. My experience with that doctor was short and stunning for a woman like me who was reaching for the future, not the past. I couldn't wait to get away from that misogynistic, Old Europe mental prison camp.

Freudians offer patients little or no feedback. When mine did, I hated every word he said. American women zip along jockeying for a place, wanting to shake off history and be free. We want to be free. We are and want to be even more productive. We want to build things, make things, own things in our own names. I ran from that psychiatrist's office screaming, "Help!"

After Michele's murder, I tried unsuccessfully to get Mom to grief counseling to help her organize her life and mind after that horrible experience, even as my stepfather's mind began disappearing into Alzheimer's. Looking back, in conversation with my brother, we ruminated on the fact that his behavior at the repast after Michele's death, was strange, weird. We blamed it on him possibly drinking too much, as he was not a drinker. But the death of your only child is painful enough to turn you into a drinker.

In the years following Michele's death, Bob began what I'll call his Alzheimer's walks. We did not really know what Alzheimer's was in the 1980s, or even in much of the 1990s. The disease entered our everyday nightmares early in the 2000's. All of a sudden, it exploded into our minds and it is only getting more and more attention because more and more seniors are becoming afflicted with it. We learned later that his walks were definitely a sort of offshoot of the disease itself.

He walked. Many a night, Mom called me to go out looking for him. I drove around Los Angeles trying to find him or to collect him after a call from police that he'd been found wandering. In the earlier days of his disease, he carried a wallet with identification, but as his disease advanced it was clear that his mind was going fast. We used to listen to his stories about serving in World War II in the South Pacific, his stories about working in the federal prison system for many years. Soon, the stories began to sound disorganized, detached. He became quarrelsome, angry. My mother didn't mention the name of any disease, so I didn't have a good sense for the longest time about his actual condition.

Eventually, Bob walked away one day and was never found again—and I mean *nothing* of him was ever found. That day he didn't wear his medical bracelet, didn't take his wallet. His last walk.

My mother's life had become solid nightmare. But even while bearing this incredible load of loss and depression, Mom refused therapy. She said she didn't want to blab her business all over the place. I assured her that she'd be in a private office with a person whose job it was to hold each patient's confidence. Nothing worked to change her mind. Eventually, I came to feel differently and proceeded with finding some help.

I found a psychologist (as opposed to a psychiatrist) who worked primarily with creative people, artists of one sort or another. I landed in his office when it became clear to me that my work life continued to be so much better than my personal life. In short, I was out of balance. I trusted either too much or not at all. I got involved too quickly and just as quickly let go. I'd walked away from the best relationship of my life out of fear of failure, and fear also that this wonderful man would pull me away from Hollywood because he had so little respect for the industry in which I worked. This man knew well the history of Hollywood's treatment of Black people. There certainly were exceptions to his distrust of the industry, but very few. And of course, my relationship with my mother had rarely given me much in the way of emotional support. There was much to work on with a good therapist.

There's a cohort of people who believe one's demons are where the artist resides. I see how constant emotional storm and stress may be in the mix of an artist's production. All of that drama, though, also wears one out. I know from my own experience that less drama and more discipline does pretty well when it comes to freeing one's creativity. Powerful emotions and thoughts have to be shaped and shaded into an expression. That takes discipline. Our raw demons drag us around, sucking the life out of heart and soul in a silent vicious circle, never amounting to anything but agony.

Through this therapy, I learned to face my demons. I had to separate my productive better self from beating my head against the wall of my failures. What were my worst demons? A neediness for love that led me down some dark-doored corridors, and a questioning of my most basic identity—I was the child of a borrowed name and DNA that remained unknown until I was an adult. During the years when these textures of love and identity are meant to be cemented in children in a positive, helpful way, I was a wandering cutie pie always standing outside looking in. My childhood left me feeling like I could not rely on the love in the room because I sensed correctly that it was not meant for me. I began to pretend love.

Room 222 had been a plum job to be enjoyed, respected, lauded, coming as it did at the culmination of that incredible decade, the '60s. Instead, early on, I found myself in a marriage that challenged my dedication to my career and disrespected my accomplishments.

I'd locked myself in two keyless rooms with my second two marriages. Neither should've ever happened. I wasn't a wife and in my heart of hearts, I didn't want to be one. That's on me and should've ended that story. But history often pushes us to do what those who came before us did—as in getting married and having children. In trying to roll myself into that history, I betrayed myself and betrayed those who married me. Both of those marriages were about binding my need to feel secure with my fundamentally incredible romantic notions about life and love. By the time I got my head on a bit straighter, the one person I should've married, if there was to be any marrying at all, had left this earth.

I spent about two years working with this therapist before we began to wind things down. I remember, in his therapist's office, the light was tempered soft, slanting in between the blades of his white plantation shutters, feeding the illusion of calm and cool. I'd certainly had days in that space that were quite far from calm and cool.

This day, Dr. M. wore a slightly washed-out pink shirt, unbuttoned at the neck. His tan jacket draped the back of his chair. He was Irish, very fair skinned with light brown hair and blue eyes. He sat behind his desk, formal, but with a casually authoritative air. Like a good parent, I'd thought many times. A good cop.

"You're strong, resilient, and you will prevail." He nodded in the positive as he said it. I didn't know if I was transfixed by the blue of his eyes and heard what I wanted to hear, or if he really did say that to me. I heard myself saying, à la Travis Bickle in *Taxi Driver*: *You talking to me?* I chuckled at myself.

I did a quick check of the room, my eyes flitting to the right, left. With a soft, slightly camouflaged cough I turned to see if there was anyone behind me. His office door was definitely closed. Of course, he'd been talking to me. He'd said that positively wonderful thing to me about me. But because I have a lingering emotional disorder called *catastrophic thinking*—chicken-little yelling "the sky is falling" for every dark cloud in the sky—I immediately discounted his appraisal before the period was even on his sentence.

"Easy for you to say. Not so easy for me to be." Internalizing this man's appraisal with grace and gratitude was a part of my therapy. "Maybe I need to write your words on my forehead, or at least on the bathroom mirror?"

"Not on your forehead or on the bathroom mirror." His eyes twinkled. "But it wouldn't hurt to write them 500 times a day in your notebook until you really internalize them. "

"That's reasonable. Like a child." I mumbled, pushing back what would've become a giggle.

This therapist, this *good* therapist, surprised me by actually engaging me in a dialogue, offering opinions, directions, digging for weaknesses in my platform that we might repair. He didn't tell me what to do but he helped me find my best direction. He seemed to have a real appreciation for my pluck, my fight, as I maneuvered through my life's swamps, three steps ahead of the snakes and crocs nipping at my heels.

On this day, my good and earnest therapist was letting me go. I was graduating, so to speak, only I wasn't ready to be let go. I settled deeper into my chair, gripped the armrests wanting to stay spinning those words around in my brain: *You're strong, resilient, and you will prevail.* I'd had enough of the big bad world to want to hide there, or at least linger in his waiting room.

Over the years of my therapy, I would time my arrival at

his office to get maximum benefit out of the quiet of his tiny waiting room. This space—a sort of faux Christian Science Reading Room—was quiet, respectful, with magazines like *The New Yorker* and *National Geographic* easy to reach. The tiny room was a place of peace, a meditative space. I timed it right all but once or twice, when I arrived before the waiting patient had gone in. I put a book in front of my face, to apologize for violating the other person's anonymity. I was definitely wrong to have arrived so early, but I felt so good in that little room. As time passed, I came to feel I owned a bit of it, using it as my personal reading room, my place of reflection.

"People who've experienced the kinds of losses that you have often end up sitting on a curb with a needle stuck in their arm. Not you. You're very strong."

That ended my brief reverie. I could see myself sitting somewhere with a bottle of wine, but a needle stuck in my arm? Me?

"I hate needles. I guess I should be grateful for that." I tried hard not to sound flippant. "Strong?" That word again. Okay.

Red flags flapping in my brain, which led directly to my usual trope.

"Wait a minute. Would you say that needle in the arm business to a white woman?"

My eyes got hot like I might cry. In all this time, I'd never detected even a molecule of racism in this man. I have a well-developed racism detector that's never in the off position, even when I'm asleep. Yes, it's exhausting but it's my spiritual survival machine.

"I'm sorry. That was uncalled for." I owed him that small apology. He was quiet.

If Michele's murder, my less than stellar marriages, the

knowledge that the man who I'd thought *for most of my life* was my father turned out to not be my father, my mother's emotional distance, changing careers mid-life hadn't brought me down, then I had to admit he had a good point. I'm nobody's wimp. Life hadn't brought my down but it sure had scraped my knees.

Soon after, I was at a dinner with lovely people who happened to be white. One person proffered that the Civil War was not about slavery. Was I shocked that a well-educated person harbored such a view, announcing it as historical fact? Yes. A thousand times, yes! But we listen endlessly to a bastardization of our own history, our own story and the truer story of this country's history. That's part and parcel of our PTSD. Sometimes it's an intentional dig, a prompt to send you off on a tangent. Sometimes it's just plain ignorance, the kind of ignorance that doesn't yet know itself.

I spent about five minutes or less on a mild mini-tangent about the Civil War and slavery, then I went on home. I was done. One more little red wagon we drag through life, the wheels often going in opposite directions like a shopping cart that goes off on its own when you try to shove it into the holding area. You release it then grab it again as it heads for someone's unsuspecting new car. That's the game we often play to even have white friends. You never know what's hiding behind some of those smiles. It may not be hatred but it's usually if not always founded in ignorance of this country's history. That's how efficient and complete American racism has been.

If my therapist wanted to jar me, he'd succeeded. I gave him a pass on that one as I reminded myself that white women of all types and kinds take Xanax, Valium, meth, over-the-counter drugs, under-the-counter drugs and on-the-corner drugs. Perhaps I should say, we gave each other a pass. Took me a few minutes to absorb how profoundly positive he was being about my prognosis. I had already survived the worst of it, more or less. I hoped.

My therapist was having similar *end of the line* conversations with all of his patients. He'd decided to retire. He'd given me cover to regain emotional flexibility, to sit down and mull over the journey I'd been on, to call the good the good and the bad the bad. He acknowledged that I'd been through some bad stuff, some by my own instigation. He'd validated my experiences, told me I was not crazy but like all others, I needed some work in various departments. But overall, I had much to be thankful for.

Do you get why I *loved* this man?

Working with creative people, he'd probably heard it all—creative procrastination, tales of woe about overindulgence in drugs and alcohol, family dysfunction, marriages good and bad, flings, divorces, and an overall adolescent take on life, liberty, and the pursuit of happiness. Probably plenty of, *Why isn't my life perfect all the time, no matter what I do?* Underneath all that morass of telling, of trying to make sense of one's journey, he'd given unconditional compassion and required only that I be as honest as possible, revealing my own frailties and weaknesses and my strengths, too.

Our last session was over. He stood and walked around the desk as I stood up from my favorite chair close to the box of Kleenex. I'd had a few cries in this room, had snatched Kleenex from the little box on the between-the-chairs table. He hugged me, professionally. I liked that. A doctor/patient professional hug. I wanted to ask him if I might somehow keep coming to see him, at a coffee shop, on a park bench. I'd take any crumbs he was willing to extend to me.

I mumbled my "thank you," then aimed myself for the exit door. For a brief moment, I felt like Tom Hanks in *Cast*

Away or Matt Damon in *The Martian*. Alone. Whatever my fear level was, I knew, intellectually, at least, that it was time to sink or swim.

21.

We insomniacs thought we heard in the middle of a night in 2009 that Farrah Fawcett had died after a long battle with cancer. By morning, as we drank our coffee, the news was confirmed. We hadn't had a REM sleep nightmare as we tried to find sleep's comfort. She fought the good fight. Practically every family in America has suffered losing someone to one cancer or another. We're terrified of its pervasiveness. She was such a bright light we began to believe that she might win. We wanted her to win, flashing her gorgeous smile on us all. She was 62 years old.

By late morning, the new shocker of Michael Jackson's death began seeping out. As if we harbored disbelief, the news began to blast out of all televisions, all radios to remove all doubt from our minds. As we tried to absorb this news, it dried on our disbelieving lips. We fought the news in our minds and hearts. How could this be? He's down there at the Staples Center rehearsing with his musicians and dancers and background singers. But the news doesn't stop. They go deep: wall to wall retrospectives of his monumental career and some mention, too, of his troubles. On this day, the brilliance of his accomplishments as an entertainer were all we wanted to hear. *He's gone. Leave the troubles over somewhere else. Let us enjoy these memories.*

227

It felt as if a black feather quilt hovered over the city. We were at a loss for words to even describe how we felt. Two minutes before that news hit, we were delighting in the fact that he was preparing to take his new show on the road, thrilled that he'd be center stage again, with his astonishing talent. He was 50 years old.

I sat on my patio staring at the yard, the pool reflecting the sky as the clouds parted to reveal the blue of blues. In the quiet, my head kept wagging side to side, thinking *what in God's name is going on in the world?*

The rumbling thunder of a helicopter approached steadily, that remarkable noise that sounds like a large living bird beating its wings against the heavens. Helicopters are a part of LA life. Police have them, as do banks, hospitals, the sheriff, athletes, and other rich folks. That sound—to this day—takes me back to Vietnam War footage from the early 1970s. It was Pavlovian for me—hear the sound, remember the war.

I sat back in my chair and stared up recognizing the markings on the bird from the sheriff's office as it rumbled across my sky. Michael was going home. I knew by the timing that it was Michael on his last journey—from UCLA Medical Center to the coroner's office way downtown. It's a fairly straight shot right across the LA sky from the West Side to downtown. I stood up, nodded, and waved goodbye.

Though he died quite young, his awesome productivity gives us many different Michael periods to listen to as often as we'd like, from his little boy prodigy time to the brilliant creator he became. But we won't see those graceful elegant moves, the sensual teases, the hardcore rhythms as his feet seemed to be enjoying a dancing life of their own. We gasped, applauded, and cried it was so beautiful. He really did take our breath away.

On that very same day that the bird with Michael's body flew over, I'd hired a roofing repair man to do what I'd been told was a small job, repairing a section of the roof damaged by the termite exterminator company when they'd tented the house a couple of months earlier. Admittedly, the roof on this old house, first built in 1924, needed to be replaced. Ancient wood shingles degrading in the California sun? Not good. The roof repair man used a torch to seal the new shingles with a kind of tar. He climbed down to collect his check and went on his way.

I poured a glass of wine and was about to head to the television when my phone rang. In those days, I still had a wall-mounted phone in the kitchen. It was my next-door neighbor alerting me that smoke was coming from the eaves of my house. I ran to the stairwell heading up to check on things. A massive plume of dark gray smoke was pushing down the stairwell. I ran back to the phone to call the Fire Department.

The fireman told me to open the gate so they could bring equipment up the driveway. He said to get out of the house immediately as smoke could be deadly. I went out to the patio to wait for them in a state of shock. The Los Angeles Fire Department arrived quickly. Soon, my street was filled with red fire trucks.

A little United Nations of humanity trooped in and took over. They were white, Black, Hispanic, male and female. Of course, being who I am, I gave that a positive nod even as flames began shooting from the upstairs. The thick smoke reminded me again of a war zone as the Fire Department crew went to work. When things work as they should, it feels good. I felt a kind of excitement that they'd arrived so quickly, were so professional. A firefighting machine had taken over my house.

I moved toward the back fence to call the insurance company as panic at the real significance of what was happening settled in. You can't know unless you've had the experience that your mind chases what's happening, trying to make order out of chaos. Slowly it seeps in that nothing will ever be the same again. It's like an earthquake.

The insurance company directed me to pack clothes and essentials. They gave me choices of where to stay temporarily until we figured out how much of a loss was involved. My next call was to my bank to stop payment on the roofing repairman's check. At least I had that modicum of good sense still lumbering around in my brain.

For the first night, I slept on a mattress on a downstairs floor trying to gather my senses. My next-door neighbor invited me to stay in their guest house for a few nights, which I took them up on. I stayed there a couple of nights running back to my charred home to collect things as I tried to figure my way through.

Finally, I was sane enough to get into my car with my suitcase and head to the hotel the insurance company had set up for me. The hotel offered all the necessities of living minus any luxury. It was purely functional, and I was insanely discombobulated—didn't know what I was doing. Is this a kitchen? Who's slept on this bed? What about this sofa? Is it clean? I felt as though I was ever so slowly entering another person's body, a person who knew how to handle all that was before me. But, for those first few days, the Denise that I know barely remembered how to breathe. I gasped my way through, reaching for whatever grab bars I could find.

A week or so later, the insurance company called to tell me they'd rented a gorgeous apartment for me fairly close to my burned home so I could roll back and forth checking on things. It had been built as a four-unit apartment building with very large units. The owner had converted it to long-stay rentals rather than leases—for folks like me, for writers and even families on vacation who wanted to live in LA in a neighborhood instead of in a hotel.

My apartment was on the top floor which of course required hauling things that I needed to live, including groceries, up the flight of stairs. I'd been plenty spoiled by the ease of driving up my driveway at home and loading stuff in and out of the kitchen door.

In my new home, there was street parking only, and that was a daily/nightly nightmare. Folks studied each other's schedules so they could get to know when a person was leaving and when a space would become available. In the evening, all bets were off. You might find yourself parking a block or more away, or sitting in the dark in your car waiting for a space to open.

Having said that, it was a pretty street with trees and flowers, a mix of duplexes and four-unit buildings, populated primarily, I learned, by conservative Jewish persons. I saw one other Black person while living on that street, and that was the actor/musician Common. He's a long way from that street now.

There was one small miracle: right next door to my new home was a wild overgrown peach tree. I say wild because it looked as if it hadn't been pruned in ages. But the peaches? Oh my God. Huge, sweet, and oh how the exquisite juice of those peaches ran down your chin, made your fingers sticky, and dripped down onto your clothes. Everyone on the block helped themselves to those gorgeous fruits. No one confronted us about taking the fruits and the tree was so overloaded, these peaches often fell to the driveway to be squashed by car traffic. That was enough to make you cry.

I had much work to do including overseeing the packing-out of the house and then the rebuild itself. The drive from the apartment to my home took about 10 minutes and believe me, I drove between those two places sometimes three and four times a day. I was having an out of body experience I didn't begin to understand at the time.

The structural damage to my home was on the second floor, from the roof to the floor. The downstairs had no physical damage but the smoke smell choked you, and oozed from the pores of the house. Every item of clothing in every closet had to be sent out to the San Fernando Valley to a cleaning company that dealt with smoke-damaged items. All bedclothes had to be tossed. Bye-bye mattress and pillows. The packing and storage company packed my Wedgewood china and pretty much everything else that I owned and took it away. My paintings and sculptures were packed and departed on a truck. And all of the books, and I have many, were packed and removed. The scent of smoke had to be removed from everything I owned.

For brief moments at the beginning of this drama, I felt homeless, utterly disoriented. My home had become the crucial part of my stability, my sanctuary. A house is a house, but it becomes so much more as you live more years of your life in it, and I'd certainly made this one into my heart-home. It is my cradle, my inspiration, the place that has allowed my creativity to thrive. My writing room was my little chapel. Many a family dinner, many a party on the patio, many a swim, many tears and many a laugh formed the spirit of this place.

Let me say this, and it is from my heart: I'm a Black woman who's had some glorious successes and some horrendous stumbles. I'm a strong person who keeps getting up. I will do what it takes to make my life work and work well. I am definitely a loner but I know the shortcomings of that posture and work to diminish the negatives.

But my home, though. When you walk in my front door, you are greeted by a sense of calm beauty. As Los Angeles homes go, especially in this neighborhood, my home is modest. The lot size is huge, though. I put a pool in, upgraded the landscaping, and put in a new modern kitchen, as the original was the size of a broom closet. I'd made this home a reflection of my spirit. Being forced to move out nearly froze that spirit for a while.

The temporary apartment had a large living room and a dining room with a huge square table, a smallish but adequate kitchen, two bedrooms, two baths, and good closets. The furnishings were antiques or pretending to be. Not bad for temporary digs. I went about trying to make myself at home. I'd hauled (with much help) my big screen TV, my silver, and other valuables that were easily moved. But making this place my heart-home wouldn't ever happen. I felt out of place, mournful and basically lost.

For the next year, I rolled back and forth from the apartment to my damaged home as the contractors began the rebuild. For the downstairs it was cleaning and painting and redoing the hardwood floors. For upstairs it was construction—new roof of course, new closets, a giant soaking tub for my bathroom, new bookshelves down and up.

One year later, the big truck of my life pulled up in front of my home. The contractor pulled a very lovely stool out and sat me on it just behind the truck near the curb in the street and told me to sit there and tell the movers what was going into the house and what was going up the driveway's hill to the garage. I was so excited I could barely see straight. Home. I was home and oh so happy.

22.

I WORK HARD AT PUSHING SOME OF LIFE'S UNPLEASANTNESS to the rear. I can forget some things so completely, I forget they ever happened, until I stumble on a tiny pebble of a memory. That's happened multiple times as I've worked on this book. Boxes of notes and photos lift like ghosts freed from hiding on the closet shelf. Memories of joys and sorrows packed away, aching for a place in my life. I open one notebook and all of that forgotten history tumbles back into my mind. Where have all of these golden days run off to? We hiked, we laughed, we got lost, we got found. Our sweat and the fog blended on our faces to soften and smooth us. We were young and strong. Now we walk on broken knees with our memories as canes to assist our passage.

I was losing people that I loved. Death is outrageous, lurking, teasing, making false promises. We are more accepting when it comes for the elderly. When it takes the young and promising, as when death took Michele, we pull out our hair, scream at the heavens in the lonely night for being so cruel, make deals and promises to kill the killer. We are helpless.

Ten years after Michele's death, my dad passed in 1990, creating an ocean of longing. To this day, a memory of him while I'm driving will bring tears to my eyes and I'll pull the car over to get myself together. His wise words trail through my mind frequently. I won't let him go because in truth his was the only unconditional love I've ever known.

After long battles with two cancers, prostate and pancreatic, my friend Rudy Lombard died. Probably, I will never let him go. He brought such richness to my life, Creole cuisine being only one form of that richness. He did all that he did quietly. I never heard him raise his voice in all the years that I knew him. He spent much of his life trying to right the wrongs perpetrated against us as a people. He's in a special category of human being.

My cousin, the musician Delbert Taylor, with whom I was very close, died. Delbert was the MC for all festivities in this house: dinners, patio parties, inside the house parties. He brought good times in the door. A few months before he landed in the hospital, he played a Duke Ellington concert at the Universal Hilton with the Los Angeles Jazz Society. He looked like Duke in his tux, tall and handsome. His performance was stunning. Our tiny remaining family cheered him on: Mom, Delbert's wife Helen, cousin Diana Hines Allen, and her husband Derek. We were all so proud. Not long after, he was in the hospital with cancer so bad he never left. The last time I visited, he didn't know me. I walked down the hall to the waiting room and just sat there crying.

My dear friend Denia Hightower was diagnosed with Alzheimer's and was placed in a care facility near her daughter and family in the Baltimore area before passing in 2024. She encouraged me forward, her ebullience, her joie de vivre more than once moved me out of an emotional squall.

My dad's partner Mildred Stevenson passed. Mildred had both street wisdom and intellectual smarts. She was a cool lady. For years when I was not able to talk with Mom,

Mildred was there to hear my woes and correct my missteps with compassion and wisdom.

Carroll O'Connor passed. Nancy O'Connor passed. So many golden days pressed in a book of memories.

And, just last year my last sibling, my brother Otto Nicholas, Jr., passed. I was running in a forest of headstones.

My getaway place, where I go to air out the sinews in my brain and heart when they're overly stressed, is universally the ocean. I'm a born Cancer. Big water and the moon align my scattered parts. The ocean teases out my stresses. I smile as they ride away on the waves.

One beautiful, sunny and bright LA Sunday morning late in 2010, I grabbed my *New York Times*, put on a Sunday dress, and headed to one of my favorite spots, Casa del Mar Hotel in Santa Monica. The house fire of 2009, the year of living in a strange non-home, then recreating my own home at the end of that travail, drifted in and out of a yesterday that I was happy to see in the rearview mirror. The joy of returning to my home had slowly eased away the trauma of it all. Being in my home again felt fresh, beautiful and inviting. In truth, it was so lovely with zero furniture, I had felt reluctant to begin hauling all of my stuff back in.

The Casa Del Mar lobby is a huge, high-ceilinged wonder. It echoes as sounds of so many different things bounce off the walls: travelers dragging suitcases to the registration desk on a sidewall, piped-in music, the clanks of coffee cups on saucers, plates onto tables, waiters and waitresses giving orders to the bartenders, delivering orders of food to the bar area tables, people moving about to and from the restrooms off the main lobby, serious folks at work in the semi-private cubby holes on the side wall, computers open and soft key punch sounds hovering. It has the feeling of an elegant and fanciful European train station lobby.

I grabbed a small table for two at a tall window, ordered a glass of champagne, and spread my *New York Times*, feeling good in this lovely place. Skimming the paper, I needed the ocean more than the news. I closed the paper and relaxed into one of my favorite low energy activities—staring at the ocean.

I felt the presence of a human being very close. I looked up to see a large guy, Black, good looking, standing there smiling at me. I was stunned because I hadn't felt him coming so close with the swell of sound in the huge space.

He introduced himself as Derrick Holmes, the owner and designer of Banneker Watches. He laid his business card on the table. I picked it up to examine it: *Derrick M. Holmes*. He went on to tell me that on the previous night, he'd been watching television in his hotel room and one of my films aired. It was Sidney Poitier's *A Piece of the Action*. My character in the film is the director of a center for delinquent youth that is named for 18th century mathematician-inventor Benjamin Banneker. A sweet coincidence. He asked if he could send me one of his Banneker watches, and I answered, *of course*.

We became friends over the next couple of years, phone chatting or texting, which he taught me to do. Tech savvy is not in me, near me, or knocking at my door. He was/is younger than I am, which cautioned me a bit. He seemed older than his years, and said I seemed younger than mine, so somehow age never became an issue.

I'd been dating but nothing had crossed over into a full-blown relationship for a while. Derrick and I grew closer as pals and eventually we evolved into a romantic relationship. When I visited him in Denver—his home—and met his daughter, Nevaeh, I was hooked. This tiny tot (at the time) was so adorable, so smart, so full of laughter and fun. She was a beautiful child inside and out and became a favorite human being of mine. She's nearly an adult now, in high school, and I hope heading in a good direction.

Derrick is a history buff. He knows more Egyptian history than even the Egyptians I know well. He'd also dug around in American history and knew the stories of Black inventors whose patented inventions we live with and use every day. Most people—Black, white, and other—do not know that the inventor of this or that was a Black man or woman. I certainly had plenty to learn in that area.

My dad was not college educated but he was smart. Derrick reminded me of him in many ways—street smart but with style, no obvious rough edges, natural intelligence and curiosity, a big embracing personality. In a different time and place, my dad would've been in an elevated position doing whatever. He'd owned and run a lucrative bar for years. He managed bars after he sold his own. He was a gambler in the numbers game, but he dressed like a Wall Street banker—conservative, handsome, immaculate. I say all of that to say, certain aspects of living off the grid make sense to me. Black folks are often forced to live off the grid. Dad wanted to be his own boss and for most of his adult life he was just that. This is as free as a Black man can be in this country to this day.

The same spirit of independence, of making a way through the brick wall of American resistance to Black men, is there in Derrick. He's more middle of the road than my dad and two generations younger. He's done something remarkable and is mainstreaming it to the marketplace. Otto Nicholas would've admired this man for breaking out on his own and making his own way.

People who work for themselves have a profoundly different energy than people who work for others. I understand

and respect that sense of freedom but also the stress of it. My drive to make the writing life work well for me is part and parcel of the same thinking. I've always wanted to be my own boss or at least to be respected, not treated like a rube, an inconsequential idiot. Working as an actor, I could not ever be in control of my own life and work. When you sign a contract to work for and be paid by others, they own you in a sense—at least for the run of the contract. Unfortunately, generally speaking, because actors are so desperate for the work of acting, that desperation is a signal that you can be treated like a nonentity, like someone who will do anything they want you to do to survive/win the game, or just be in the game. As a writer, I'm my own boss, nearly completely. If a writer has a deal to write a book, you have a boss but still, you have infinitely more freedom than an actor might.

We began, Derrick and Denise, with me wearing one of his watches as we strained to keep him and his business afloat. I'd headed into a work stream that I hoped and prayed would lead to a deal for a film of my novel, *Freshwater Road*. The book had been optioned by a television producer. A ton of work followed that netted out to a lot of work with negative results.

Derrick began spending as many weekends as possible in LA as our relationship deepened. Then he began working from here—staying for longer than weekends. My pals welcomed him. He certainly pushed me out of the nest a bit as he began to see that one of my favorite activities was hiding from the world. Writing suited that part of me way more than acting did. While I had loved my years as an actor, as I grew more serious about my own personal growth, my love of acting waned. The work had become repetitious. I felt zero challenge beyond trying to keep my looks from sagging and trying to create a financial nest egg of sorts. In time, age con-

quers all. *Heat* was the best last job I could hope for. I loved
the show and certainly loved Carroll and Nancy. I'd spent my
career trying to wiggle into more substantial work. I made it
halfway there with my character on *Heat*. That was it as far
as I was concerned.

Derrick and I took smallish road trips up and down
California. You can spend a lifetime discovering California,
with a landscape so varied, so big and so extraordinarily beautiful. We drove the coast route, Highway One, we drove the
inland routes north and south from San Diego to north of
San Francisco. We loved Hearst Castle and Carmel, the cows
in Fresno, the artichokes in Monterey County, the Aquarium
in Monterey, stops along the way to do that favorite non-ac-
tivity of mine—sit and stare at the ocean. Never got him as
far as the wine country or Mendocino, but we'll get there.

In LA, we attended events, drank too much, ate too
much, entertained pals with good food and good conversation. We went to films, one of my favorite things to do. We
swam at sunset and listened to good music—thankfully he
loved some of my oldies from the '60s and '70s. He listens to
rap. I don't hear the musicality of it; I just hear a lot of talking
with a beat. Having said that, I've watched *Straight Outta
Compton* three or four times. I love it.

My *Straight Outta Compton* story opened my ears and
eyes to something in our history in this country that's not
unique, but I'd forgotten the gist of it. I had invited some
pals to go with me to a screening of *Compton* at the Academy
of Motion Picture Arts and Sciences.

The Academy auditorium was packed when we arrived.
We found three seats midway down the left side aisle, settled
in, and I did my usual *how many Black people are in this room
to see this Black film* scan of the audience. There were just a
few Black people, which is more often than not the case for

Academy screenings. I'm thinking, *all of these white people are here to see this film about Black kids from the "ghetto" who became famous performing rap music.*

The film began. As the music in the film blasted from the speakers, the primarily white audience began singing along with the guys making the music in the film at the top of their lungs. I'm looking around the huge auditorium, white people are singing, heads bopping and knees bouncing up and down. I'm sitting there like the square fuddy-duddy stunned that the music has already become a part of white culture. I whisper to my pals what I'm noticing and they are having a similar response. White folks already had the memo in their happy hands: Black folks changed the world of music once again and white folks were off to the races. I had to catch up with *my* own culture.

Derrick of course knew the music well. That was helpful as I tried to get inside of it. Tried is the operative word. I'm stuck on Al Jarreau, The Emotions, Al Green, Otis Redding, old Motown, Curtis Mayfield, Aretha. I still listen to Laura Nyro. My fallback is jazz—John Coltrane, Duke Ellington, Charlie Parker, a nostalgic nod to my dad and my brother, both loved jazz most of all.

Derrick's excellent cooking packed about 20 pounds on me, which I've now thankfully lost—and I hope they stay lost. His shrimp and grits, his salmon croquets, his steak. I eat no more red meat these days, but I remember how good that steak tasted when I did. Rudy first taught me and I'm sure many others that gathering around to enjoy a meal prepared with love is the height of richness and comfort. Big special dinners were like that in my Grandma Waddy B.'s house, but I was too young to understand the real meaning of those moments. Rudy brought this to my understanding: good fellowship, good conversation, the sharing of life all ride in on the same platter that holds a meal prepared with care and love. That's the way home dining used to be before we began staring at the television while eating, or staring at our phones, or eating on the run. Or at least, that's the cultural memory we have, whether we actually experienced it or not. The idea was sold to us. Derrick understood that way of being in the world. Gather around a big table to talk, eat, drink, enjoy.

During the COVID lockdowns, that dreary dark time, Derrick and I texted and talked, but did not see each other for three years. Derrick intuited what my *running in a forest of headstones* losses have left in their place in my heart and soul. A profound loneliness. I lean into him when my way is clouded. I talk with him about my dad, about the others I've lost. There's room for that conversation between us. His advice and encouragement helped stabilize me as my dad's used to. We're an odd coupling in a way but oddness or difference doesn't particularly bother me. I'm comfortable not being like most other people in this way. I try to figure how we can be so congruent considering the age difference. He reminds me that his mom was the same age as my mom, both born in 1921. His mother passed some time ago. I'm wondering if having an older mother gives him insights into the aging woman that I am. Or perhaps he's just an older soul.

Top: High school graduation, age 16, eager to get out of Milan, Michigan and head to Ann Arbor for college. I appeared on my first *Jet* magazine cover around the same time.

Middle: Trying out my brother's bike in the backyard of Grandma's house, Detroit 1950.

Bottom: Even as a baby, my light skin and blue/hazel eyes set me apart from my parents and brother in ways I struggled to understand.

Mom, top row left, and Dad, top row right, with friends in early 40s Detroit.

Opposite page: Top left, Mom, sometime in the early 1960s. Top right, in the light jacket, is Harold Mullins, the man who my mother informed me, when I was in my early 30s, was my biological father. Lower left are my grandparents on Mom's side, John Jones and Ethel Jones. Right center, is my great-grandmother, Etta Hines. Right bottom is Eliza Clarke, my great-great-grandmother.

Me with my dad, Otto Nicholas, Sr., at the reception hosted by Jacquie and Clarence Avant at their home in Beverly Hills when I married Bill Withers in 1971. (Credit: Howard Bingham)

With Mom when I took her to Paris in 1981, in the aftermath of my sister Michele's murder.

Top: My brother, Otto Nicholas, Jr., and me, wearing shoulder pads like I was trying out for the Detroit Lions.
Below: I love this shot of Otto after an especially successful day fishing.

Left: My sister Michele Burgen at Nepenthe in Big Sur, CA, 1975
Below: Despite her youth, Michele became an accomplished pilot.

Left: Us two sisters on Highway One heading to San Francisco, 1975.

With Rudy Lombard in the 1970s in his town, New Orleans, which I also came to love, in the garden of the famed Commander's Palace restaurant.

This portrait captures how I looked and felt in my early years in Los Angeles when I was first becoming nationally known while appearing on *Room 222.*
(Credit: Gene Trindl)

In 2000, I made a life-changing trip to Egypt, where I'm pictured here with a group of local children.

With the "Tight Ends Hiking Club," a group that included actor and writer Anna Deavere Smith, center, and Loretta Devine, at bottom.

Director and friend Asaad Kelada, who organized my visit to Egypt as well as other memorable trips, including to his home in the south of France.

At a dinner in honor of Mrs. Rosa Parks at my home in LA. Bottom row, left to right: myself, Anne Johnson, Mrs. Parks and her assistant, Jan Galanter, Mom. Top row, left to right: my cousin, Delbert Taylor, Shirley Jo Finney, Rod Gaines, Doug Galanter.

Left: This program, designed by B. Patitucci, was produced for the second anniversary of the Negro Ensemble Company, which was my chief professional focus between the Free Southern Theater and *Room 222*.

Right: Layne "Shotgun" Britton gave me this photo of himself when he did makeup for me on *Room 222*, where I did my best to expand this Southern white man's racial consciousness.

Being made up while Gil Moses plays his guitar in Holmes County, Mississippi, 1965. We were preparing to perform in a half-completed community center, being built to replace a structure burned down by the Klan.

A 20th Century Fox publicity still for *Room 222*: from left, Howard Rice, Lloyd Haynes, me, Karen Valentine, and Michael Constantine.

With Sidney Poitier as he officially calls an end to production on the set of *Let's Do It Again* in 1975, one of my best movie-making experiences.

Winning Emmys for the PBS production *Voices of our People: In Celebration of Black Poetry,* which I co-produced with Charles F. Johnson.
Top row: Charles F. Johnson, Jim Washburn, Brock Peters, Robert Hooks.
Bottom: Tracee Lyles, me, Janet MacLachlan.

With the great Curtis Mayfield while he visited the set of *In the Heat of the Night.* His song "Keep On Pushing" was an indelible part of the Civil Rights Movement while I was in Mississippi with the Free Southern Theater.

A publicity shot from *Capricorn One*, in which I played the wife of an astronaut, during the period I was trying hardest to find good roles in the movie business in the 70s.

Much of my screen work ended up having Civil Rights Movement themes. With Danny Glover in the 1985 PBS film *And the Children Shall Lead.*

With the great Carroll O'Connor on the set of *In the Heat of the Night*, the TV series he produced, starred in, and often wrote and directed, in Conyers, Georgia, 1990.

The Longwood Writers Workshop, which I established in 2018: from left, Hattie Winston, Charles F. Johnson, Denise Billings, me, Otto Stallworth, Gwendolyn Williams. (Credit: Karine Simon)

Sidney Poitier, me, and Charles F. Johnson, the executive producer of *NCIS*, grinning so hard we had to put our faces in traction to straighten them out again, while Sidney looks handsome and cool.

Left: At the big publication party for *Freshwater Road* at the Ebell Club in Los Angeles in 2005. It was a packed house of actors and writers and an unforgettable celebration.

CROSSROADS THEATRE COMPANY PRESENTS

BUSES

A World Premiere Production by
DENISE NICHOLAS

Above: At a book event for the launch of *Freshwater Road* in Washington, DC—it was during this trip that the *Post*'s rave review was published on the cover of its book section.
Left: The program for *Buses,* the award-winning play I wrote when I went back to school at USC, 20 years after dropping out of University of Michigan to join the Free Southern Theater. (Credit: Crossroads Theater)

One of my favorites—another image from this shoot appeared on the jacket of the first edition of *Freshwater Road*. (Credit: Mary Ann Halpin)

23.

"I will kill you."

I said it to the nurse's back as she did a hurried sidle out the examining room door.

Had she heard me? If she did, didn't she have the right to report a death threat? A near obligation? Say she did that, and reported me to her boss, the doctor who owned the clinic. And he, not knowing what had actually transpired between his nurse and myself, would surely take the word of a trusted employee over the word of an on-again, off-again patient. She more than likely would *not* tell him her part in this attitudinal skirmish—that she'd been rude, disrespectful, nearly unconscionable in dealing with me behind the closed door of the examining room.

The clinic, though located in a low-income area with scads of drive-through fast-food eateries within steps of the door, had a fine reputation because of the lead doctor. The parking lot told the entire story. It was a showroom for late models from Lexus, Jaguar, Land Rover, and the odd limo, engine humming smooth and tactful. It was a scene from a comedy, but not funny to those of us trying to stay age-worthy in this town of eternal youth.

In the waiting room, coffee with Styrofoam cups, various

fake sweeteners, fake milk, and a plate of discount cookies from Ralph's Market sat on a small table near the check-in counter. When folks offer you coffee and cookies, they're trying to take your mind off the wait. And wait you did, along with all ages of women, primarily white but not exclusively (obviously), come to get their wrinkling faces plumped up with Botox, Restylane, Juvederm, or any one of a number of other expensive fillers designed to slow the jawline droop, the ribbed neck, the overall sag associated with the general progress of time. Of course, nothing really stops time. If you continue using the fillers, sooner or later you begin to look like a specimen from Madame Tussaud's Wax Museum. When I'm watching television these days, I find myself searching for faces that express, that move. Too many do not move at all. (Then there are those blindingly white teeth that require sunglasses to converse with a person who has recently bleached theirs. That's kind of new.)

As often happens with aging women, your spiritual and mental self will not only keep right on aging, but also usually getting better. But you lose count of your body's plumped-up age, and the two end on disparate tracks, creating an odd inner confusion.

"Mrs. Miller, the doctor will see you now." The named woman stood, thin and attractive in the SoCal way that women work so devilishly hard to achieve, often obliterating parts of themselves, remaking themselves in fear of fading youth flying away. Sweet Bird.

I watched from my corner seat, sipping my unremarkable coffee, passing on the cookies, waiting my own turn to get my face "filled" with anti-gravity, anti-wine consumption, anti-years fillers.

Mrs. Miller followed the nurse through the door leading to the examining rooms. I knew from experience that she'd emerge on the back side of the clinic with little ice packs on her reddened face, head to the desk to pay, and put on her big sunglasses as the office assistant slid her Platinum American Express card through the machine. She'd sign, then exit through the backdoor to the jammed parking lot, climb into her humongous Land Rover, and disappear into the frenetic traffic of an area of the city she wouldn't be caught dead in for any purpose but the joy of seeing a few years disappeared from her face. Is there any grace in this? I'm as frail as everyone else in this amazing and sometimes shallow town.

Black people, generally speaking, age gracefully in terms of skin wrinkles and droops. Melanin works. With my infusion of European genetics, I inherited some Caucasian issues: extremely delicate skin, hyperpigmentation, slight jaw droop, off-brand coloring—neither Black, white, nor brown really, but an alchemic blend of all three.

In the examining room, the young white nurse glanced at my chart, at my clothes, my bag, my diamond rings, and I guess she had a mini-meltdown. There she was in her Nurse Betty shoes and uniform and there I was, a grand-assed Black woman who had the audacity to come in for filler and who didn't look anything like the age I'd honestly written on the registration forms one must fill out before seeing the doctor in the first place. I could almost see the smoke curling out of her ears.

"Nurse, how long will the wait for the doctor be, approximately?" My manners were on display.

She didn't answer my question. Instead, she repeated it in a mocking, snarky tone.

Where'd that come from? I thought. I was actually too stunned to speak for a moment.

Then, as is typical of Black people continually caught off guard by the disrespect served cold on a multitude of platters, I pressed on, even as queasiness grew in my stomach. She continued preparing the anesthesia to administer to my face. The thought of that woman putting a needle anywhere near my face made the bile rise up in my stomach.

"The doctor will have to administer that." I did a fake dig around in my purse to focus on anything but the situation.

"*The doctor will have to administer that.*" She mocked me again, adding a Southern lilt this time. I have no Southern accent. Was she trying to give me one? In her small mind, did she attribute a Southern accent to all Black people? Or was she saying that she *wanted* me to have a Southern accent, be a Southern Black person?

Dizzying thoughts on warp speed raced through my mind. *Should I get up and leave? Should I knock her upside her bleached blond head? Should I scream for help?* And who in that desert of self-absorption would come to my assistance? I smoldered for a few minutes more.

"Get the fuck out of here."

I do not know where the words came from but there they were, hanging in the chilled air of the examining room.

"I will kill you."

Did the devil make me say it? Whatever, those words popped out of my mouth like they'd been resting and waiting for an opportunity to serve.

She left the room. The door didn't slam. I was shaking. She'd rattled me. I said something I'd never said in my life to a perfect stranger. I threatened another human being. I could land in jail. I had no weapon, no way to harm anyone except my hands and very strong legs. The words were the weapon. I felt as if I'd already done the deed by the whisper of those words. Soon, I felt diminished, as if my sense of whom I was and what I stood for had been sullied. Those words put me on her level. She wanted to break me down and she succeeded. On the other hand, I doubt she'll be so crude again with another Black or brown patient.

These encounters happen so frequently we tend to keep stepping without even a modest response, but that skullduggery digs holes deep in our self-esteem. It made me think of all the like encounters I'd had in recent years.

When my novel *Freshwater Road* was published, a woman at a book event—from out of nowhere—asked: "What made you think *you* could write this book?" My jaw dropped. Was it an attack or an inquiry? I couldn't tell. It felt insulting, but was it really?

A conversation I had with another woman began in total innocence and ended with me nearly running in the opposite direction. This one took place at a spa. I sat down for dinner with a woman who'd exhibited what seemed to be a modicum of warmth. We chatted about the spa's programs. I was leaving the next day and said, "Be so glad to get home and jump into my pool." It was hot as blazes in SoCal. She turned her head to face me and said with a fair amount of surprise, "*You* have a pool?"

"Sure." I scarfed down my remaining lettuce leaves and excused myself to go pack. What if I'd said, "I can't wait to get home and sleep in my own bed." Would she then have said, "*You* have a bed?"

I'm thankful that for the most part, I've been lucky enough to be able to read the folks I've been around, to remove myself if I sense these kinds of diminishments coming. I've been around any number of white folks who'd never even consider such aggressive rudeness. The genes for beauty, intelligence, compassion, productivity, creativity or any other positive human trait do not rest in any one ethnicity, and anyone who says they do has lost his or her mind already.

That's what racism is, folks.

Regarding the aforementioned spa: I'd checked in to lose a few pounds, to regain my sanity after a long siege of work, and to detox myself off coffee and wine. The program at this spa promotes calming your entire digestive system, tamping down your taste buds by fasting on green juice, deepening your meditation techniques, learning the extraordinary value of veganism. What little food you eat is raw, green, and extremely healthy. I loved every headachy minute of it. I had not been able to sit quietly and read for a year. While at this spa for a week, I read *The Warmth of Other Suns* by Isabel Wilkerson between the classes offered and our exercise walks around the property. I felt like I was in a kind of peaceful heaven, a paradise behind the gates where there's no traffic, no helicopters, no pressing responsibilities except to take care of oneself, something we all need more of, whether white, Black, brown, or everything in between.

Near the end of my week there, I'd bonded with many people in a gentle way. One knows that one rarely makes deep and lasting relationships at these places, but there's definitely bonding in a good supportive way. There were a couple of people who remembered me from my television days. A couple of others were interested in my writing. None of it was over the moon. Just kindnesses really. I appreciated it and listened to the life vignettes of others with interest, too. It's a kind of bonding reciprocity.

On this day, I approached a woman from whom I'd felt kindness during our stay, to speak to her. Another woman was standing with her, older, a multi-visit person. You have to wonder about people who go to this kind of spa 25 or 30 times with no overwhelming health issues. Hanging out at the weekly rate there was seriously strange. The older woman saw me approaching with a smile on my face and said loudly to me, in a weirdly accusatory tone, "I thought you were someone important!" It was a shocking thing to say, especially in this environment of peace, tranquility, and spiritual awareness. She must be a slow learner on the spiritual side of things, having trouble getting to a really good place of peace and love for others. It takes time, I guess. I stared her down and responded quickly. "I most certainly am an important person, lady!" Her face contorted, her mouth dropped open, and she slunk away. She'd obviously gotten away with her rudeness with others.

On another insane occasion, I went in for my pap smear and breast checkup. I'd gone to see this female gynecologist after changing from a male doctor whose fingers got a little too frisky. I'm on the examining table, indisposed. The pap smear was completed. The cursory breast exam came next. She examined one breast. No lumps. She checked my chart then asked, out of nowhere, "What are you?"

The question threw me off. What was she getting at?

"Excuse me?"

"What race are you?" She'd turned away from me.

"I'm Black?" I said it with a soft question, because I hadn't figured out yet what was going on.

She seemed to ruffle, get irritated. She pulled off her rubber gloves and slammed them on a side table.

"Well, you don't *look* Black." She exited the room and never checked my other breast. I don't have clue what was going through her highly educated mind, but it was extremely disconcerting.

Remembering that little awkward moment as I'm writing about it, I'm laughing. Thank God, I'm laughing. Some people want to continue believing that their definition of you, their estimation of who you are as a person, a human being, is all there is. When you are outside of their narrow thinking about you and they can't figure things out, they get miffed. They want to own and define your image, your being. That's racism.

During the Obama Administration, my racial/rudeness Geiger counter was on 24/7. Remember Governor Jan Brewer of Arizona wagging her finger in his face on the tarmac? To a sitting President of the United States of America? She didn't feel she had to respect him regardless of his position as President of the United States of America because he was not white.

President Obama's exterior remained calm, holding on to his cool dude persona no matter what. Perhaps he's not a seether. Perhaps the continual assaults roll off him like the proverbial water off a duck's back. I seethed for him and for Mrs. Obama, too. I know they didn't need me to be their stand-in seether, but seethe I did anyway. I wondered during those days if Mrs. Obama was as cool as the President. Somehow, I don't think so. I wanted to be inside her head. Just once.

There was news footage of a White House luncheon following the Second Inauguration. Mrs. Obama was seated next to House Speaker John Boehner. I remember a distinct eye-roll she gave him that raised the hair on the back of my neck. I cheered her. Was that her *I will kill you moment*? A sort of Black girl moment of *you must be out of your mind coming at me like that*. That's when the misplaced self-importance of some people, the hateful chicanery, the out-and-out rudeness and ignorance, has been aggressively pointed toward you, your husband or your significant someone, for no reason one time too many.

That's a tipping point, a flash point, an enough-is-enough moment, a point when rage and impatience with the lack of civility bubbles up to the top of the pot and is on the verge of spilling over. You stand there stirring, praying, lowering the heat. Smoke comes out of your ears, your heart rate increases, and because more often than not, you're outnumbered, you have no backup, you must adjust the mask you constantly wear to make nice, to act as if nothing bothers you, as if it's all like "water off a duck's back." Until you have one of those moments that will not be quelled, not stuffed back down your throat.

I eventually saw the doctor that day at the clinic. I said nothing. He said nothing. I was given ice packs for my throbbing face, went to the counter to pay, put my big sunglasses on and my baseball cap, exited out the back door, and got into my Benz and headed for the freeway.

24.

My late brother, Otto, Jr., was my go-to guy for memory excavation about everything we experienced as youngsters. My memories are often fuzzy, slippery, and often more poetic than journalistic. Some of them are perhaps too painful to keep in the chest. Otto's were crystal clear and definitive. He and my journalist pal Ed Boyer were my unpaid research assistants for all things Detroit.

As in *Freshwater Road*, the city of Detroit becomes a character in pretty much everything that I write—either in opposition to other places or in my attempts to repair the image of the city—a city often disparaged for all sorts of things. Detroit always was and remains Motown, and so much more.

For this memoir, we began the same way: me calling either one of them and asking if they remembered this or that. They both remembered everything. It stunned me. Perhaps when you stay in the same city for your entire life, as my brother did, you remember so much more because the reminders are there to see every time you walk out the door. He never left the womb so to speak. Ed Boyer did migrate to Los Angeles, but journalists constantly do research to support their stories, so in a sense, Ed never left Detroit either.

He's a walking textbook of Detroit history.

My life experience has been significantly different: I've lived in Detroit, Milan, Ann Arbor, New Orleans, briefly in Jackson, Mississippi, New York City, and, of course, the home I found, Los Angeles. Every time I've moved, a Mack truck of memories is tossed into the grinder of time and place passing.

When I began writing about the Detroit my brother and I experienced in elementary school, I had *bupkis* in my memory bank beyond a couple of muted memories of those days. All the teachers were white while we were in elementary school. I remembered an assembly teacher called me out for talking. The white girl I was talking with got no scold.

Otto opened the door for me. We took music lessons; he played drums and I crucified the violin. That lasted five minutes because the screeching sounds coming from my playing made everyone in earshot ready to take the violin and toss it. Other gaps he filled in for me—as elementary school children, we were taken to the Detroit Institute of Arts, the Detroit Symphony and even the Michigan State Fair. He reminded me that we stood staring at the cow made of butter trying to figure out why anyone would make a cow out of butter.

To his eternal delight, one of his Christmas presents when we were quite young was an entire Lionel train set, which he laid out under our grandparents dining room table. It really was a marvelous toy. His interest in Lionel trains was born there and never left him. By the time he passed in 2023, his Lionel trains took up nearly his entire basement. I was always fascinated by the details—stores, cars, little people walking around, homes. I was relegated to many forgettable dolls and doll houses. I played with them but there was nothing there to hold my interest.

On one of his trips to Los Angeles, he wanted to visit the Allied Model Train store on Sepulveda. Off we went. We browsed the store and it was easy to see that he already had everything they offered for sale. It was fun for me to watch the salesman watching and chatting with my brother. I knew he'd been to train shows, had been featured in *Model Trains* magazine and usually was the only Black guy attending those shows. The salesman was impressed, and I was so proud.

His other passion was gardening. His double-lot yard in Detroit was a thing of beauty. Here in So Cal when we have good rains, the spring breaks out in super blooms of wildflowers on the mountains. I sent him photos of a super bloom and he thought they were of a painting. I have that passion as well. I think that comes from Grandma Waddy B. because her yard was perfection at all times. We spent many days in that yard as little ones, flowers everywhere.

In 2018, Otto made his last trip to Los Angeles for our very first family reunion. Our late cousin Diana Hines Allen and I got things organized, and it was just fine. It was grand to spend time with folks who were merely names mentioned from time to time by elders. Our cousin Jesse Hines, a Dayton native now settled in Texas; his wife, Veronica; his sister, Donna Westbrook, and her husband Gary from Georgia; Shelly Hines; Sue Hines. My guy Derrick brought his daughter and we all had a good time.

Missing and missed were Gabriella and Bianca Hines, Jesse and Veronica's daughters.

We swam, we ate, we drank and swapped memories. It was on this trip that Otto's health issues became clear. He had heart disease, which had killed our dad. These men were major meat eaters and hard liquor drinkers and so it is and was. They both wearied of me yakking about a healthy diet.

They were ardently opposed to a healthier diet and let me know it.

When *Room 222* was canceled in 1975, and Mom and Bob retired to Los Angeles, I was ecstatic to have them because in those days, I had zero family in California. They lived briefly in my home as they searched for a permanent home. I believe two things prompted this move, three if you include the weather.

My dad had never stopped supporting my decisions to do things that put my prospects for a successful life in doubt—becoming an actress, marrying a man or two I probably should've stayed away from. He believed in me no matter what I decided to do. His cautions were never to diminish my journey but to remind me to protect myself. He knew I had a habit of throwing caution to the wind and he knew I paid the price. Mississippi was a horror, as I've written; death was in the small print at every turn.

As my television career blossomed, I think my mom wanted to enjoy the fallout. I sometimes think that she saw herself in ways I saw myself—but in my case, I was able to take the bull by the horns and make it real, make it happen. She didn't have those opportunities, and though she was a strong-willed person, she was basically living the life that others had lived—get married, have children, and consider yourself lucky.

It wasn't long after she arrived in Los Angeles that she told me that Otto Nicholas was not my biological father. While I was a grown woman living comfortably in my own home, I was still in recovery from the nightmare that my marriage to Withers had become. I was definitely fragile. The information she dropped on me that day sent me to my bathtub, where I sat crying for two days. When I emerged, I spoke to

Dad. He calmed me down, and he talked frankly and honestly with me about some of the issues that had shaped his relationship with Mom. He never wavered for one second in his love and support of me until the day he died. I miss him every day of my life. And he never disparaged her—except he did offer one dollop of knowledge that clarified something in Mom for me. He said she was a very jealous woman.

I left it at that. I know well that Dad was a handsome guy in his youth and probably gave her the fits because he was a man of the streets. Elegant in appearance, always driving a beautiful car (like me!) and loving jazz, jukeboxes, and the night life. I'm sure an aggressive woman or two gave Mom a serious eye-roll on occasion.

For much of my life, I felt as if my mom held me aloof. Our relationship teetered between benign and tortured, back and forth between warm and fuzzy and strained, uncomfortable. We've struggled to find a groove, a way of coexisting with a positive undertow. Let me rephrase that. I've struggled.

I thought for a good while that her distancing began when I hit puberty and blossomed. It's not uncommon for women to have modest jealousies of their daughters based on looks, life's possibilities compared to the lack of same for the mother's early years. Certainly, coming from abject poverty in southern Ohio, navigating the Great Depression on an empty stomach, among other deficiencies, laid the groundwork for extreme insecurity and need. One could say she gave as good as she got. She evolved into an emotionally frugal person. Later, thinking through the new information about my paternity, that frugality more than likely deepened the moment I was born. I was born a problem. I was the baby embodiment of the man with whom she'd had an affair, the man who fathered me and then walked away, leaving her to deal with it all by herself. Or, perhaps she pushed him away because she certainly was not free. I have no doubt that she loved me, but it was a sparse, uneasy love.

During times when there was congruency, we enjoyed a few wonderful experiences, all of which I set up and financed. I treated myself to a vacation in Aruba and took her with me. We hit the exquisite white beaches during the day, walking in the warm shallow water that went out quite far. At night, we hit the restaurants and bars. She loved Aruba. Much of the population there is racially mixed—Dutch and African. We both pretty much looked like everyone on the island. I realized then that she probably paid a price as a Black youngster being as beautiful as she was, with exquisite hair and a soft voice. She could've passed for at least 50 other ethnicities if she'd chosen to. In her youth, often folks who were able to pass did so in order to get away from the horrid pressure of racism in America.

Another of my attempts to smooth the field of play between us was when my sister-girl Marcia Stevenson and I planned a trip to the California wine country. We packed Mom up to go with us. We had a fabulous time, wine tasting in Napa and Sonoma, driving on to Mendocino, riding the Skunk Train through the incredible forests of Northern California. She was for a brief period a *girlfriend mom*.

My last big trip with Mom came after Michele's murder. Mom called me sounding very dark and pained and told me she was ready to put a gun to her own head. I immediately got busy setting up a trip to Paris. Mom didn't want to go but I was able to talk her into the travel. My pal, the late Barbara Smiley, and me and Mom headed for Paris. It was me trying desperately to drag Mom away from the sorrow of losing her youngest, most gifted child. It was a fool's errand, but when has that ever stopped me?

In Paris, we lived large, staying at the Hôtel de Crillon overlooking the Place de la Concorde, visiting museums, touring Versailles on a cold damp day, walking the Left Bank, lunching a Les Deux Magots, visiting a World War I cemetery. Although Mom's father, John Jones, is buried in the Veterans Cemetery in Dayton, she wanted to be in the area where he'd spent some of his time during the war. She had death on her mind and I couldn't dislodge it.

We drove to Epernay and Reims. I found rooms for us at a 16th century chateau anointed by Relais & Châteaux as a place of exquisite dining, quiet country pastoral living. It was definitely old with a modest musty aroma.

Our first tour was to Moët. We drank so much champagne and giggled so much in that tasting room, I'm sure the staff thought we'd gone bonkers. Mom loved it! Then back to the chateau to enjoy a five-course meal that was so rich, we spent the night running to the bathroom.

The next day we ached for a normal old fashioned American sandwich. Off we went to Reims to the Cathedrale Notre-Dame de Reims, enjoying the modern stained-glass windows done by Marc Chagall. We found sandwiches made, of course, with baguettes—excellent bread to soak up the champagne and mitigate the richness of the food at the Chateau. It was a glorious trip that included shopping for rain gear at Samarataine department store in Paris.

I've pieced together a sort of rough-edged picture of Mom's early life. Her father was a biracial man who looked white. Actually, very much like me, he had European DNA on both sides. In the one photo I have of him, he looked as if he could've been from England, Spain, Italy. He came home to Dayton after fighting for his country on foreign soil during World War I to face a level of racism that would've dissolved me into a profound depression. He could find work because bosses thought he was white. When they discovered he was married to a brown-skinned woman, they fired him. My Grandma Ethel shared those stories with me when I was too young to understand the horror of it all. When he died in the 1930s, the family bent under the pressure of racism and those miserable economic times. Grandma Ethel told me that the only food they had for days at a time was a bowl of oatmeal.

In November 2020, in the midst of the raging Covid-19 pandemic, my assistant Susan Garrison-Sirotta, my pal Aaron Williams, and I began moving my mom from her longtime apartment to my home. Susan and I had been "masking and gloving up" every Sunday to clean Mom's apartment for the previous few months. It became our ritual, nerves on high alert getting into the less than sanitary elevators during the pandemic, hauling cleaning supplies, food, whatever was needed. Mom had become housebound at least two years before the pandemic hit. I'd pick her up and bring her to my home for lunch, dinner, whatever was going on, not paying too much attention to her apartment. She began feeling insecure in my home, not able to sit comfortably after lunch or dinner, always ready to go back to her apartment immediately. I couldn't figure it out. That was new because in years past, we'd always hang out on the patio or here in the house after a luncheon or a special dinner. I now believe that her rapidly mushrooming insecurity about being anywhere but her apartment was early dementia, she recognized that something was changing but early on, couldn't figure out what it was.

When I finally began really checking her apartment, I saw things were unraveling. I asked Mom on multiple occasions if she wanted me to send a cleaning person over to help. She'd say she "had someone" over and over. I saw no evidence of that but she insisted and when she insisted, it was ironclad. By the time Susan and I began our Sunday morning cleaning ritual, that "someone" hadn't made an appearance in quite a long time. I'm thinking years. The place was a total mess. It became clear that Mom could no longer care for herself or her apartment. I began feeling in my bones that the move would be inevitable but I hadn't accepted it in my heart. My brains were firing. My heart was in denial, still.

During the time before I decided to move Mom to my home, Susan and I did marketing for her, cooking healthy meals, generally trying to bring things up to a standard that resembled normalcy. We had arranged caregivers who came and went, but there was no supervision. Mom's diet had gone to hell and she'd been a stickler for healthy eating. Thus at 102 years old, she continued to have the blood pressure of a 30-year-old. But, the dreadfulness of her apartment was vast and getting worse: Mom was incontinent; she was basically living on cookies, milk, coffee with an occasional meal. Giving her a shower—as Susan and I did—became our challenge because she simply didn't want to get wet. These tics and obsessions were so out of the norm for her—this lovely woman who *always* dressed beautifully, was immaculate in personal care and in her living space. I was befuddled.

When earlier she'd complained to me about losing memory, I put it off to her age. She made an appointment with her primary care doctor and I went with her. He gave her a perfunctory one-page test, which she passed easily. My mother knew for a while at any rate how to hide her memory loss. She fooled a lot of people for at least two or three years as the disease progressed. His sort of offhand treatment of the issue fed into my stance: I didn't accept that she had dementia because I didn't want to. Her friendship group died off which left her isolated. She lost her hearing and refused to wear a hearing aid. That in itself is a marker for dementia.

I knew with no other family now in the Los Angeles area,

that I would be totally and exclusively responsible. And, here I am . . .

Mom began doing things that could cause her great harm—to say nothing of perhaps starting a fire that would burn the entire building down. She'd put cups of water on the stove and turn the burners on, walk out of the kitchen forgetting to turn burners off. We removed the knobs from the stove. She no longer changed her sheets, vacuumed the carpets, or took garbage to the incinerator down the hall. Things continued piling up in all the wrong directions.

I hemmed and hawed for months before taking the bit between my teeth. When I took it, it was with my substantial will and my strength focused on making things better for her. This decision came quickly on the surface, like plunking money down on a bet at the last moment, your stomach tap dancing in fear and a kind of resignation that prepares you for a loss. But you roll the dice and hold your breath. My brain snapped clearly into the moment I was facing. Her current situation was not working for anyone, least of all Mom. And me trying to keep track of what was going on in her apartment, what was going on in my home, and what was going on with my apartment building until 2018 when I sold it. And running a writing workshop at the same time was a major load for me, a single woman. If you'd like to know how it feels to lose your mind, come walk in this girl's size nines.

Mom had been living in that apartment since the mid-1970s, so imagine how much stuff was in every corner, closet, cabinet, box, drawer. She'd never thrown anything—not a sheet of paper—away. At least that's' the way it looked and felt as we began hauling stuff out of there via the elevator. Thank God my home has a two-car garage and I have only one car.

Before the big move, my mind raced through my remaining options. The dilemma was mine and mine alone. Could

I afford to place her in a facility that I'd find acceptable? Not really. The care facilities here in Los Angeles that I'd find acceptable start at about $6,000 per month. The high-end facilities start at about $10,000 a month. That would clean me out pronto and leave me on the corner with a cup. Mom had the potential to live at least five more years. I visited a few care facilities that were on the lower end financially, but hear me, I wouldn't put anyone that I cared for into any of those places unless there was no other option. So here I am caring for a 103-year-old with dementia, extreme hearing loss, and who still refuses to wear her hearing aid which means of course that folks have to yell for her to hear. It irks me because it reflects that same emotional selfishness that I experienced as a child and an adult.

There's good news in this for my own longevity—if I don't kill myself caring for others. Sound cranky? Sometimes I am. Sometimes, I sit in my office and cry. It comes in waves. It calms. It revs up again and the waves are bigger, stronger, knocking me down. I get up and go at it again.

Classify the care Mom gets here in my home as Cadillac or Mercedes Benz care. Classify the care level at the cheaper places I visited as equal to a battered, paint-splotched Volkswagen from 1969. I made the call. Mom will be living in my home until one of us croaks. I called my late brother in Detroit to tell him the news. I'd asked Mom on three or four occasions before the big move if she'd like to live with me. She craftily didn't answer clearly. Finally, the last time I asked her, as I was on my hands and knees spotting her carpet after the carpet cleaner guy didn't do a great job, she said yes. We packed that place up so fast and moved her happy hips over to my home so fast even my head was spinning.

That was only the beginning.

Moving a 100-year-old person with dementia who's been

living in the same place for years and years is more than a notion. She was disoriented for months. I expected that and did my best to deal with it. I had to be front and center with her for quite a long time until she began to relax in her new environment. My face was the only thing familiar to her. Since I work at home now, I'm able to be around to supervise the caregivers, to check in with her during the day. Even with help, it's the biggest, most stressful thing I've ever done. She falls periodically. I've had to call my neighbor to help get her up and Mom is a small lady. But lifting her up off the floor is more than I could do alone. What stunned me and informed me about dementia is this—my mother has been coming to this house for 40 years. I've given her multiple birthday celebrations here, many dinners and lunches, etc. She has no memory of any of it. She has no memory of ever being in this house. It's a stab in the heart to realize that the memories that were so carefully built do not exist anymore for her. Even photographs of her in those celebrations do not prick her memory.

As time has gone on, she's acclimated to the space as she began owning the rather large chunk of my home that I basically handed over to her—a bedroom, a large bathroom that can accommodate her walker bumping around, a huge "social" room with a flat screen, comfy furniture, books, music. It was my old office and exercise room. The treadmill's gone now and I moved my writing room/office downstairs to the TV room, which is not ideal because of the traffic and the caregivers going up and down as they work to care for her while I try to concentrate on this book. She still falls periodically. And in the still of the night when I'm snoring, I hear in the soundtrack of my dream someone yelling, "Help!" I leap out of the bed and race to her space and find her on the floor. I now sleep with one ear open, never fully relaxing for fear I'll miss her yell for help. It's not good.

The kindness, the love that I needed from her all those years ago is now on full display. She's shrewd enough to know that she's fully and completely dependent on me. Perhaps, somewhere in the depth of dementia, she feared I would not be the person I am in caring for her, some mother/daughter revenge fantasy. That's not who I am. There was plenty in her parenting that helped the best parts of me develop.

The overarching situation of my birth influenced so much of what went on back then. Her scandal. She lived through it. I lived through it with stipulations. I needed help. The only words she spoke after announcing to me that my dad was not my real dad (whatever the hell that means) were, "I'm so glad I'm not carrying that guilt anymore." She relieved her guilt by breaking my heart.

Much later, when going through some of her papers, I discovered that as my brother and I backed away from chasing the murder of our sister, Michele, going back to the trajectory of our own lives as best we could, Mom kept fighting the good fight. I found letters to district attorneys in New York, Chicago, and even here in Los Angeles where Michele had no presence. She wrote and wrote trying to get something positive from the authorities, some modicum of appreciation for her pain, our pain, our loss. If the NYPD dropped the ball, that was it. We don't even know when they threw in the towel, stopped searching. There was a wall that neither I, nor she even made a dent in.

It took two years of searching to find helpers for Mom that fit into the energy of my home. That was entirely too difficult— me trying to have a life, trying to write as I interviewed helpers, got rid of helpers who didn't fit, kept searching and finally almost by accident found two ladies to help care for her. Without them, I'd lose my total mind. We have Mom in a California program that helps to pay for her care as she is very low income.

For a brief while, we had family in Los Angeles. Our Dayton cousin Delbert Taylor, arranger, conductor, king of the piano, lived here in Los Angeles and married Helen. We spent many holidays around the table. Another cousin, Diana Hines Allen, also from Dayton, lived with her husband in the Sacramento area and visited for holidays. A few other cousins have passed through Los Angeles on extended visits giving us a big family feel. Cousin Carl Farley lived here in LA for a while but moved on. Both my niece and nephew lived in my home for extended stays but eventually returned to Detroit. We're down to almost zero on family. Delbert died young. His loss felt huge. We loved him so—big personality, a tall great-looking man who always brought fun and music to the room. My brother and sister both are gone.

The excellent part of dementia, if there is one, is that people forget the bad and the good. The mind becomes nearly an empty vessel with leaks. Mom does not know her first born, her son, has passed. Her doctor advised me to not tell her. What would be the point? She's mostly calm with periodic flare ups of confusion, of tiny memory pieces floating to the surface that she tries so hard to grasp. Caring for her is a 24/7 nonstop job. When I took this on, I had not a clue as to how devastating it would be relative to my own life. I'm trying hard now to punch out time for myself—to see a film, a play, have lunch with pals. Everything must be arranged so that there's someone here with her because she cannot be left alone for longer than a few minutes.

My fatigue is profound. I'm pushing myself for more energy by exercising more and eating a very healthy diet. Except for wine. I'm calling the wine a necessary adjunct to a healthy diet and most importantly, my sanity.

Writing this memoir peeled back my tough and my tender

skin, making me feel naked to the rough winds of my own life's doings. So often during this process I felt as if the first go-round had been enough. Please, must I dig around these bones again? The work forced me to confront so many things that I'd rather have left to the dust bin of history. Now, having faced the worst of it, in some small way it feels as if many things have been put to rest for all time. Here's hoping.

When I began writing as a second career, the public part of my life began to slip away. Earlier, that life as a working actor flung me widely and rewarded me greatly. It landed me in a sweet spot of comfort with memories to ride on and nightmares to pick at. So many of my actor pals spin yarns of their dreams to become actors beginning practically at birth. Acting opened a door that led to me fulfilling my writer-lady dream—a door I'd tapped on for years with no ability to crack it open enough to squeeze in.

As a young person I floated dreams of being so many different people—I worked in international relations to heal the world of its most egregious insanities; I became a femme fatale of the silver screen; I cured America of its racial skullduggery for all time; I became a writer of readable, interesting books. But no matter where my dreaming took me, in my mind I was heading toward writing. Thank God I arrived in this space before I got too old and my brains too soft to do the work. Changing careers has been a struggle that I've cherished.

On the father issues: after learning a little about the phantom dad, I got a copy of his death certificate here in Los Angeles. That's when I discovered that he and his family lived for years no more than 15 minutes from my home. I drove over there, parked and stared at the small cottage house with bougainvillea vining up the porch walls. I knew only that he married an Italian woman, they had children and he died. He never reached out to me though we lived so close. It never occurred to me to reach out to him. I didn't even know he existed for years. Also, I never saw myself as the kind of person who goes knocking on the door of a total stranger asking to be acknowledged. That's a tried-and-true way to get your feelings hurt.

I wondered if my mother ever saw or spoke with the phantom since we all ended up here in Los Angeles. She was a master of secrets and would not unzip those lips to reveal that to me or anyone else. Now whatever memories she had of this man are gone.

The phantom's niece Shelley Mullins and her son Adam gave me all the information that I have about the phantom dad. I've thought more than once that I may have been at a stoplight in a car right next to his or passed his children on a street or in a restaurant. Shelley tells me that years ago, there was talk in the shadows of their family about me being his child as they watched me on television.

Mullins is about as Irish as one can get. Putting my DNA test from 23andMe and other information together, I know now that I'm Irish and Nigerian. Of course, when that little bit of information became a part of my self-knowledge, I harked back to my trip to Nigeria in the early 1980s and how a group of locals there laughed till they fell off their stools when I said I was Black. What in God's name would they have done if I offered that not only was I Black but I was also Nigerian. I giggle when I think about it.

The phantom is buried in San Luis Obispo, California. I thought of driving up there to pay my respects—by speaking to a stone. I stopped myself from that Hollywood silliness. He hadn't earned that kind of behavior from me.

My dad, Otto Nicholas, Sr., has no stone and he rarely leaves my mind for very long.

In 2018, a few pals expressed interest in a writing workshop. I was in need of that kind of support for my own work, so I began pulling them in. Hattie Mae Winston, Dr. Otto Stallworth, Denise Billings, GW Williams, and long-time friend Charles Floyd Johnson came to my dining room table for the Longwood Writers Workshop. We began with an intensive on the basics as taught by Janet Fitch in the workshop I attended for four years, the workshop that taught me the beauty and the difficulty of writing well and helped me to produce *Freshwater Road*. I attempted to get my writers on the same or very close to the same level, so that all understood the nomenclature, the dedication required, the beauty sought.

We decided that memoir would be our format, because each person at the table had an interesting life story to wrestle down to the page. Nothing about this little venture has been easy but it has certainly been fulfilling. They've worked hard as I drilled into them the idea that writing is rewriting, that writing the senses gets you inside the reader, that bad writing can sink a good story idea, that good writing sings, that pacing matters, and more. Five years after we began our workshop, our anthology, titled *A Gathering of Voices,* was published early in 2025.

Writing this memoir in my life's current hurly-burly circumstance—managing the care of my now 104-year-old mom, nearly floating down the little hill I live on as five atmospheric rivers flooded my basement repeatedly, stuffing cotton in my ears and wearing a noise block headset as neighbors on both sides did concrete work that went on and on, having knee replacement surgery one year into this book's life and most of all, feeling the pain of loss when my brother Otto died in April 2023, which left me sans any siblings. It's been quite a time.

As for me, now that my memoir is completed, I'll get back to the novel I've been working on. A love story.

Acknowledgments

Otto Nicholas, Jr. (July 27, 1941–April 12, 2023)
Ed Boyer
Doug Seibold
Margarita Sweet
The Longwood Writers Workshop: Denise Billings, Charles F. Johnson, GW Williams, Hattie Winston, Dr. Otto Stallworth

Emotional Support:
Dr. Sandra Roussell
Madelyn Murray
Gale Hollingsworth
Retired Judge Veronica McBeth
Kynderly Haskins
Teresa Wallette
Evelyn Tolliver
Avis Lang

Susan Garrison-Sirotta
Aaron G. Williams
Sonia Paredes
Brent Sudduth

Caregivers for Mom:
Rene Ramos
Beverly Jenkins
Debra Jones

About the Author

DENISE NICHOLAS is a writer and actress who has starred in numerous films and TV shows, including *Room 222*, for which she earned three Golden Globe nominations, and *In the Heat of the Night*, for which she also wrote several episodes. She is the author of the acclaimed novel *Freshwater Road* (Agate, 2005). She lives in Los Angeles.